Published by Stackpole Books
An imprint of The Rowman & Littlefield Publishin
4501 Forbes Blvd., Ste. 200
Lanham, MD 20706
www.rowman.com

Distributed by NATIONAL BOOK NETWORK
800-462-6420

British Library Cataloguing in Publication Informatic

Library of Congress Cataloging-in-Publication Dat

ISBN 978-0-8117-3804-0 (hardcover)
ISBN 978-0-8117-6810-8 (e-book)

♾™ The paper used in this publication meets the mini
Standard for Information Sciences—Permanence of P₂
Z39.48-1992.

Contents

Prologue

On a hot August afternoon in 1914, two brothers sat with friends at a lunch counter in Atlanta. Newspapers warned that Europe was on the verge of war, but few people on this side of the Atlantic saw that as a concern. It might be something to talk about over lunch, but it was too far away to affect them. To some, it wasn't even worth a lunch conversation.

The two brothers didn't see it that way. One of them, Kiffin Rockwell, stunned his friends by announcing that he was going to set out for Europe and fight for France. His brother Paul was not surprised. He planned to go with Kiffin. Kiffin and Paul's friends didn't know quite what to make of this announcement. Germany had not yet declared war on France, but the newspapers made it clear that war was inevitable. In 1914, many Americans felt this was simply another European power struggle that was none of America's business. Kiffin had no such doubts. He was already convinced this war would be fought for "the cause of all humanity." The rest of America wouldn't come to that conclusion for another three years.

Within days, Kiffin and Paul took a train to New York and caught the first ship to Europe. When they arrived in France, they immediately joined the French Foreign Legion. Neither had ever been to France before. Kiffin didn't know a word of French. Paul had studied the language in school but discovered that he had difficulty understanding the language as it was spoken in France, and the French had even more problems understanding him. (One suspects the French were not accustomed to hearing their language spoken with a thick Southern drawl.) Paul's war ended early due to battlefield injuries, but Kiffin slogged it out in the trenches until the summer of 1915, when he was wounded during a bayonet attack. That wound made it difficult for him to march, so he transferred to the newest, most "high-tech" form of warfare—a branch of the service where you didn't have to march because you could fight sitting down. He became an aviator. Kiffin was a founding member of an elite military unit that was known as the Lafayette Escadrille. The unit was a squadron of American fighter pilots who voluntarily flew for France long before the United States entered the war. Kiffin was the first American pilot in that unit to shoot down an enemy plane. To this day, the Lafayette Escadrille and Kiffin Rockwell are remembered with honor and gratitude by the people of France.

During the war, the exploits of the Lafayette Escadrille were heralded in newspapers around the world. Articles about the pilots appeared in papers that ran the gamut from the *New York Times* to the *Chickasha Oklahoma Indian Reservation Daily Express*. There were seldom more than a dozen pilots in the escadrille at any one time, and throughout the course of the war only thirty-eight pilots served in the unit, but its fame was such that after the war more than five thousand impostors publicly claimed to have flown with this prestigious group.

Paul and Kiffin Rockwell may have been the first Americans to leave the United States to fight for France, but they were by no means the only ones to volunteer. Some Americans were already in France, studying at French universities or working at jobs that ranged from practicing medicine to driving taxis, and they joined the Legion too. Forty-three Americans joined the Legion in August 1914, and many more would follow. Many of those who followed were inspired by the publicity given to the Lafayette Escadrille.

The volunteers came from diverse backgrounds. Millionaire playboys, poets, architects, scoundrels, soldiers of fortune—a wide range of Americans gave up their civilian lives and volunteered to serve in the Foreign Legion for a penny a day. Many joined because, like Kiffin, they firmly believed they were fighting to save civilization. Some joined for adventure, others for a variety of reasons. There were even one or two who fit the stereotype of joining the Legion because they had been jilted by a lover. All had a story worth telling.

These men were not saints, by any measure. They had all the faults and vices that you would expect from any group of young men adventurous enough to voluntarily enter a war in a foreign country. When not at the front they drank, brawled, and engaged in romantic escapades. When Jim McConnell was killed, three women arrived at his funeral dressed in black, each believing she was his one and only. Two more wore black to a memorial service held for him in North Carolina. Still, he behaved better than his fellow pilot Bert Hall. Bert actually was married to at least five different women during his life, but as far as we know he was never married to more than two at any one time. These were side issues, however, irresponsible behavior engaged in when the men were temporarily released from the stress of combat. Most of their time was spent at the front, in one of the most brutal and frustrating wars ever fought. It was not the glorious war they had expected. Indeed, it was not the kind of war the politicians and generals who started it had expected. A few of the volunteers were stressed beyond their limits and deserted or (very rarely, in this war) were discharged for medical reasons. The vast majority served with honor until they were killed, wounded so badly they could no longer serve, or miraculously survived until the end of the war.

What kind of a man was Kiffin Rockwell? Why would he leave the life he knew to go to a country he'd never seen and fight in a war his friends thought was of no concern to America? This book tells the story of Kiffin Rockwell as it has not been told before. He has sometimes been romanticized into an almost mythological figure, a wealthy southern aristocrat who fearlessly fought for the ideas he held to be true. Kiffin wasn't wealthy, he wasn't an aristocrat, and he wasn't fearless. He was an idealist, however, and he fought relentlessly for a cause he believed in. Like most human beings, he had a number of virtues and a few faults. He was an aggressive pilot, but he knew fear. No sane man could dive into a dogfight against multiple enemy aircraft—a firefight with no cover and incoming fire from all directions— without feeling fear. Kiffin was brave. He overcame his fear, and he voluntarily flew into combat day after day. The stress of that combat took its toll.

This book is based upon thousands of original source documents, including letters, photographs, unpublished histories, interviews, and period newspaper and magazine articles. It brings a new perspective to the life of Kiffin Rockwell and the men with whom he served. It is the story of an extraordinary man who slogged through the mud and trenches on the ground, and who took to the sky to engage in a new kind of warfare. The aircraft he flew may seem quaint and almost comical by today's standards, but the death he faced was just as real as death has ever been.

The Education of an Idealist

I do not feel that I am fighting for France alone, but for the cause of all humanity, the greatest of all causes.

—Kiffin Rockwell

IF YOU'VE EVER EATEN AT AN OLD-FASHIONED LUNCH COUNTER, IT'S EASY to imagine the restaurant in Atlanta where Kiffin and Paul Rockwell had lunch with two friends on August 2, 1914.[1] The booths, tables, and counter seats were jammed with hungry customers. Voices were raised to carry over the background of conversations, clattering dishes, and shouted orders. An occasional laugh or call to a waiter rose above the general din. Large fans hung from the high ceiling, providing welcome puffs of air. The weather was a bit cooler than the normal August heat, with temperatures in the low eighties, but the humidity made it feel like a sauna. As is always the case during Atlanta summers, there was a chance of afternoon thunderstorms.

The customers had a new topic to talk about that day. The bold head-line of the *Atlanta Journal* announced, "Germany Declares War and Then Invades Luxemburg!" Germany had just declared war on Russia. The invasion of Luxemburg, which lay between Germany and France, made it clear that France was next. A seemingly trivial squabble in a remote backwater of Europe had somehow erupted into a major war.

For most of the diners, the war talk lasted only until their food was served. After all, this war had nothing to do with the United States. The kings and queens in Europe had been going to war for centuries. There would be exciting headlines for a few months, and then there would be a peace treaty in some city with an unpronounceable name. In the meantime, the newspaper also described events that might actually affect the people of Atlanta. There was a rousing battle in Congress over plans to protect cotton farmers. Rebel forces under General Carranza were advancing on Mexico City, and the Boston Braves, in last place on July 4, were suddenly dominating the National League despite their manager's preseason complaint that "I've got sixteen pitchers and they're all rotten!"

At Kiffin and Paul's table, the war talk did not die so quickly. Paul was a reporter for the *Atlanta Constitution*, and he had followed the growing crisis with great interest. Neither he nor Kiffin believed the United States could stay out of the war, and they earnestly tried to sway their two friends to their point of view. Kiffin was particularly adamant on this point. He felt the United States was duty bound to help France, just as France had helped the Americans during the Revolutionary War. Lafayette and Rochambeau had come to America's aid in the infant country's hour of need. Now it was time for Americans to repay the debt. Unexpectedly, Kiffin went beyond just talking about the war. He suggested that they travel to France and join the fight. Paul quickly seconded the motion. One of their friends, R. L. Mock, said he would join them. A reporter sitting at an adjacent table overheard the conversation.[2] The fourth young man agreed with their sentiment but would not commit himself. He then turned the conversation to the previous night's poker game.

To Kiffin and Paul, this was not just idle talk. After lunch, they continued their conversation and made definite plans to go to France. When Mock discovered that they were serious about going, he backed out.[3] The next day Kiffin wrote a letter to the French Consul in New Orleans, offering his and Paul's services. He asked whether they should report to New Orleans with the French reservists who had been called up or go directly to France to enlist.[4] On the following day (Tuesday, August 4), they learned that fear of German warships was disrupting shipping between the United States and Europe. There were still a few berths available on the American Line vessel SS *Saint Paul*, which was bound for England, but other ships were canceling trips to Europe. The *Saint Paul* would depart from New York on Friday. Without waiting for a reply from the French Consul, the Rockwell brothers hurriedly packed their things and departed. They made a quick stop in Washington to secure passports, and on Friday morning, August 7, 1914, they departed from New York harbor bound for Southampton. They were on their way to war.

What type of a man decides to go to war in an afternoon? And how does he convince his older brother to go with him? To travel thousands of miles to defend a country neither one of them had ever seen? In fact, the events that shaped Kiffin's life began long before he was born.

Near the Atlantic coast the border between North and South Carolina angles downward, becoming as much an east-west division as a north-south border. Marion County lies on the South Carolina side of that line. The county was named for Francis Marion, the famed "Swamp Fox" of the Revolutionary War. Several rivers meander through the county. Cypress and sweetgum trees lean over the rivers, their branches draped with Spanish moss. Falling leaves stain the water with tannic acid, giving it a distinctive "blackwater" appearance. One of these rivers is called the Little Pee Dee River, and it joins the larger Lumber River near Nichols, South Carolina. The area around Nichols is dotted with cypress swamps, which feed the rivers. In between the swamps are large "islands" of arable land. The Ayres family has been prominent in this area since before the Revolutionary War. The area is still studded with farms belonging to Ayres descendants today. In the late 1800s, a man named Enoch Shaw Ayres grew tobacco and cotton on one of these farms.

In later years, Paul Rockwell would reminisce about his grandfather Ayres's plantation named "Beechwood,"[5] but estate records show that it could better be described as a family farm. Perhaps it had once been a plantation, but the division of land between heirs and the ravages of the Civil War had left Enoch with a farm. Enoch knew very well what the ravages of war were like, having served as a sergeant in the famed "Kershaw's Brigade." He had seen action in several major battles, including Bull Run, Second Manassas, Antietam, and Gettysburg.[6] He lost a brother in that war, and he carried bitter memories of it for the rest of his life. He also lost both his parents and a sister to a smallpox epidemic that swept through Marion County during the war.[7] Enoch proudly declared that he was "unreconstructed" because when the war ended he refused parole and never signed an oath of allegiance to the United States government. He simply got on his horse and rode back home. In his mind, he had fought a just but impossible battle against a tyrannical federal government that had invaded his homeland and threatened his family.

After the war, he and his brother Thomas divided their father's land, as they were the only two surviving male heirs of the five boys born to William and Mary Ayres.[8] Enoch resumed farming and preached at the Bear Swamp Baptist Church in Lake View, South Carolina, where he was referred to as "the pope." He married Samantha Tyler, and together they raised nine children. Their fourth, Loula Ayres, was an intelligent, headstrong, and progressive child. She attended Chowan Baptist Female Institute in Murfreesboro, North Carolina, earning an AB degree in 1886.[9] The fact that the daughter of a South Carolina farmer attended college in the 1880s is probably a reflection of how independent she was, as well as an indication of how successful Enoch was at farming. A farmer who knew him at the time said he got better results from his acres than anyone else in the community.[10]

Just across the state line, near Whiteville, North Carolina, lived another Confederate veteran, Henry Clay Rockwell. The Rockwell family also had a long history in America, having descended from a deacon who fled England with his congregation to escape religious persecution and landed in Massachusetts in 1630.[11] A Rockwell had served on General Washington's staff, and Rockwells fought during the War of 1812. During the Civil War, Henry Clay Rockwell had been a captain in the Fifty-First North Carolina Regiment. He met Enoch Ayres in 1863 when they were both involved in the Battle of Charleston. Fighting continued around the city until General Sherman captured it in 1865. Rockwell's and Ayres's units were withdrawn long before the city fell, but not before the two became close friends.

After the war, the two men and their families often visited each other. Rockwell had married Sarah Jane Powell and they had five children. Their third child, James Chester Rockwell, was born on the twenty-first of January 1868. He was frail but precocious and was considered a child prodigy. He sometimes attended the academy of Professor W. G. Quackenbush in Laurinburg, North Carolina, but was largely home schooled and self-taught. His father died when James was only six, but James persevered with his education. He was a voracious reader with a special interest in poetry, and he sold his first poem to the *Augusta (Georgia) Chronicle* when he was eleven years old. By the time he was sixteen, he was writing and selling pamphlet-length poems, having partnered with his older brother William to open a publishing company called "The Rockwell Publishing Company." His poems and essays were published by Walter Hines Page, among others.

Tragedy struck the young man in 1886 when his older brother William died. Never a strong man, James's health failed, and he went to a resort in the foothills of the Blue Ridge Mountains to recuperate. There he met a Baptist minister named Murchison, who inspired him to leave the Presbyterian Church and become a Baptist. He enrolled in the Southern Baptist Theological Seminary at Louisville, Kentucky. While studying to become a minister, he married his family friend and sweetheart, Loula Ayres, on February 29, 1888.[12]

Their first child, Paul Ayres Rockwell, was born on February 3 of the following year, in Nichols, South Carolina. James Rockwell continued to be plagued by health problems and he was advised to move to the mountains, so he accepted a position with a Baptist church in Morristown, Tennessee. On September 5, 1890, Loula gave birth to a daughter, whom they named Agnes. The climate in Morristown did not help James's health, so shortly after Agnes was born he accepted a position as the first resident pastor in Newport, Tennessee.

Newport was a quiet town, located along the Pigeon River in eastern Tennessee. About fifteen miles from the North Carolina border, Newport is located in the misty blue foothills of the Great Smoky Mountains. When the Rockwells moved to Newport the population was just under one thousand. A brief logging boom had collapsed, but the city had a thriving tanning company and the Stokely cannery (later to become Stokely-Van Camp) was growing rapidly. The first Baptist Church of Newport was founded in 1876, but until they hired James they lacked a resident pastor and only held services once a month.[13] James proved to be a very popular pastor, and his sermons were said to hold the congregation "spellbound."[14] A tall man with black hair and a bushy black beard, people sometimes said they felt as though they were listening to one of the apostles. While he was pastor, the church built its first parsonage, which the Rockwells moved into. On September 20, 1892, Loula gave birth to their third child: Kiffin Yates Rockwell.[15]

Things were going well for the Rockwells. Their family was growing, the church was growing, and the congregation loved Reverend Rockwell. Then James contracted typhoid fever. He died on September 4, 1893.[16] He was twenty-six years old, and he died less than three weeks before Kiffin's first birthday.

Loula Rockwell was in a terrible situation. Her husband had sometimes joked that "all preachers have in this world are babies and books," and that is precisely what he left her. Paul was four, Agnes was two, and Kiffin was not quite one year old. To make matters worse, they were living in the parsonage, which she would have to turn over to the parson hired to replace her late husband. The obvious solution, and the one most women in the 1890s would have chosen, would be to go back to her parents' house. Loula didn't want to surrender her independence, though, or her ability to infuse her own ideals into her children. Paul and Kiffin spent many summers with their grandparents, and Loula probably accepted financial help from them, but she found a house in Newport and stayed there. She turned down an opportunity to teach at Carson-Newman College in Jefferson City, about twenty-five miles from Newport, because it would require too much time away from her children.[17] Instead, she found a job teaching in the Newport elementary school system, a job that allowed her to earn money while staying near her children.

For Kiffin and Paul, it was an idyllic childhood, despite the loss of their father. They spent summers with their grandfather, who became a father figure to them. On his farm and the surrounding lands, they went swimming and fishing, and they learned to ride horses. They both learned to shoot at an early age and spent many hours hunting. And they especially liked to listen to their grandfather tell stories about the marches and the battles he fought during the Civil War. Sometimes other veterans joined his grandfather, and the boys listened to tales of the "lost cause." The boys also learned about ancestors in both the Rockwell and the Ayres families who had fought in previous wars. Not surprisingly, Paul later recalled that their favorite game was "playing at war."[18]

The stories Kiffin's grandfather told the boy had a great impact on his personality. His mother tried to raise him to be a scholar, but his heart wasn't in that. Throughout his life Kiffin searched for adventure, especially thrilling military adventures like his grandfather had described. He was idealistic, sometimes to a fault. He was firmly convinced that he knew what was right and what was wrong, and he was willing to fight for his beliefs. He could be critical of people who did not share his convictions, but he was loyal to his friends. And whenever a situation didn't live up to his expectations, he always felt things must be better somewhere else—a better school, a better job, or a better military unit.

The boys spent the school year in Newport. Newport may have been a sleepy little town, but compared to their grandfather's farm it was a booming metropolis. There were other kids to play with in Newport, and the town was rural enough to have open fields, horses, and other ways to have fun. Years later, when friends reminisced about the Rockwells, they often focused on the fact that Kiffin was fearless and headstrong and wouldn't give up. His skills in horseback riding especially impressed his friends, not surprising in an era when cars, motorcycles, and airplanes were unknown and boys envied anyone who could ride a fast horse. Some of the events his friends remembered were as follows:

When Kiffin was four years old he attempted to ride an untamed Shetland pony on his grandfather's farm. The pony threw him to the ground again and again, but he wouldn't give up. By the end of the day, he had mastered that horse.[19]

When Kiffin was around 8 or 10 years old he began to demonstrate "indomitable will, unfailing courage, and small boy generalship." A friend had a Shetland pony named Dandy that would go into a "hump-backed, stiff-legged lunging and plunging act that wouldn't quit" if somebody tickled his flank. None of the other boys in the neighborhood could stay on him when he did this, even the boys who were fourteen years old. Kiffin, however, would stay on Dandy's back until the horse became exhausted and stood still, panting, with his tongue hanging out. Kiffin would also be panting and sweating from the exertion, but he was still seated on the horse.[20]

One day Kiffin was riding a larger horse named Kentucky Chief when the horse suddenly bolted for the stable. It was headed for a Dutch door and the top half of the door was closed, so the horse could run under it but there was no room for a rider. As the horse reached the stable Kiffin reached up, grabbed an overhanging beam, and let the horse run out from under him. He seemed totally unconcerned by this near disaster.[21]

Kiffin didn't always escape unharmed. When he was ten, the local newspaper reported that "Kiffin, the little son of Mrs. Loula Rockwell, fell while playing last Saturday and broke his ankle. Dr. Smith who has been attending the little fellow says he is getting along nicely and is able to be out again."[22]

The *Newport Plain Talk* newspaper, which was published weekly during the years the Rockwells lived in Newport, provides insight into what life was like in the small rural town where Kiffin grew up. Seemingly trivial things, like the fact that Loula built an addition to her house,[23] her sister came to visit,[24] and an automobile was seen in town,[25] were exciting enough to be newsworthy. The fact that life in Newport was quiet didn't mean it was idyllic, however. A short, matter-of-fact article in the *Plain Talk* also described a smallpox epidemic that was sweeping the area, so victims and suspected victims had been quarantined in the town jail.[26]

Newport opened a new "Newport Grammar School" in 1898, the year Kiffin started school. Kiffin's mother Loula helped organize the school and she began teaching at that school the year it opened. She soon became the principal. This was a remarkable achievement for a woman in that era, particularly in a conservative small town like Newport. In fact, after she left it would be a hundred years until Newport had another female principal.[27] Kiffin grew up "on strict orders from his mother," according to family friends. Kiffin and Paul were extremely close to each other, but while Kiffin was daring and athletic, Paul was what was known as a "sickly child." In addition to the normal run of childhood diseases, he caught pneumonia frequently and once had a bout with typhoid fever—the same disease that had killed his father.[28] According to family lore, when Paul was fourteen doctors were so convinced he wouldn't survive his latest case of pneumonia that they suggested Loula have Paul measured for a coffin.[29] Given the poor health and untimely death of her husband, Loula had good reason to worry about Paul's health.

Loula was not a woman to sit passively and worry. She wasn't satisfied with the results Paul was getting from the doctors in Newport, so she began looking into what today we would call "alternative medicine." She became interested in the practice of osteopathy, which was founded by Dr. Andrew Taylor Still, MD, in 1892. While not rejecting traditional medicines and surgery for the treatment of disease, Dr. Still emphasized a focus on the whole patient and founded the concept of "wellness." He believed problems with a body's structure could hamper its ability to fight disease, and he developed exercises and manual techniques to correct his patients' body structures.

Loula set a new goal for herself. She enrolled in the Kirksville College of Osteopathic Medicine in Kirksville, Missouri, a school founded by Dr. Still. In February 1904, she left Newport and moved her family to Kirksville so she could study osteopathy and place Paul under the care of Dr. Still.[30] At the time, it required two years of study to become a doctor of osteopathy (DO). In 1906, Paul graduated from Kirksville High School and Loula graduated from Kirksville College with her DO degree.[31] She never stopped worrying about Paul's health, but he no longer suffered from periodic bouts of pneumonia. Loula moved her family to Asheville, North Carolina, where she went into partnership with Dr. W. Banks Meacham.[32]

In Asheville, Loula rented a large rambling house at 142 Hillside Street. Originally built as a farmhouse in 1832, the city had expanded to the point that the house was now on its outskirts.[33] As the name implies, it was built on the side of a hill, overlooking the city of Asheville. The terrain and climate of Asheville were similar to that of Newport, but the city was much larger, with a population of more than fifteen thousand. It was a perfect place to raise a family, except that Loula's children had reached the point where they began leaving home.

Now that Paul had graduated from high school, Loula expected him to go to college. She had spent years preparing both boys for a life of scholarship,[34] but that wasn't what they wanted. Paul spent a few months in Asheville, and then he got a job with a surveying crew, scouting out possible railroad routes. He spent the winter of 1906–1907 surveying in Tennessee, North Carolina, and South Carolina. When summer came, he wandered up to New York, where he got a job as a ticket-taker on Coney Island. That job, and the urging of the people he worked with, convinced him that maybe he should go to college after all.[35]

In the fall of 1907, Paul enrolled in Wake Forest College. Wake Forest wasn't entirely to his liking, so the next year he transferred to Washington and Lee University in Lexington, Virginia. He listed his major as "history," but he took as many language courses as he could, as well as courses in politics, economics, and similar subjects.[36]

Agnes lived with her mother and Kiffin in Asheville until she graduated from high school in 1908. That fall she entered Wellesley College in Massachusetts,[37] leaving Kiffin the only child still at home. He attended high school at Asheville's Orange Street School, where a teacher described him as "a handsome, intelligent, chivalrous boy of fifteen, immaculate in person as in honor, impatient of the tedium of school routine, restive, though ever courteous under restraint; with serious deep-set, grayblue eyes, aglow with enthusiasm over tales of daring adventure; breaking rarely into surprising light of merriment."[38]

One aspect of Kiffin's personality that the teacher did not mention was his self-confidence. His mother jokingly referred to him as "Senator Smart" or "The Senator" because he looked like someone who was used to being in charge. Someone who knew what he wanted, and knew how to get it. In truth, he did not yet know what he wanted to do with his life, and he would explore several blind alleys before he found it, but that indecision was not apparent to others. When Kiffin's teacher wrote that he was "impatient of the tedium of school routine" and enthusiastic over "tales of daring adventure," she hit the nail squarely on the head. Kiffin had listened to his grandfather's tales of daring adventure for years, and he yearned for his own adventures. He also missed his brother Paul. Several people who knew them commented on how close the two brothers were, and years later Loula wrote that "probably few brothers were ever so close and dear to each other as these two."[39] Surprisingly, although Paul was four years older than Kiffin, Kiffin was "the directing head in his association with Paul."[40]

There are no records that explain why Kiffin decided to go to the Virginia Military Institute, but it's not hard to understand why it would appeal to him. It was located within walking distance of Washington and Lee University, where Paul was studying. VMI admitted students as young as fifteen, so Kiffin would not have to endure the "tedium of school routine" while waiting to graduate from high school. Best of all, it was a *military* institute. Uniforms, marching, drill, encampments—Kiffin could begin having his own adventures.

It's possible the idea of attending VMI took root when Paul came home from Washington and Lee for Christmas in 1908. It appears to have been a hasty decision, as in late January 1909 Loula wrote to the superintendent of VMI to let him know that Kiffin would "probably call upon you Saturday," and she asked that they consider admitting him to the Fourth Class. She thanked the superintendent for having sent a catalog and a letter (there had obviously been at least *some* prior planning), and she explained that although Kiffin had missed the fall semester, she thought the work he had done in Asheville would enable him to catch up. She went on to make several suggestions as to what classes he should take and what order he should take them in, fulfilling her role as a doting mother and ex-schoolteacher. She added that Kiffin was very anxious to attend military school, and she thought it would be best to do it soon because he was growing very tall and had a tendency to stoop.[41] (She underlined "stoop," possibly prompted by her concern, as a doctor of osteopathy, about the effect of his posture on his health.) The letter also said that if, after consulting the boy, the superintendent felt he was not ready to enter the Fourth Class, he could simply send Kiffin home. Kiffin must have made a good impression, as he signed into VMI on February 1, 1909, and became a Fourth Class cadet, popularly known as a "rat."

The education Kiffin received at VMI was significantly different from his Asheville high school experience. Often called the "West Point of the South," VMI emphasized muscular development and physical health as well as academics. Daily schedules were tightly controlled, with specified times for studying, eating, sleeping, bathing, exercising, and other activities. Rules were defined by a comprehensive book of regulations and were strictly enforced. The academic curriculum was surprisingly modern, with science and technology emphasized more than ancient languages and classic literature. VMI's *Official Register* (essentially a student handbook) stated that its primary objective was to teach cadets how to learn and proudly declared, "The Virginia Military Institute was the pioneer in this state in the effort to attain this great end of education through the instrumentality of the sciences rather than through classical studies."[42]

Although the environment, uniforms, and marching at VMI were distinctly military, the school was not exclusively focused on preparing students to serve in the army. The United States did not at that time have a large standing army, and VMI graduates did not necessarily go into the military. In fact, Virginia residents attending VMI had to promise to serve in the capacity of a teacher within the state for at least two years after graduating. The cost for tuition, room and board, and all incidentals except uniforms was $365 per year (the equivalent of about $10,000 today).

Kiffin enjoyed his time at VMI, finishing the year with a class ranking of 42 out of 120 despite the fact that he missed the first semester and began the second semester "out of sync" with his classmates. He was ranked ninth overall in German and scored in the top 20 percent in English.[43] He also managed to endure the all-too-common hazing by upperclassmen. In the early 1900s, hazing was common at many universities and fraternities in the

United States. At VMI, first-year students, or "rats," were routinely beaten with bed-slats, broomsticks, flats of bayonets, and other cudgels. A student who attended VMI a few years after Kiffin described the hazing in a letter to his father:

> Am getting along very well to be where I am but I don't like this place for they have almost killed several boys (rats) up here the last week. . . . It will certainly make a man out of you but I [would] rather not be a man if this was the only way of being one. One boy got a broom handle broken over him this morning and fifteen of as hard a lick as a great big stalwart man could hit with one of those short steel swords called bayonets. . . . They took my roommate ____ and laid him across two chairs and told him to say choo and just keep it up and as he was saying choo they almost strangled him by pouring water down his throat.[44]

Kiffin was allowed to visit his brother for lunch on Saturdays, and Paul was outraged when he saw the bruises on Kiffin's body. Kiffin laughed off his brother's concerns, saying, "It was all in the game and the best way to make men out of rats was to haze them."[45] In the end, it wasn't the beatings, waterboarding, or strict discipline at VMI that caused Kiffin to leave. It was a desire for action.

Kiffin wanted to take part in exciting battles like the ones his grandfather had described. The marching and drill at VMI didn't satisfy that desire. More important, he recognized that although VMI could help prepare him for a career in the army, it did not appear to him that there was going to be any military action in the foreseeable future. The Civil War had ended nearly fifty years earlier, the Spanish-American War had decisively eliminated whatever threat Spain might have presented, the Indian wars were over, and neither Canada nor Mexico seemed poised to launch an invasion. However, there did seem to be at least a possibility that the navy might see action. The US Navy's "Great White Fleet" had just returned from a trip around the world ordered by President Teddy Roosevelt, and he seemed intent on using the navy to project US power abroad.

It is not clear how Kiffin obtained an appointment to the US Naval Academy at Annapolis, but in the fall of 1909 he entered Werntz Preparatory School to study for the Naval Academy entrance exams. At this school he met many other students who were studying for exams, as well as midshipmen who were already enrolled in the Academy. They convinced him that it was not likely the navy would see action any time soon, and they also gave him an idea of what life was like in the peacetime navy. It was not something that appealed to Kiffin. He had already asked his mother to help him change schools twice within the past year, so he wrote to Paul and asked him to intercede with her.[46] Paul succeeded, and on November 23, 1909, Kiffin enrolled at Washington and Lee University. He joined the Sigma Phi Epsilon fraternity, where Paul was already a member, and they were both members of Theta Nu Epsilon. (ΘNE was a "secret" fraternity, originally begun as a chapter of Skull and Bones.) The two were once again inseparable.

Paul later described Kiffin at this point in his life in a letter:

> He was bright enough not to have to grind in order to learn his lessons, and had plenty of time to mix with the other students. A good judge of human nature, he did not quickly make friends with people and accept them into his intimacy; but he was never discourteous to anyone, and when he deemed someone worthy, he was a real and devoted friend. Therefore, he was very popular and well liked among his fellows. Tall and handsome, with clear blue eyes, a graceful dancer and of a pleasing manner, he was much sought after by the girls, but he was not of a sentimental nature.[47]

Kiffin returned to Washington and Lee in the fall of 1910, but Paul did not. Paul wanted to enter the US Consular or Diplomatic Service, and since he had already taken all the modern language courses offered at W&L, he decided to move to Washington, D.C., and put his education to use. He spent the winter of 1910–1911 in Washington, but apparently diplomatic work was not forthcoming because in the spring he moved to Atlanta, Georgia, and became a reporter for the *Atlanta Constitution*.[48]

Kiffin completed the 1910–1911 school year at Washington and Lee but couldn't decide upon a major. At this point his mother told him he "needed to learn the worth of a dollar."[49] Kiffin agreed to go to work, with the assurance that his mother would help him get back into college once he decided what he wanted to do with his life. He teamed up with three friends and organized "The Southern Press Bureau." This company helped newspapers publish special advertising editions. Kiffin hit the road and traveled westward through the northern United States and southern Canada, selling the idea to local newspapers and helping them produce the special editions.

Kiffin spent two years traveling across the country, eventually settling in San Francisco. He liked San Francisco and started his own advertising company there.[50] Kiffin obviously had a flair for advertising, as the company grew to employ twenty people, but he missed his family. In the fall of 1913, Kiffin left San Francisco and returned to Asheville. He spent a few months with his mother and then traveled to Atlanta to see his brother.[51] He arrived on New Year's Day 1914.

At the time, Paul was living in the Sigma Phi Epsilon fraternity house at the Georgia Institute of Technology. He had stayed up late the night before, celebrating the New Year with his fraternity brothers, and he was sound asleep when Kiffin arrived. As he gradually regained consciousness, he had the uncomfortable feeling that someone was staring at him. He opened his eyes and saw Kiffin looking down at him with an amused expression on his face.

They spent the next few days catching up on the past two years. Resolving never again to part company, they rented an apartment on West Peachtree Street. Their attempt to publish a paper they called "The Commerce of Greater Atlanta" failed miserably, but Paul kept his job with the *Atlanta Constitution* and Kiffin found a job with the Massengale Advertising Agency. Britt Craig, another reporter for the *Atlanta Constitution*, wrote about meeting the two of them that spring:

> Not quite three years ago I stood on the corner of East Hunter Street and Whitehall and talked with a solemn, whimsical young man. . . . He carried a leather wallet that contained bills owed by bad debtors of the advertising concern with which he was then employed. It was a sunny day and the young man was reluctant to ply his business of collecting bad debts. He preferred to linger in this sunny spot and comment upon passing events and shopgirls, for it was in the shopping district. He had the solemn mien of a newspaper humorist, but there was the wistful glow of a dreamer in his eyes. . . . It was Kiffin Rockwell, and his brother Paul was standing with us. Now, of the two Paul was the more popular. Care-free, debonair, impulsive, he was the sort of fellow who made friends easily. Paul laughed when there was occasion. Kiffin smiled—reluctantly, it sometimes seemed. It also seemed that Kiffin

said the funniest things—whenever he said them—by reason of the fact that you hardly expected Kiffin to say anything funny. Kiffin was quiet, retiring—almost timid. Paul was laughing, gay. Kiffin meditated a lot, Paul laughed a lot. They loved each other devotedly, and were as nearly inseparable as brothers ever are.[52]

Several people who knew Kiffin at this time described him as serious and contemplative. One writer also described him as "quick to anger and visibly intolerant of those whose standards of conduct he felt did not measure up. To Kiffin there were no shades of gray; the world and everything in it was white, or it was black."[53] He made a strong impression on others. Many people described him as being at least six feet, four inches tall, but his 1914 passport lists his height as six feet, one and a half inches.[54] Back then, passports did not include a photograph,[55] but they did include a description. Kiffin's was as follows:

Age: 21
Height: 6' 1½"
Forehead: high broad
Eyes: blue-gray
Nose: straight
Mouth: medium
Chin: square
Hair: brown
Complexion: fair
Face: long

For Paul and Kiffin, the spring and early summer of 1914 were filled with the excitement of new plans, a new apartment, a new job, and being together again. The only shadow came in late June, when their grandfather fell ill. They returned to Asheville for a few weeks to be with their mother during this difficult time. Their grandfather, Enoch Ayres, died on July 26, 1914. He left an estate valued at $14,400, the equivalent of about $350,000 today. Not an insignificant estate for a family farm, but a far cry from the fortunes of men whom Paul and Kiffin were soon to meet. The estate was divided equally among Enoch's surviving children, and Loula received $1,960 ($50,000 in today's money).[56]

When Kiffin and Paul returned to Atlanta, Europe was on the verge of war. This led to the fateful conversation at the lunch counter. In the midst of their frantic packing for New York and beyond, Kiffin made time to visit his boss, St. Elmo Massengale, to tell him he was leaving for Europe. Massengale, who had a very high opinion of Kiffin, tried to dissuade him. "I asked him if he realized he might be killed," Massengale later wrote. "He said he was not afraid at all—that he believed whatever happened would be for the best. That God knew when and where his time would come, whether here or there, in peace or war, and that he thought his duty was to go."[57]

For Kiffin, this must have been an easy decision. He had spent his entire life yearning for adventure. He had briefly attended three different colleges, traveled across the country, and established an advertising business in San Francisco. Now he was more or less settled in Atlanta, collecting bad debts. The biggest war the world had ever seen was erupting in Europe, undoubtedly with cavalry charges, bugle calls, and all the excitement his grandfather had described. It was a war that he was clearly convinced would be fought between the forces of good and evil. It was a chance to fight for what he described as "the cause of all humanity, the greatest of all causes."[58]

2

War!

The lamps are going out all over Europe. We shall not see them lit again in our lifetime.

—Sir Edward Grey

World War I was nothing like the war Kiffin expected. He was not alone in this, as almost no one anticipated the protracted stalemate, massive casualties, and outright butchery that characterized the "war to end war." There had been incidents of trench warfare and stalemate during the American Civil War, the Boer War, and the Russo-Japanese War, but no one saw them as evidence that modern firepower had made cavalry charges and mass infantry assaults obsolete. Those were "brush wars," conflicts that occurred in far-away places. Those wars weren't being fought by Europe's well-trained armies. Occasionally a fiction writer would try to imagine what would happen when the science of the Industrial Revolution was applied to the problem of annihilating humans from a neighboring country. In *The Human Slaughter-House*, for example, German author Wilhelm Lamszus imagined a war so devastating that the soldiers would go insane because of the mass carnage that surrounded them.[1] That was simply fiction, of course. Somewhat more troubling was the warning given by retired general Helmuth von Moltke to the German Reichstag in 1900. General Moltke had been the hero of 1870, leading Germany's armies in a series of rapid victories that defeated the French army and created a unified Germany. His words carried a lot of weight. "The age of a cabinet war is behind us," he told the assembled lawmakers. "All we have now is people's war." He predicted that a future war between major powers would not be won by one or two campaigns, because neither side would admit defeat until it had been crushed as a nation. "It may be a war of seven years' or of thirty years' duration—and woe to him who sets Europe alight, who first puts the fuse to the powder keg."[2]

Despite these warnings, virtually all the politicians, soldiers, and populations in Europe expected the war to be short, glorious, and, of course, victorious for their side. In the capitals of the warring nations, excited crowds thronged the streets, cheering the bellicose speeches of politicians and showering soldiers with flowers as they marched off to war. They had no idea they were welcoming a cataclysm that would last four years, kill seventeen million people, and leave twenty million wounded. Nor did they realize that many of the soldiers they cheerily sent to the front would disappear into the face of the earth, their bodies shattered beyond all recognition as they were buried, unburied, and reburied by successive explosions. If they were lucky, their remains would eventually be placed in a cemetery with a cross, one of thousands, labeled "Inconnu" (Unknown). Inconnu, inconnu, inconnu—row after row after row.

When Kiffin and Paul decided to go to France, all this was in the future. The cheering crowds, the screaming shells, and the bitter remorse had not yet begun. Austria-Hungary had declared war on Serbia to avenge the killing of their archduke, but the rest of Europe had not yet plunged into war. Not quite. But a complex series of treaties and alliances, combined with miscalculations, misunderstandings, and a few outright lies, inexorably dragged one country after another into the war. On Saturday, August 1, the day before Kiffin and Paul made their fateful decision at the lunch counter, Germany declared war on Russia, and France began mobilizing for war with Germany. On August 2, when Kiffin and Paul decided to fight for France, Germany demanded Belgium allow her troops free passage to attack France. Belgium refused on August 3, the day that Kiffin and Paul wrote to the French consulate in New Orleans. (Amazingly, they were not the only Americans to offer their services to the consulate that day. Edgar Bouligny of New Orleans went there in person and volunteered.)[3] This was also the day that Germany declared war on France and sent troops into Belgium. England gave Germany an ultimatum: withdraw those troops within twenty-four hours or England would declare war. That evening the British foreign secretary, Sir Edward Grey, watched the street lamps being lit outside Whitehall. He turned to a friend and said, "The lamps are going out all over Europe. We shall not see them lit again in our lifetime."[4] On August 4, the day Kiffin and Paul boarded a train for New York, England declared war on Germany. That was also the day President Wilson announced that the United States would remain neutral in the European war. The following day, Kiffin and Paul demonstrated their thoughts on the matter by stopping in Washington, D.C., to get their passports. This was the day the German Army began bombarding the forts at Liege, Belgium. On August 7, Kiffin and Paul boarded the SS *Saint Paul* in New York and set out for England. The French launched their first attack against Germany that day, in the Alsace region, roughly two hundred miles south of where the Germans were attacking. Why were the first battles so far apart? And why did the Germans begin the war by attacking Belgium instead of France? To understand these actions, and the subsequent four years of stalemate, we need to look at the war plans.

German war plans were based upon the fact that Germany was facing a war on two fronts. Russia and France were bound by treaties to come to each other's aid if either was attacked by Germany. France had a modern army, excellent communications, and excellent railroads. Germany knew that when war came, France would attack within days. France had also built an impressive series of forts along the border with Germany. Attacking France along this border would require a long, costly siege.

Russia lagged far behind Germany and France in terms of infrastructure. It would take Russia weeks to gather her army and march it to the German border, but once it arrived it would be a vast, virtually unstoppable force. People often described the Russian Army as a "steamroller." Defending against this attack would require the entire German Army, leaving Germany vulnerable to an attack by France.

In 1905, a German general named Alfred von Schlieffen had devised a bold plan to overcome these obstacles. His plan counted on the Russians taking a long time to mobilize. Germany would only deploy a small force in the east to slow down the Russian advance when it finally materialized. Similarly, Germany would only deploy a small force along the French border. This force would not attempt to attack the strong French fortifications. Instead, it would wait for the inevitable French attack. Schlieffen expected the French to drive this force back, but the German troops would slow the French advance and wear it down in the process. The main German force would sweep north through Belgium, bypassing the French fortifications, and then turn south to catch the French Army from behind.[5] The French would be caught between two German forces and destroyed. With France knocked out of the war, Germany could concentrate all her forces on defeating the Russian Army. It was a risky plan at best, and it virtually guaranteed German troops would be forced to fall back along the eastern and western borders, subjecting German lands and German people to temporary occupation by the enemy. It also meant that Germany would violate Belgium's neutrality, which could bring England into the war. Nevertheless, the German General Staff felt it was the only way to win.

French plans were heavily influenced by the humiliating loss they had suffered in their war with Germany in 1870. In that war the German Army had marched across the border and quickly encircled the French Army. The immediate French reaction to that loss was to aggressively build forts along the German border. They also took a long, critical look at the way they had fought in 1870. They began that war by going on the defensive, letting the Germans decide when and where to attack. From that moment on, the French never regained the initiative. The war had been a series of German attacks and French retreats. Not only was that a losing strategy, but it also ignored France's best weapon—the spirit of her people. The will to win, the élan vital that had carried a ragged throng to victory when they stormed the Bastille, had not been used against the invaders. This led to major changes in French military doctrine. The "doctrine of the offensive" came to dominate French thinking at their war college. General Ferdinand Foch was one of the foremost advocates of this doctrine, spouting phrases like "The will to conquer is the first condition of victory," and "A battle won is a battle in which one will not confess oneself beaten." Foch clearly understood the realities of modern warfare, however. He condemned the idea that morale alone could lead to victory as an "infantile notion." He lectured on the elements of firepower, the need for protective cover, and other practical considerations.[6] Unfortunately, the inspiration provided by his attack philosophy was much more compelling than his lectures on reality. The students of Foch soon emphasized the doctrine of the offensive to the point of absurdity. Colonel de Grandmaison, French chief of operations for the General Staff, was famously quoted as saying, "For the attack only two things are necessary: to know where the enemy is and to decide what to do. What the enemy intends to do is of no consequence."[7] Tragically, during the brief moments between when they leaped to attack and when the spark of life left their writhing bodies, millions of French troops would soon learn that what the enemy intended to do *was* of consequence.

As the doctrine of the offensive came to dominate French military thinking, their war plans placed very little reliance on the border forts and focused on attacking Germany directly. In this plan, known as Plan XVII, their forces would sweep around the German fortifications at Metz and head straight for Berlin. They did not ignore the possibility that the Germans would attack through Belgium; in fact, they felt it would be easier to defeat the Germans if they did this. If the main German attack took the "long way around" and marched through Belgium, the forces guarding the border with France would be weak. The French attack would then smash through those forces and swing northward, severing the German right wing from its base and rendering it powerless.

While France and Germany were putting these plans into action, Kiffin and Paul departed from New York aboard the SS *Saint Paul*. They had not taken time to notify their mother before they left Atlanta, so Kiffin wrote to her from their hotel in New York City the night before they shipped out. Paul had already written to let her know their plans, so Kiffin's letter focused on explaining why they were going to war. He tried to convince her that it was the right thing to do: "You have always told me that you wanted me to live my life without interference, and this opportunity is one that only comes once in a lifetime." Kiffin said it would be "a great opportunity" for Paul because it would get him "into the line of being a good short story writer." He closed his argument by saying, "You know I have always been a great dreamer and I just couldn't keep myself from this trip, for I felt the call of opportunity. You have always said you had great faith in my future and now is the time for you to prove it, by not worrying about me."[8] The letter was not entirely successful in convincing Loula, as she almost immediately started trying to get them sent home.

Kiffin and Paul's voyage to England was uneventful and pleasant. The passenger list included a duchess, two or three lords, and a number of military officers as well as the famous author and columnist Irvin S. Cobb. Kiffin and Paul got to know Colonel Sam Reber, the chief of the US Army's Aviation Department, during this voyage. At the time, the entire Army Aviation Department consisted of 44 officers, 224 men, and 23 aircraft. Also on board was a man who claimed to be a Hungarian officer in the Red Cross, but whom Kiffin suspected of being a spy. Apparently the British shared

Kiffin's concern about the Hungarian, as the ship was ordered to stop before it got to Liverpool. A British cruiser pulled alongside and sent over a boarding party that arrested several Germans and the Hungarian.

The arrest of the suspected spy delayed their arrival until Saturday, August 15. Kiffin and Paul hurried to London, and then, somewhat surprisingly, they stopped to see the sights. They had been in such a rush to get to France that they didn't stop to say good-bye to their mother, but now they paused to spend ten days sightseeing in London. Kiffin wrote a long letter to his mother describing some of the sights they were seeing. Then, on August 25, Kiffin and Paul were once again in a hurry. They stored their trunks in London and hurried across the channel to France. The reason they seemingly stopped for sightseeing was divulged in a newspaper story two years later. The delay was the fault of the man who claimed to be a Hungarian Red Cross official. Kiffin and Paul were "detained" by the authorities (probably just warned not to leave the country) for ten days because they had been "found in company with a German spy" and the police needed time to check their story.[9] Kiffin undoubtedly neglected to mention this fact to his mother because it would have caused her to have even more doubts about their trip.

In France, a lot had happened since Kiffin and Paul left New York. The German right wing had effectively crushed the Belgian Army and was marching almost unimpeded toward France. The forts at Liège delayed them for a few days, but the Germans brought up massive 420 mm (16.5 inch) mortars nicknamed "Big Berthas," which quickly reduced the forts to rubble. The Germans were marching to Paris on schedule.[10] The British Expeditionary Force held up a portion of the right wing for two days at Mons, but they were forced to withdraw the day before Kiffin and Paul landed in France.

Farther south, the French were being stopped dead by the German left wing. Plan XVII was proving to be a disaster. The German Army had grown significantly since Schlieffen first developed his plan, and the Germans had been able to strengthen their left wing as a result. The primary reason for the failure of the French attacks, however, was that at this point in history technology strongly favored the defense, especially if the defenders had time to dig in and prepare fire pits or shallow trenches to protect themselves. No amount of élan vital would enable unprotected infantry and cavalry to stand up to the concentrated fire of machine guns, clip-fed rifles, and quick-firing artillery. It wasn't for lack of trying. On one day alone, August 22, the French Army lost twenty-seven thousand men who were killed trying to execute Plan XVII.[11] The only good news for the Allies was that the Russians had mobilized a portion of their army faster than expected and, rather than wait for full mobilization, this force was attacking East Prussia much sooner than the Germans had expected.

Paris was still optimistic. The French had not yet grasped the fact that the fighting in Belgium signaled the onslaught of a massive German right wing, and in France the battles on the German border were being portrayed as victories. Kiffin and Paul arrived in Paris and found a number of other Americans had already volunteered to fight for France. These Americans were already in France when the war broke out and they were eager to serve. In fact, so many foreigners had flocked to French military offices, offices already overwhelmed by the massive effort of mobilizing the French Army, that the minister of war announced that foreign volunteers would not be accepted until August 21.

Even after that time, there was a problem. Before Kiffin and Paul departed, President Wilson had announced that the United States would remain neutral in this war. He further emphasized this decision by declaring that Americans "must be neutral in fact as well as in name . . . must be impartial in our thought as well as in action" and must curb "every transaction that might be construed as a preference of one part of the struggle before another."[12] Most of the Americans who were willing to fight for France cared very little about what the president said, but he had the legal power to back up his words. A law passed in 1907 said any American citizen who took an oath of allegiance to any foreign state would forfeit their American citizenship.[13] To enlist in the French Army, they would have to take an oath of allegiance to France. A similar oath prevented them from joining the British Army.

Several Americans went to the American Embassy to see what could be done. Ambassador Myron T. Herrick was a holdover from the Taft administration, and he did not see eye to eye with Wilson on this issue. He dutifully read the applicable passages of the law to the young men and then slammed his fist on the table and said, "That is the law, boys, but if I were young and in your shoes, by God I know mighty well what I would do!"[14] He then suggested the risk to their citizenship would be much less if they joined the French Foreign Legion. The Foreign Legion was a famous (and infamous) unit that had been specifically created to allow foreigners to serve in the French military. Individuals who joined the Legion (or the Légion Étrangère, as it was officially titled) did not have to take an oath of allegiance to France. They only had to promise "to serve with faithfulness and honor" and to "follow the corps . . . wherever the government wishes to send it."[15]

Thanks to Hollywood, the stereotype of the Foreign Legion is a mixture of scoundrels and heartbroken romantics, fighting desperate battles in desert outposts. That is partly true, as the Legion had long served in Algiers, but they also fought in Mexico, Africa, the Crimea, Indo-China, and multiple European locations. The Legion did not ask questions about the backgrounds of its volunteers; it did not even care whether they enlisted under an assumed name. This made it a refuge for anyone trying to start a new life, including criminals. Technically it was an organization of mercenaries, although the harsh discipline and the salary of one *sou* (roughly 1 penny) per day meant a recruit really had to be down on his luck to seek his fortune in the Legion. Because of its reputation for tough fighting, the French Army considered the Legion an elite unit; yet in some ways it was also scorned by the army. Civilians tended to lie low and hide their valuables whenever the Legion camped nearby.

To the Americans eager to serve France in 1914, the Legion was exactly what they were looking for. Dozens of men enlisted when the recruiting stations opened on August 21, and they were joined by Kiffin and Paul on August 27, the day they arrived in Paris.[16] Normally, enlistments in the Legion were for a period of five years, but the Americans were allowed to enlist for the duration of the war only.[17] Skeptical recruits were assured the war would not last longer than nine months.[18] Forty-three Americans volunteered during those first few days, and they comprised a very diverse group. One of them, René Phélizot, was a big game hunter, a profession that back then combined the prestige of an arctic explorer with the fame of a professional athlete. Another volunteer was Alan Seeger. A graduate of Harvard University, he was already recognized as a rising poet. He would soon write the prophetic "I Have a Rendezvous with Death," which would become one of John F. Kennedy's favorite poems. Kenneth Weeks was an MIT graduate who went to France to study architecture but soon became known as a playwright and essayist. By 1914, he had published five books of plays, short stories, and essays. Already a wealthy man, he would share whatever comforts and luxuries he could find with his fellow legionnaires.[19] Fred Zinn was a recently graduated civil engineer from Galesburg, Michigan. An unassuming man, his IQ registered at the genius level (168).[20] When he graduated from the University of Michigan in 1914, he used his meager savings to travel to France as a graduation present to himself before settling down to a life of engineering. In Paris he joined the Foreign Legion, after which he saw a lot more of France than he'd bargained for.

Bill Thaw was born in Pittsburgh, Pennsylvania, the son of a prominent businessman and multimillionaire. He dutifully attended Yale for two years before deciding that college and business were not for him. He dropped out of school and learned to fly at the Curtiss School of Aviation. He purchased a Curtiss Model E Hydro flying boat and soon made headlines by flying *underneath* all four of New York City's East River bridges. After successfully competing in air races in the United States, he traveled to France to participate in the Schneider Trophy competition on the French Riviera. Newspapers referred to him as "the playboy of the Riviera."[21] A large, impressively built man, he had an imposing face that somehow looked as though he had been born with a moustache. The war erupted while he was in Paris. Thaw volunteered his services as a pilot but was told that France already had all the pilots she needed. He then donated his plane to the French government and enlisted in the Foreign Legion, at a penny a day.

Bert Hall came from a very different background than Bill Thaw. He was born in Higginsville, Missouri, and named Weston Birch Hall by his father, who had served as an orderly during the Civil War. Like Kiffin's grandfather, he was an "unreconstructed" Confederate. Bert worked at a number of jobs before the war—farmhand, railroad worker, circus hand, chauffeur, political "muscle," and merchant seaman. He was a compact man with a smile that looked as though he was about to make a wisecrack (which he frequently did). Bert was not known for telling the truth if he could invent a better story. As an example, he claimed to have once been a human cannonball with a circus. He actually had worked for a circus, but as a marketer—someone who put up posters and called people to see side shows.[22] Bert was driving a taxi in Paris when the war broke out, and he was one of the first Americans to join the Legion. Just why he volunteered has never been clear, as he was not one to be carried away by sentiments and ideals, but it may have seemed like an interesting adventure.

The volunteers were sent by train to a French training center at Rouen, about seventy miles northwest of Paris. The first train left Paris on August 25. The volunteers hadn't been issued uniforms yet, so they were still dressed in civilian clothes.[23] There was one American who did not make the trip to Rouen, however—one who, according to some accounts, was dismayed to discover that he could only serve France by joining the Foreign Legion. Gervais Raoul Lufbery had been born and raised in France. His father had been born in the United States but moved to France, where he married Raoul's mother. She died when Raoul was an infant. His father soon remarried, left Raoul and his two brothers in the care of French relatives, and took his new bride to Wallingford, Connecticut. As Raoul grew up, he took a series of odd jobs and wandered through North Africa, Turkey, Germany, and the Balkans. In 1906, he decided to pay a surprise visit to his father in Connecticut. Raoul landed in New York at almost the exact time his father boarded a ship to France. He missed his father then and never saw him again in his life.[24]

Raoul wandered across the United States, joined the US Army and saw action in the Philippines, and eventually wound up in India. There he met a French exhibition pilot, Marc Pourpe, who was in need of a mechanic. Raoul had never worked on an airplane before, but he was a quick learner, and the two men spent 1913 barnstorming across Europe and Africa. Pourpe made headlines with a series of flights from Cairo, Egypt, to Khartoum, Sudan, and back, a feat that was only possible because Raoul preceded him every step of the way by train, camel, or foot with essential tools, parts, and fuel.[25] In 1914, they returned to France to buy a new airplane. Then the war broke out. Pourpe immediately enlisted as a pilot in the French Army, and Lufbery tried to enlist as his mechanic. Much to his surprise, he was rejected because he was not French. He was American. Raoul had always considered himself French,[26] but because his father was an American citizen who resided in the United States, Raoul was a US citizen.[27] Lufbery had to enlist in the Foreign Legion, and he was then detailed to Army Aviation to serve as Pourpe's mechanic. In the years to come, this same process would be used by many Americans who enlisted in the Legion and then went directly to pilot training.

When the first American volunteers reached Rouen, they were billeted in an old machine shop. Some of the men were issued partial uniforms, depending on available supplies. Bert Hall wrote of receiving stiff, tan-colored fatigues and a pair of ankle boots that hurt his feet.[28] Others received less, and by the time Kiffin and Paul arrived on August 28 they received no uniforms at all. Kiffin wrote his mother and described the conditions in Rouen:

> Paul and I are here drilling with the American corps and about sixteen hundred other foreigners from every land. I think Paul wrote you about our joining. As it is very hard to get letters through and we are not allowed to write much about what we are doing, will only tell you that both of us are well and feeling fine. It is, of course, a little rough, but it will make men of us both.
>
> We left Paris Friday morning and arrived here in the afternoon. Since then we have been living the army life, except that we have not yet gotten our uniforms. The American branch is quite a mixture, but there are several fine fellows. Yale, Harvard, Michigan, Columbia, Cornell and several other schools are represented by graduates. There are two or three college professors and two lawyers. We drill about six hours a day and have three hours that we do what we please.
>
> This will be the last letter I shall write you for some time, as they don't like for us to write letters, and they read them all and don't send them if one talks too much. Everyone uses postcards and I will "follow suit" after this. We do not expect to be here much longer but guess mail will be forwarded from this address.
>
> We both hope that you will not worry, as this is a great thing for us to do.[29]

One aspect of Rouen that Kiffin didn't mention in this letter was the chaos that was beginning to envelop the town as the German right wing bore down on it. It was now obvious that a very large German force had swept through Belgium and was marching toward Paris. When Kiffin and Paul arrived in Rouen, the Germans were ninety miles away. Four days later, they were within sixty miles. The French had given up their attacks along the German border, and the Russian Army that had excited everyone with its early attack had been soundly defeated at Tannenberg. Paris was being bombed by German aircraft, and the French government would soon leave Paris and move to Bordeaux. David King, another American volunteer, described the atmosphere in Rouen that Kiffin hid from his mother:

The city was teeming with a marvelous, heterogeneous collection: wounded from the British Army, stragglers from the Belgian Army, refugees, French reservists, British Army Service Corps units—all wandering around the streets aimlessly, some terribly depressed, others hilarious and singing, and a good portion of them drunk.[30]

On the morning of September 1, roughly two thousand Foreign Legion recruits, including the Americans, were loaded into French *Hommes quarante, Chevaux huit* (Men: forty, Horses: eight) boxcars and evacuated to Toulouse.[31] Toulouse was located near the border with Spain, where they would be safe from the German onslaught.[32]

While the volunteers were traveling to Toulouse, the first cracks began to appear in the German advance. German infantrymen had marched more than two hundred miles in the hot August sun, with full pack and combat equipment, and had fought multiple battles against British, French, and Belgian troops along the way. They were exhausted, and they were outrunning their supply lines, so they were also weakened by hunger.[33] The closer they got to Paris, the more French resistance they encountered. Units turned to face attacking forces and left the flanks of their neighboring units exposed. French and British reconnaissance aircraft gave early proof of how important airplanes would be in this war when they revealed these gaps in the advancing German line.[34] The fact that the General Staff had strengthened the German left wing may have worked against them, as, instead of giving way when the French attacked and drawing the French armies farther away from Paris, they had stopped the French attacks on the border, where they could more quickly be redeployed to meet the advancing right wing. Schlieffen had planned on the French pushing the left wing back and clearing the way for the right wing, like a "revolving door."[35] Instead, these French troops were rushed northward to help stop the German attack in what became known as the "Battle of the Marne." The German advance stalled, and they began to dig in to defend against the French attacks. Both sides repeatedly tried to outflank each other, and they dug in when each attempt failed. The so-called Race to the Sea ended when they reached the English Channel. The exhausted armies faced each other across a makeshift series of trenches and foxholes that extended all across France and Belgium, from the Swiss border to the English Channel.

It's hard to comprehend the vast number of troops, the fierce fighting, and the staggering casualties that resulted from these battles. The French are believed to have lost 329,000 men killed, wounded, or taken prisoners in a little more than a month. The Germans lost almost 300,000 men on the Western Front during the same period, and an additional 67,000 men on the Eastern Front. Accurate figures on Russian and Austrian casualties are virtually nonexistent, but they have been estimated at roughly 550,000 and 400,000, respectively. Add in British and Belgian casualties, and the opening campaigns of World War I resulted in more than two million men killed, wounded, or captured. To put this total into perspective, the American Civil War was the bloodiest war in US history. During that war, the Union suffered 600,000 casualties while the Confederates lost 490,000, resulting in total casualties of almost 1.1 million men. The first five weeks of World War I caused nearly twice as many casualties as the four years of the American Civil War.

This was the kind of war that Kiffin and Paul had entered.

3

Life in the Foreign Legion

We are the famous Legion, that they talk about so much.
People lock up everything, whenever we're about.
We're noted for our pillaging, the nifty way we steal.
We'd pinch a baby carriage, and the infant for a meal.

—FOREIGN LEGION MARCHING SONG

THE TRIP TO TOULOUSE WAS LONG, SLOW, AND HOT. CONSIDERING THE military situation at the time, with the desperate rush to move combat units to the front, it's amazing anyone even thought to evacuate a group of untrained recruits from Rouen. Expediting transportation for them was not at the top of anyone's agenda. Thus, the train creaked and groaned its way south, frequently being shunted onto sidings to let northbound trains carry troops to the front. It took more than four days in the hot August sun to make the trip, averaging less than eight miles per hour. As might be expected when wooden boxcars are used to transport horses on one trip and soldiers on the next, neither of which have had frequent opportunities to bathe, the atmosphere in the cars was pungent, to say the least.

A "Forty and Eight" boxcar, meant to hold forty men or eight horses, measured 20.5 by 8.5 feet. Narrow shutters at the top of each side could be opened for ventilation, and the sliding center doors were often left open as well. These provided some relief, especially when the train was moving. Occasionally the train would stop at a station, and the thirsty recruits swarmed the platform trying to get a drink and fill their canteens. The train seldom stopped long enough for everyone to get water before officers began herding troops back into the boxcars. Although forty men was supposed to be the limit, on this trip some cars were packed with as many as fifty-six men. That meant there was only enough room for about half the men to sit down at any one time, and no room to stretch out unless men lay on top of each other. In the rush to evacuate Rouen, each man was issued an industrial-sized can of corned beef. They were told to form groups of four and share one can each day. A few recruits were too suspicious to share. They opened their can on the first day and tried to make it last. The meat soon spoiled in the sweltering heat of the boxcar. The first deaths due to food poisoning occurred on the morning of the fourth day.[1]

When the train finally arrived in Toulouse, officers formed up the tired, sweaty recruits and marched them through town to the training camp. Most were still wearing the rumpled remnants of civilian clothes, carrying the few military items like canteens they had been issued in Rouen. Some were wearing partial uniforms, but they were tan canvas training fatigues, not the blue coats and red trousers of the regular French Army. None carried rifles. To their surprise, the townspeople began to shout insults and hurl rotten fruit at them. The recruits who could understand French soon realized they were being mistaken for German prisoners. The howling mob paid no attention to the officers who tried to correct them, so the recruits double-timed to the security of the training camp.[2]

The next day all recruits were issued coarse canvas fatigues, a heavy blue greatcoat, stiff hobnailed boots, wool shirts, and two sets of long underwear. Socks were not issued, but if a recruit requested them, he would be given a handful of small muslin squares. Theoretically, if wrapped around the foot in the correct overlapping pattern, these would prevent blisters. They were also given a knapsack, blankets, an 8 mm Lebel rifle, bayonet, cartridges, and a mess kit along with emergency rations: twenty pieces of hard tack, two cans of "monkey meat,"[3] and a small bag of sugar and coffee.[4] When deploying, they also carried a pick, a shovel, a canteen, and 125 rounds of ammunition.[5] All told, this equipment tipped the scales at about seventy pounds and had to be carried on the soldier's back.[6]

Training primarily consisted of bayonet practice and long forced marches with full pack. Bayonet practice involved running across a half-mile wide field and stabbing a straw dummy. Little time was spent on rifle practice, and almost no time was spent learning how to dig trenches, erect barbed wire obstacles, or emplace machine guns. This was, after all, the era of the "doctrine of the offensive." Recruits were taught that the use of deep trenches was tantamount to hiding from the enemy. Their training handbook stated, "From the moment of action every soldier must passionately desire the assault by bayonet as the supreme means of imposing his will on the enemy."[7] In any event, the Model 1868 Lebel Rifle issued to the recruits was an ungainly weapon for shooting, but when fitted with a bayonet it made an intimidating six-foot-long spear. The rifle held eight tapered rounds in a tubular magazine, which made it difficult to load and prone to jamming. When the war started, most units had already replaced these with more modern, clip-fed versions of the Lebel, and the Legion would eventually follow suit.

A typical training day started at four in the morning, with a breakfast cup of coffee. Recruits soon learned to save bread from the previous day to supplement this coffee. Marching and bayonet drill followed, with lunch served at 11:00 a.m. Lunch was the heavy meal of the day, consisting of soup with meat, bread, a cup of coffee, and one cup of red wine. More training and drill followed, with the final meal at 5:00 p.m. Typically this was some sort of a goulash made with meat, lentils, beans, potatoes or rice, and another cup of coffee or wine. The bread was stamped with the date it was made, and troops could refuse it if it was more than ten days old. There was no guarantee it would be replaced with a fresh loaf, however, so refusal usually meant going without.[8] The men were free to go into town from 5:00 until 9:00 p.m. After the war, Paul Rockwell wrote a detailed history of his time with the Legion in which he said recruits who had money could skip the evening meal at the barracks and enjoy dinner at "one of the various restaurants for which Toulouse is famous."[9] This, of course, assumed that the penny-a-day recruits had the money to pay for dinner and weren't too tired to go into town. Paul did admit that even the millionaire's son Bill Thaw soon ran out of the money he had with him when he enlisted.[10] Kiffin sent a postcard to his mother that opened with "Have been so busy for the last four or five days that I haven't had time to even write a card. Have been getting up at four A.M. and working as much as fourteen hours a day."[11] Kenneth Weeks wrote his mother that he had not had a bath for a month and he slept fully clothed, as he had somehow missed the blanket issue.[12]

One morning the recruits awoke to the sound of a military band. Looking out the window, they saw several hundred experienced legionnaires of the Second Regiment, newly arrived from North Africa, marching across the courtyard in an impressive parade.[13] The veterans were there to drill with the recruits and show them how things were done in the Legion. The recruits were further buoyed when they were finally issued regulation French Army uniforms: a blue jacket, red breeches, short black leggings, a red kepi (hat), and a nine-foot-long blue sash to be wound around the waist.[14]

If the experienced trainers and new uniforms were a boost to morale, payday was definitely a letdown. They were paid every ten days, so the recruits were expecting a windfall of ten cents. On their first payday, they discovered they were actually paid seven cents and issued a small bag of tobacco, for which three cents was deducted from their pay. Of course, they had to sign a receipt for these wages, "just as if we were getting a million dollars out of a bank," as Bert Hall put it.[15] The tobacco was no bargain, either. David King described it thus: "Considered as firewood it wasn't bad. Every ten days the Government issued a package per man, called *Scaferlati des Troupes*. It was mostly the stalks of tobacco plants, and you had to spread it on a handkerchief, pick out the longer pieces, and chop them up before you could possibly roll it into a cigarette. Hardly worth the trouble as it was poisonous stuff, anyway."[16]

The recruits who didn't smoke were at first outraged by being issued tobacco as part of their pay, but they soon learned they could sell their tobacco to others at a good price.[17]

The training was intended to last for six months, but the enormous losses suffered by the French during the opening weeks of the campaign created a desperate need for replacements. On September 12, it was announced that the veteran legionnaires would soon be sent into action, and a call went out for volunteers to accompany them. Because of the short time they had been in training, only recruits with previous military experience would be considered. Amazingly, almost all the Americans had previous experience. Many described exploits during various revolutions in South and Central America. David King announced that he had gained military experience at the Columbia Institute Military Academy in New York. He neglected to mention that he was seven years old at the time.[18] One recruit gravely said he had served five years in the Salvation Army.[19] Kiffin, Paul, and Bill Thaw claimed to have seen service with the Mexican Army. The sergeant recording this information became suspicious and asked why, with so much prior experience, were they so terrible at drill? Bill calmly replied that they had been engaged in guerilla warfare, where drilling was not required.[20]

Training intensified now that they were destined for the front. On Sunday, September 20, Kiffin celebrated his twenty-second birthday, probably with a forced march and bayonet practice. Even with the intensified training, Kiffin found time to write to his mother. He mentioned the hard training and the fact that his feet were sore from the forced marches, but mostly he tried to get her to stop worrying about her two sons and to understand their feelings. "I know you must think me selfish and inconsiderate of your feelings, but I am not," he wrote. "You expect great things of me and I want to do great things, and can see a great future before me. If I am killed in the attempt to attain that future, I have at least done my best; that is all any of us can do."[21]

A few veteran legionnaires who were thought to be of questionable loyalty were sent to Morocco. There were many Germans in the Legion, but those with long service who were assumed to be loyal were retained. Among them were two Austrians who soon committed suicide. One stabbed himself with his bayonet, and the other smuggled a cartridge out of the firing range and blew his brains out. He left a letter stating that, as much as he loved France, he could not march against his native land.[22]

On September 30, 1914, the men formed up and marched to the railroad station. This time they were in full uniform, and René Phélizot proudly carried an American flag. It was the same flag he had carried through the streets of Paris, dressed in civilian clothes, when the Americans informally drilled before being allowed to enlist.[23] He would keep this flag with him throughout his time in the Legion, carefully wound around his waist underneath the blue sash of his French uniform. After lots of photographs and bewildering delays, the men boarded the "Forty and Eight" boxcars that were waiting for them. This time there was better organization and planning. Forty men, no more and no fewer, were loaded into each car.[24] They were heading off to war.

The troops had no idea where they were headed, but after a little more than two days in the boxcars they were herded off the train at Camp de Mailly. This was one of France's largest training camps, located about eighty-five miles east of Paris. The camp had been on the edge of the fighting during the Battle of the Marne. The iron shutters at the train station were riddled with shrapnel. Several buildings were missing roofs or were completely destroyed by shell fire.[25] The fields and woods where they trained were littered with discarded equipment—broken rifles, rusting bayonets, abandoned haversacks, canteens, mess kits, French kepis, and German spiked helmets. (The kepis were cloth, and the spiked helmets were leather. Steel helmets wouldn't be used until late 1915.) In the days to come the recruits would probe deep into the forests during maneuvers or while searching for firewood, and they would occasionally find the rotting corpse of a dead soldier that had been overlooked by the burying details. The camp was close enough to the front that they could hear the rumble of shellfire, like thunder in the distance. One day Fred Zinn and an American named Dennis Dowd captured a German soldier they found hiding in the woods, too weak from hunger to resist. He told them that at least forty other Germans were still in hiding, trapped behind the lines when the fighting swept farther east. Their officers had told them the French killed prisoners, so they were afraid to surrender. He seemed greatly surprised when they took him back to camp and fed him. He ate ravenously and gave away all the buttons on his tattered uniform to the curious soldiers who gathered around him, some of whom spoke German fluently. Eventually, of course, he was taken to a POW camp.[26]

The legionnaires stayed in Camp de Mailly for two weeks doing advanced training and conducting maneuvers. They were assigned to squads, and these became the teams in which they would train, work, and fight for as long as they remained in the unit. The Legion tried to keep soldiers who spoke a common language together, as many of the troops could not understand French and depended upon their buddies to translate their officers' commands. The tallest men, including several Americans, were assigned to the Ninth Squad. In addition to Kiffin and Paul, the Ninth Squad included Bill Thaw, Alan Seeger, Dennis Dowd, two Englishmen, and seven other men.[27] This squad was led by Corporal Weideman, a German who had spent many years in the Legion and who took a genuine interest in the welfare of his squad. Unfortunately, Corporal Weideman was not well liked by his superiors, so his squad often got stuck with the worst details.

Camp de Mailly was where the American legionnaires were first introduced to the bane of soldiers in every army during this war—lice. Called "cooties" by the British and "Monsieur Toto" by the Legion, lice infested the bedding in camps, rest areas, and front-line dugouts. In no time at all, everyone had lice. The lice lived in their clothing and fed off their blood, leaving itching welts like mosquito bites. Occasionally units would be marched to delousing stations, where the troops would shower while their clothes were fumigated, but the relief was only temporary. As soon as they got back to their barracks, the lice would return. "Shirt hunts"—men sitting in a group with their shirts on their laps, picking lice out of the seams while they discussed the issues of the day—were a common sight. When the weather turned cool, Bert Hall began wearing three shirts at once. He claimed he could obtain temporary relief by taking off his shirts and putting them back on in reverse order. The lice would now be on his outside shirt, and it would take them the better part of an hour to burrow down to his body.[28]

Kiffin only found time to write his mother once during the time they spent at Camp de Mailly, and he apologized for the fact that the intense training had kept him too busy and too tired to write more often. He said what little news they did hear was bad. He was convinced the Allies would eventually win, but he was beginning to realize it would be a long war.[29]

Early on the morning of October 18, the legionnaires began marching toward the front lines. It was a sunny morning, and they began the journey singing marching songs. Soon the road led through the remains of a vast battlefield, and the troops fell silent. They passed torn-up fields, shattered woods, and blackened villages. Sometimes they'd pass a house where an outside wall had collapsed and all the rooms and contents could be seen by everyone who passed by, a view that somehow seemed almost indecent. They passed villages where entire blocks of houses and streets were reduced to gray-brown rubble. They realized that when the people who had fled the village returned, it would be impossible for them to even tell where their house had once stood. All landmarks were gone. They also passed graveyard after graveyard. Crosses marked spots where the dead had been hastily buried. A kepi hanging on a cross indicated a French soldier; a spiked helmet indicated a German.[30]

As the day dragged on their muscles began to ache, their feet hurt, and their packs felt like they weighed even more than seventy pounds. In some cases they did weigh more, and soldiers began throwing away items they now considered unimportant. Souvenirs, hairbrushes, extra bars of soap—all became dispensable. Soldiers made deals with their buddies: "I'll carry a mirror if you carry a razor."[31] Still, the long weeks of training paid off. Their officers gave them a ten-minute break every hour, normal practice for the Legion on the march, and they reached their destination for the day in the early afternoon.[32] Not a single man had fallen out during the fifteen-mile march.

They marched an additional thirty-five miles over the next two days. The fourth day was a killer. The men were roused from their exhausted sleep at 4:30 a.m., issued the standard cup of coffee, and on the road by daybreak. The road led up the side of Reims Mountain. They trudged uphill, their aching muscles screaming with each bone-jarring step. The day turned hot and they sweated in their wool uniforms. The straps of their packs and equipment dug deep into their shoulders. Those who had not yet mastered the art of wrapping the cloth strips that substituted for socks had long since seen their feet turn from blistered to bloody. Men began falling out by the side of the road.

Bill Thaw and David King were two of the soldiers who fell by the wayside. The millionaire's son Thaw detested marching even under the best of conditions, and his feet were now shredded. As Bert Hall wrote, "His feet were swollen up like Zeppelins, and they were not like Cinderella's feet at the beginning, either."[33] Thaw and King decided to wait for the ambulance, which was rumored to be following the column. Instead of an ambulance, the commander of the Second Regiment, Colonel Passard, came riding up on his horse.

"What are you doing there?" he demanded.

"Our feet are cut to ribbons, Colonel." King replied. "We're all in."

The colonel drew a large revolver from his holster. "March!" he commanded. By double-timing, Thaw and King were able to catch up with their section.[34]

The exhausted troops stumbled into the village of Verzy around 1:30 in the afternoon. The plan had been to march them to the front lines that night to relieve a regular French Army unit, but after watching the legionnaires trudge into town, that unit's commander decided the relief could be postponed. The men were quartered in houses and barns throughout the town. They were close enough to the front lines that rifle and machine gun fire could be clearly heard. Most of the Americans were billeted in a hayloft, a spot they felt was especially attractive until Fred Zinn stumbled in. Fred was well liked as an individual, but he was infamous for his snoring, which could wake a regiment. His fellow Americans pleaded with him to sleep somewhere else, and even threatened him with their bayonets, but the exhausted Zinn refused to leave. He finally gained grudging acceptance when he promised them that if he snored, they could wake him by beating his face with their hobnailed boots.[35] His friends slept soundly that night, although how much sleep Fred got is unknown.

Two days later, a convoy of motor buses arrived to take the Second Regiment to their combat sector, an undisclosed location somewhere to the east. The men were relieved to be riding instead of marching to their next destination. Except for the Ninth Squad.

When the legionnaires left Camp de Mailly, it wasn't just troops who made the trip. They were followed by a long supply train of mule-drawn wagons carrying tents, cooking gear, ammunition, and other equipment. Now this convoy had to travel to their new duty location. There were valuable supplies on these wagons, and somebody needed to guard them. That somebody was the Ninth Squad.

At 4:30 in the morning of October 26, 1914, Corporal Weideman formed up his squad. Due to a planning blunder somewhere in the supply chain, no rations were issued to the men. Each man was simply given a half-cup of cold coffee. They then began marching, guarding the supply train. It was a pleasant morning and their route took them in a semicircle around the city of Reims. The city was being shelled by the Germans. Portions of the city were on fire, and they watched shells explode against the ancient Reims Cathedral. Gradually they left the city behind. The hours dragged by as the men marched. Other than the requisite ten-minute break every hour, there were no stops. Lunchtime came and went with no food. Dinner time passed and still no food. Even Corporal Weideman, who had spurred on his men throughout the day, developed blisters and began to lag behind. One of the mule drivers started a rumor that their destination was Fismes, and they would stop there for the night. Corporal Weideman admitted that he did not know where their destination was but said he hoped to get orders in Fismes. Night fell.

The convoy reached Fismes after dark, but no one had any idea where the Second Regiment was. Finally a courier rode up on a bicycle with orders for the convoy. They were to proceed to the town of Cuiry-les-Chaudardes near the Aisne battlefield. Reluctantly, the convoy headed out of town. As the troops and the mules grew even more exhausted, the convoy began taking ten-minute breaks every twenty minutes. The men collapsed on the ground and slept during those ten minutes. Finally, at 11:00 p.m., the convoy halted for the night. Kiffin, Alan Seeger, and Dennis Dowd appeared to be in the best shape, so they were posted as guards. Everyone else slept. The Ninth Squad had just marched 56 kilometers (35 miles) in one day, the longest march that would be made by any unit in the Legion during World War I.[36] And the next morning they got up at 4:00 a.m. and began marching again, still with no food. A few hours later, they finally staggered into Cuiry.

The town was under sporadic shellfire, but the men of the Ninth Squad ignored the shellfire, collapsed in a barn, and fell asleep. Later they would find the kitchen and get something to eat, but first they slept.

Two nights later they moved into the front-line trenches. Front-line troops were generally relieved at night, when it was less likely that the enemy would spot the relief and shell the exposed men and doubly occupied trenches. The men were warned against smoking or talking during the relief, both of which would draw fire, and they were told to secure their canteens, mess kits, and other loose equipment so it wouldn't rattle during the march. At first they followed a newly constructed military road. Then the route descended into a wooded marsh. There, as David King described it, they struck one of the horrors of the war: "Mud. Liquid mud—full of treacherous roots. Mud like chewing gum—squelching—sucking our boots off. Mud with a stench obscene and putrid—Black mud—black night. Somebody down. Up again, cursing foully."[37]

Finally the path angled up, out of the marsh, onto relatively dry ground. A few miles later they came to a hill. The rudimentary trenches and foxholes they were to take over were near the crest of this hill, overlooking the ruined village of Craonnelle. The legionnaires waited quietly as the French troops they were relieving slipped out of their holes and headed for the rear. Then the legionnaires crept up the hill and took over the position. There was no barbed wire in front of this line, so every night a few of the men had to crawl in front of the French positions to man what the French called *petite poste* (small lookout posts that would provide advance warning of an attack). That first night, Kiffin was chosen for *petite poste*.

When dawn broke the scene looked almost peaceful. The village of Craonnelle, which lay between the French and German lines, was in ruins, but the "no-man's-land" between the lines was not the barren wasteland it would become later in the war. There were still trees standing and the grass was green. There was, however, a sickening, sweetish smell in the air. The veterans knew what it was. They pointed to the dead bodies lying in no-man's-land.[38]

Paul Rockwell was in a small trench, just large enough to hold eight men, and he was worried about Kiffin. Kiffin had come back from *petite poste* just before dawn and was in a nearby shelter, but Paul didn't know that. Paul climbed out of his trench and began to creep forward, looking for Kiffin. Before he had gone ten feet, he heard a hiss as a sniper's bullet zipped by his ear. His first thought was "What in the dickens is someone shooting at ME for?" but he instinctively dropped to the ground and snaked his way back to his trench.[39] Later that day, Paul and Charles Trinkard found a sunny spot to clean their rifles. Behind them a young Belgian volunteer sat on the bank, dangling his feet in the trench, as he rearranged the contents of his pack. Paul saw the Belgian's legs stiffen as Charles called out, "*Homme blessé!*" (Man wounded!) The Belgian had been shot in the head and toppled over without a word.[40] Clearly this was not the kind of war they had trained for. There had been no heroic charge with bayonets. No struggle to impose their will on the enemy, no shouts of "*Vive la France!*" There was just a momentary carelessness that resulted in a man being killed by an unseen enemy.

This also was not the kind of war their officers and non-coms were prepared for, despite their years of experience in the Legion. These veterans carefully selected a location for the battalion kitchen a few hundred yards behind the trenches, hidden from the enemy's view by a steep hill. An airplane flew over while they were setting up the kitchen. This attracted some attention, as airplanes were a novelty back then. This was, after all, only eleven years after the Wright brothers' first flight at Kitty Hawk. Most of the men had never seen an airplane before the war. Their first reaction, at least according to pilots, was to shoot at anything that flew over them. They had no idea of how to tell friendly aircraft from hostile ones. This airplane dropped no bombs and was quickly forgotten until dinnertime, when ration parties arrived to pick up food and carry it to the troops in the trenches. Then German artillery pulverized the kitchen with a short, intense bombardment. The plane had spotted the kitchen, and the artillery waited until dinnertime to cause the most damage. Fourteen men were killed and thirty were wounded.[41] The next day the kitchen was moved a few miles farther back.

Following the kitchen debacle, the men learned to hide their activities from aerial observation and to take cover when a plane flew overhead. In late October, Bill Thaw took cover with a number of other men as a plane circled their position. As he watched the plane, he said, "Well boys, one day a lot of us will be flying up there too. It'll be a bunch of Americans flying."[42] He had not given up on his dream of flying for the French, and he broached the subject to French officials whenever he had an opportunity.[43]

Trench life settled into a routine. When things went according to plan, the troops spent six days in the front lines, followed by three days in the rest trenches and four days at Cuiry. Things seldom went according to plan, of course. King wrote that he had spent twenty-eight days in the front line before being relieved.[44] And whoever came up with the term "rest" trenches clearly had a twisted sense of humor. The rest trenches were a second line of defense, still within artillery range of German batteries but far enough back to not be plagued by snipers or machine gun fire. While the men were "resting," they were assigned to work details such as digging trenches. They also carried supplies to the front lines and often worked on the lines at night—stringing barbed wire, excavating dugouts, and generally improving the position. They marched back to their rest trench just before dawn to get some sleep.

One advantage to being in the rest trenches was that they were closer to the kitchen, so the men generally ate better. Bert Hall described the problems of hauling food to the front line:

> The Foreign Legion is not particularly well fed at any time—coffee and dry bread for breakfast, soup with lumps of meat in it for luncheon, with rice to follow, and the same plus coffee for dinner, and not too much of anything, either. But in our case all the grub had to be brought in buckets from the relief post, four miles away, by squads leaving the trenches at three A. M., ten A. M., and five P. M., and a tough job it was, what with the darkness and the mud and the shell holes and the German cannonade, to say nothing of occasional snipers taking pot shots at you with rifles. I got one bullet once right between my legs, which drilled a hole in the next bucket in line and wasted all our coffee. As you can imagine, quite a lot of the stuff used to get spilt on the way, and then the boys carrying it used to scrape it up off the ground and put it back again, so that nearly everything one ate was full of gravel and, of course, absolutely cold. More than once when the cannonade was especially violent we got nothing to eat all day but a couple of little old sardines; and, believe me, it takes a mighty strong stomach to stand that sort of treatment for any length of time. As far as we Americans were concerned, who were mostly accustomed to man-sized meals, the net result was literally slow starvation.[45]

It was impossible to bathe in the front-line trenches, and shaving was very difficult. Kiffin and most other legionnaires let their beards grow when they were in the lines. It became a mark of distinction. The French nickname for infantry soldiers during World War I was *poilu*, meaning "hairy."

As the fall turned into winter the men suffered from cold weather, especially when it rained or snowed. They began to realize that trench warfare had come to stay. From November on, temperatures frequently hovered around zero degrees (Centigrade).[46] They gradually improved their trenches to become a permanent position protected by barbed wire, as did every other unit on both sides from Switzerland to the sea.

Boredom set in as well. The men spent hours huddled in the front-line trenches and dugouts with nothing to do. Bert Hall complained, "We could not play cards as cards were scarce and we had no money. Playing cards without money is not a man's game."[47] Hall was an expert at playing cards for money, a skill that would later arouse suspicions among his fellow pilots. The suspicions probably also arose from Hall's penchant for embellishing the truth. One day he told an especially spellbinding tale while he and others were engaged in a "shirt hunt." It left the others sitting in awed silence—until one of them spoke up.

"Bert, you know that's a damned lie."

Bert's reply was disarmingly honest: "Well who the hell said it wasn't?"[48]

One encouraging development was that the mail service improved and the men began to receive letters and packages regularly. Even men without close relatives might receive mail, as many French women adopted such soldiers as their *filleuls*, or "godsons." The women in turn were referred to as *marraines* (godmothers). If a soldier was very lucky, his *marraine* might be young and single, but usually this was purely a platonic arrangement that brought much-appreciated letters and packages. It was not unheard of for a soldier to have multiple *marraines*.

At night, sentries were sent out to man the *petite postes* and warn of German attacks. Often patrols were sent out as well, to reconnoiter German positions, eavesdrop on enemy conversations, and make it clear that the French "owned" no-man's-land. The Germans did the same thing, and several legionnaires were killed or wounded in the fights that occurred when opposing patrols met.[49] David King participated in a particularly memorable fight of this kind:

About midnight the moon began to show through the clouds and my heart skipped a beat. "Christ—here they come!" Stealing silently up the slope in skirmish order were ten or twelve shadowy forms. A warning hiss from Sergeant Morlae, and we retired to our lines to report. "Everyone up—Load—Commence firing!" . . . The enemy replied. A gale of bullets whistled overhead, and we could see the flashes of rifles towards the left of the line. This went on for half an hour; then firing stopped, and an old Legion sergeant volunteered to go out and reconnoiter. Half an hour later he came back convulsed with mirth. The enemy we had seen proved to be twelve cows grazing between the lines, of which nine had paid the full penalty. The firing came from another battalion of the Legion that had come up and occupied the edge of the woods in front of us, forming one side of a V with our own lines. Naturally, these trenches were dubbed *les Tranchees des Vaches* [the cows' trenches].[50]

For the next few days at least, the legionnaires had fresh beef for dinner.

In late November, the legionnaires saw what at that point in the war was a rare sight—combat between two airplanes. A French two-seater attacked a German two-seater and their observers traded fire. It ended when the German plane plunged out of the sky and crashed to earth.[51] Bill Thaw learned that the French plane came from a squadron that was commanded by Lieutenant Fèlix Brocard, a man he knew from his prewar flying days. The next time the legionnaires pulled back to Cuiry for a few days' rest, Bill obtained permission to visit his friend, even though it meant hiking twenty miles. Bert Hall and Jim Bach accompanied him on this trip. While they were there, Bill pleaded with Lieutenant Brocard to use his influence to get him transferred into aviation. Bert and Jim asked to be transferred to aviation also, assuring Lieutenant Brocard that they were both experienced pilots. The lieutenant promised to see what he could do.

Back in the trenches, life dragged on. Kiffin wrote to his mother on November 14, ostensibly to reassure her that he and Paul were all right: "We are still at the front, but have been most of the time in the reserve trenches and therefore in no danger." In the second paragraph, he broached the real reason for the letter: "The French Army pays only one cent a day and we are both broke. We left the money we brought over locked up in our trunk, and we have no way of getting at it. When we do get into a town, we will need to buy a few things, so if you will send us $5 or $10 a month it would come in handy."[52]

In late November, Paul was returning from a *petite poste* just before dawn when something alerted the Germans. They illuminated no-man's-land with flares. At the same time they loosed a volley of rifle and machine gun fire in his direction. Shells began falling as he sprinted toward the safety of a trench. A shell exploded behind him and slammed him into the trench, while shell fragments or frozen clods of dirt grazed his shoulder. He knew his shoulder ached, but he didn't know that his collarbone was broken. Several days later, when they were being relieved, he discovered that he couldn't pick up his pack.[53] He was sent to a hospital to recuperate from his shoulder injury and from frostbite on two of his toes. Later, "inflammatory rheumatism" set in.[54] That was a blanket term for what is now diagnosed as a number of diseases that can cause joint pain, including rheumatic fever. Paul would spend months recuperating, and each time he thought he was ready to go back to the front, a new complication would arise. Neither he nor Kiffin knew it at the time, but his days in the Legion were over. Kiffin would have to soldier on without him.

December 1914 was a lonely month for Kiffin. He sent a postcard to his mother on December 1, telling her that Paul had been slightly wounded, not seriously, and he assumed Paul had already written to her.[55] He couldn't tell her more, as he had not heard anything from Paul himself. His mother addressed a number of letters to Kiffin and Paul in which she complained about how cold it was in Asheville, how she had heard it was even colder in France, and how she and other women were knitting socks and other warm things to send to them for Christmas. She advised them to wrap several layers of newspaper under their clothes to protect their chests from the cold "and maybe bullets." She also suggested that if they were captured, they should beg to be sent back home, as maybe the Germans would do that to avoid the expense of keeping them as prisoners.[56]

On December 3, Loula forwarded Kiffin a note from the National Collection Agency. Kiffin had signed up for a correspondence course in 1913 and had been sent a typewriter and a "Library of Advertising." Apparently Kiffin had stored these in Atlanta when they left for France, and in the excitement of his penny-a-day job with the Legion he had not kept up with the payments. Loula warned him that "it was a mistake to ignore obligations like this," and "if you live to get back these folks could hurt you in more ways and at times you would not suspect." She also lamented that the war news was not good: "How I long for it to be over, how I long for my boys!"

She closed with "I do hope some rest will come to you all at Xmas. I do pray for peace."[57]

Kiffin wrote back on December 10, saying he had spent twenty-one of the last twenty-four days in the trenches. He said the American bunch had dwindled, with only fifteen Americans left in his unit. They had fixed up their trenches to the point where they could now have a fire at night, when the smoke wouldn't show. (Visible smoke drew shell fire.) He suggested that a little jam and peanut butter might make a nice Christmas present, and, not surprising considering David King's description of the French tobacco, he asked for American cigarettes. He gave his best wishes for a Merry Christmas and a Happy New Year to everyone at home.[58]

Kiffin was far from being the only legionnaire who felt blue at Christmas. On December 23, Kenneth Weeks wrote to his mother, "There are long days of inactivity that become monotonous to despair, and an attack, an ambuscade, a lively cannonade are really welcome. When not at that there are trenches to make, and I have become a 'miner'—a day labourer. In fact, I have learned all the labours: cook, miner, tailor, woodcutter; the soldier's life is not all uniform and glory. It is uncommonly hard, but forced labour is better than idleness here."[59]

Bill Thaw had a reason to celebrate. On Christmas Eve, his transfer to Aviation finally came through.[60] Ironically, both Bert Hall and Jim Bach received their orders to Aviation several days before Bill did. Despite their claims to Lieutenant Brocard, Bert and Jim knew nothing about flying.

Kiffin spent Christmas Day in the reserve trenches. He was not in the front lines and made no mention of a Christmas truce, although legionnaires stationed at other points of the line described an unofficial truce to bury the dead and exchange cigarettes.[61] Kiffin's unit was scheduled to dig trenches from 11:00 a.m. to 4:00 p.m. on Christmas Day, the same as they had done the previous four days, but Kiffin wrote his mother that he and several others managed to slip off to a farmhouse where they talked and drank coffee instead. They returned in time to enjoy a Virginia ham that was given to them by an American doctor in the Legion. The mail had become congested and only two Americans received packages, but they shared them, so everyone had candy, nuts, cheese, and other delicacies to eat.[62]

Kiffin also wrote to his brother Paul to describe his Christmas activities, but that letter was decidedly less cheery. In it he complained that he wasn't able to enjoy the treats much because he'd had an awful cold for the past week and felt perfectly rotten. He also said that they had been overwhelmed with knitted socks, mufflers, and other articles sent by well-meaning civilians. He was writing to thank those people for their generosity, but he told Paul that the woolen goods were only "lice traps," and he did not want to load himself down with them. He also wrote, "The English expect to be transferred to the English Army soon; they took the names of all the English, and I gave my name. Rapier has promised to get me transferred and told me to write you to stay where you are if you don't get reformed and that he and I would get you transferred. I had rather stay with France but this is such a damn rotten outfit that I figure I had better get out if I can."[63]

4

The Fortunes of War

There is no romance to the infantry. It is only a matter of being a good day laborer.

—KIFFIN ROCKWELL

KIFFIN'S COMMENT ABOUT WANTING TO GET OUT OF THE "DAMN ROTTEN outfit" would not be the last time he complained to his brother about the unit he was in. He would express similar sentiments several times during the war. In part, it was a normal form of "grousing," the time-honored tradition of soldiers complaining about their circumstances. In Kiffin's case, it also stemmed from his idealistic quest to save humanity. He didn't feel as though he was helping to win the war in the Second Regiment. The exciting battles his grandfather had told him about, the bayonet charges he'd practiced at Toulouse, and the thrill of "imposing his will on the enemy" were not happening. He wrote to Paul:

> There is no romance or anything to the infantry. It is not a question of bravery, it is a question of being a good day laborer. . . . As far as fighting goes, we are always in danger of our lives but don't get a chance to protect ourselves, as this is mostly an artillery war. Of course, the infantry sometimes does fierce fighting, but seldom, and I believe it possible to go through the war without ever taking part in the kind of fighting we imagined we would do. You take a few days ago: a battle was raging on every side of us, and we were in a very advanced position. Our artillery near us did the most damage of any. It simply raked the valley, yet we didn't fire a shot. We sat with our rifles in our hands underground, ready to go out any minute and fight, but that was all.[1]

The letter he received from his mother couldn't have helped his mood:

> It is useless to tell you the anxiety I live under. I know the strain on both of you is great. I pray daily for peace. May it come soon. We have had such bad weather as never before and Asheville is dull. Times are hard everywhere and no money to be had. A great reaction will come after a while. The South will learn not to depend upon cotton and tobacco but upon the necessaries of life, grain, meat, etc. But it is hard now.[2]

Kiffin may have been dissatisfied with his life in the Second Regiment, but he did not regret his decision to fight for France. Whenever he complained to Paul about his current situation, it was because he didn't like the outfit, or the officers, or the sector where they were fighting. He always felt that somewhere there was an outfit that was doing more fighting, that was better led, and that was focused on driving the hated Boche (slang for German soldier) out of France—in short, a unit that was just as enthusiastic and idealistic as he was.

Kiffin celebrated New Year's Day 1915 by marching six miles to the rear and taking a bath, the first time in three months the army had given his unit a chance to bathe. The next day they were inoculated against typhoid.[3] While that seems like an unremarkable event today, in 1915 it represented a major advance in medicine. In previous wars there were times when more soldiers died of typhoid than died in battle. A vaccine for typhoid was developed in the late 1800s, and by World War I soldiers were routinely vaccinated. The serum used in 1915 was not as refined as the modern vaccine and it left the soldiers sore and feverish, so they were given two days of rest—actual rest this time. These were the first days off Kiffin had been given since he'd joined the Legion. Then they marched back to the front.

This time they moved into a different portion of the Craonnelle sector, a section where the French lines included portions of the town itself. All buildings in the town had been demolished by shell fire and the inhabitants had fled, but the cellars beneath the collapsed buildings provided shelter from the German fire. Streets were barricaded at the edges of the French positions, and vicious firefights broke out around these barricades. The legionnaires scrounged shotguns from the local countryside which proved effective,[4] though controversial, in defending these barricades.[5]

The ruins of a once elegant chateau, the Château de Blanc Sablon, lay between the French and German lines. The shattered house was surrounded by the remains of a wooded park, all of which was surrounded by a thick stone wall. This chateau was used as an advanced outpost by the French. Kiffin's unit arrived in Craonnelle in the middle of the night, after a three-hour march in the rain, and was immediately sent to relieve the unit in the chateau. Naturally the Ninth Squad was selected for guard duty along the wall. Corporal Weideman placed three men at the left end of the wall, two men in the middle, and the remaining four members of the squad at the right end of the wall, where a dugout provided a small level of protection. The wall was about five hundred yards long, so it was thinly held at best.

Kiffin and Alan Seeger were the two men assigned to guard the middle of the wall. The wall itself was about eight feet high, but a shell had knocked down a portion of this structure. A wooden door was propped against this hole, held in place by a ladder, as an improvised barricade. Kiffin and Alan stationed themselves by this door so they could peer around it and periodically climb the ladder to look over it. The night passed quietly with no sign of German activity, and the squad began to feel safe in their new position. Shortly before sunrise, Corporal Weideman asked Kiffin and another man to go back to the chateau and pick up rations for the guard detail. As they returned with the rations, the morning half-light gave them their first glimpse of the surrounding terrain. The German front lines formed a semicircle around the chateau, so they were exposed to fire from three sides. In places the German lines were less than fifty yards from the wall they had guarded.[6] Worse still, the German positions were on rising ground, so they could look down into the French positions.

As Kiffin and the other man looked with astonishment at their lines, the first "crack" of a German sniper rifle shattered the morning silence. A bullet whizzed by Kiffin. More shots rang out as they crouched and ran for the meager protection provided by the wall. They hugged the wall as they carried the rations to the dugout where the rest of the squad was waiting. Kiffin wrote, "All that day we crouched in little dug-outs and cursed our officers for putting us in such a death-trap without more men and without telling us the real situation."[7]

Kiffin got no sleep that day, and the next night he and Seeger were again guarding the hole in the wall. At 10:30 p.m., January 5, Alan started to whisper a message. Something thumped to the ground by Kiffin's feet. It sputtered sparks for a moment and then went quiet. "What's this?" Kiffin asked as he picked up the heavy object. Seeger peered curiously at it and then jumped back, saying, "Good God! It's a hand grenade!" Kiffin threw it over the wall. Fortunately, it was a dud, or they would have both been killed long before he threw it. After a moment of confusion, Seeger ran to alert the corporal while Kiffin kept watch at the door. Moments later, Alan came running back with Corporal Weideman, who shouted, "*Garde à vous, Rockwell!*" (Protect yourself!) as another grenade landed beside Kiffin. Kiffin leaped over the ladder and hit the ground beside the corporal as the grenade exploded. They both shouted, "*Aux armes!*" (To arms!) As they got up, a German raiding party knocked the door aside and rushed through the opening. Realizing they were standing in the open, Kiffin and Weideman rushed for the cover of some nearby woods. A rifle flashed, and Kiffin dove for the ground. Corporal Weideman thumped to the ground beside him, and Kiffin knew by the way he hit that he was dead.

Kiffin crouched and ran the rest of the way to the woods with bullets whistling past him in the dark. He lay in the woods and watched, not daring to move or make a sound. More Americans rushed to the wall to help but they came under fire from the German raiding party, from Germans in the nearby trenches, and from additional German raiders who had slipped over the wall at another point. Ferdinand Capdevielle of New York had his scalp grazed by a bullet, and Fred Zinn was hit in his right hand. These reinforcements did not know where the American sentries were, and they expected additional legionnaires to come rushing in from the other side of the Germans. They could not fire for fear of hitting their own men. The German raiding party smashed Weideman's head with their rifle butts to make certain he was dead, stripped off his jacket with its insignia and other identification, and slipped back to their lines without a shot being fired at them.[8]

Kiffin was badly shaken by this attack. In addition to the fact that he was very nearly killed, he felt he had failed in his first real experience under fire. It was only by sheer luck that the Germans hadn't killed him with the two grenades they hurled at him or with the volleys of rifle bullets fired at him. It certainly wasn't because he was prepared for their attack and had taken the appropriate action. An NCO whom he admired and respected, a man who had helped show him the ropes when he entered the Legion, had been killed, and Kiffin hadn't even fired a shot in response. He was also outraged that they had smashed Weideman's head, viewing that as an act of senseless violence.

From a dispassionate, military point of view, it could be argued that this was a typical trench raid, no different from the raids the French often launched against the Germans. Corporal Weideman's jacket would give the Germans useful intelligence information about the unit they were facing, and it could be argued that smashing his head was a more humane way to ensure that a downed enemy was dead than the traditional bayonet jab in the belly. However, Kiffin was not open to dispassionate logic. About two hours later, Kiffin heard the Germans mocking Corporal Weideman's last words as shouts of "*Aux armes*" rose from the German trenches, followed by laughter. Kiffin wrote his sister, "It practically froze the blood to hear it. Up until that minute I had never felt a real desire to kill a German. Since then I have had nothing but murder in my heart, and now no matter what happens I am going through this war as long as I can."[9]

Kiffin resumed his post for a short while but asked to be relieved, as he was too shaken up to continue. He went back to the dugout and filled out a report on the incident. By then his nerves had calmed enough to return to guard duty. They had not calmed enough to let him sleep the next day, however. He went four days and four nights without sleep. He concluded his letter to Agnes by saying, "Nothing could be worse than those four days and nights. The uncertainty of it all—lying in the rain and mud, eternally watching and listening, knowing that everywhere men were prowling, trying to slip up on one another in the dark and kill."

In addition to the hatred and uneasiness, the attack at the wall left all the new recruits wondering whether the Legion's officers and experienced veterans actually knew what they were doing. The weeks of training that had nothing whatsoever to do with the kind of war they were fighting, the fatal mistake of locating the kitchen too close to the front lines, and the almost criminal stationing of a single squad to guard a five-hundred-yard wall so close to the German trenches had shattered the recruits' faith in the veterans. Even if there had been more men, the position itself was a death trap. The new recruits began to regard the veterans as "ignorant mercenaries." The veterans in turn did not like being questioned by the recruits and accused them of only being in the Legion *pour la gamelle* (for the food bowl—that is, for free food). This insult implied that a recruit was so worthless he had only joined the Legion to keep from starving. It was particularly galling when hurled at the Americans, many of whom came from wealthy backgrounds and had forsaken a life of luxury to voluntarily fight for France.

In the meantime, life in the trenches dragged on. Kiffin's life was a series of days in the front lines and days in the reserve trenches. Sometimes he was sent back to the place where Corporal Weideman was killed, but his officers again posted only a handful of sentries along the wall, apparently having learned nothing from the raid. Kiffin wrote to Paul that he had spent eight days at the location where Weideman was killed.[10] He told Paul that the English soldiers were going to leave the next day, but he had decided to stay in the Legion rather than transfer to the British Army. Later, on January 19, he wrote that he had just gotten back from spending four days in "the village death trap." He had a total of five hours sleep during those four days. One night he spent fourteen hours crouched by the wall in sleet and snow. There were four men and a corporal guarding the wall that night, and they were threatened with court-martial if anyone left their post for any reason. Kiffin's unit escaped without casualties, but a few hours after they were relieved there was an attack on the unit that replaced them.[11]

In the same letter, Kiffin said he was in excellent physical health, but the mental and physical strain was breaking him down, along with everyone else in the outfit. He advised Paul to "get out of the whole thing yourself," and he also asked Paul to see whether there was any way he could get Kiffin transferred into a regular French Army unit and out of the Legion. "It is no good," he wrote. "The officers are no good. It is just luck that I am not dead owing to their damn ignorance and neglect."

Kiffin repeated this request three days later. Paul was recovering from his November injuries and had been talking about returning to the front. Kiffin was adamant that he should not do that:

> In regard to your coming back to this regiment, I will say for the last time, don't be a fool. If you try hard enough you won't have to. There are at least one third of the men who left Camp de Mailly that have gotten out of the Regiment, if not out of the French Service, and there are not five here but would change if they could. You have not the physical or mental make-up to stand this life. Something I have realized for months but didn't realize before we joined. If you come back you will be no good inside of a month and it will be harder to get evacuated the

second time so you will suffer a lot and finally reach the point where they will have to send you back. I know what I am talking about. I told the boys you were trying to come back and not a one of them but said that they thought you had more sense.[12]

If these words sound harsh, remember that Paul had multiple illnesses and almost died as a child. Their father also had a weak constitution, and he died at the age of twenty-six. Paul's twenty-sixth birthday was only a few weeks away. He was slowly recovering from his broken collarbone and infectious rheumatism, but he was not yet well. Later that spring Paul contracted bronchitis, further delaying his return to duty.[13]

Loula, of course, had not been idle while her boys were in France. In addition to trying to find a way to get them sent home (something they would learn about later), she struggled to find a reliable way to send them packages and money. The US Post Office would not accept any packages addressed to military addresses in the war zone,[14] possibly because they feared that doing so would violate the neutrality provisions stressed by President Wilson. She tried sending them a Christmas package through the Red Cross, but it never reached them. In a letter dated January 11, 1915, she described a new connection: "It is a comfort to me that you have a friend in Mrs. Settle's cousin in Paris." She later referred to Mrs. Settle's cousin as "Mrs. Peloux."[15] She was in fact the Vicomtesse du Peloux, a member of the French nobility. (France was a republic, so they were "noble" only in that they were descended from pre-republican nobility.)[16] Loula closed the letter in an emotional outburst:

Now I was not ashamed that you had joined the French Army, but hurt that my boys had done a thing that looked like they did not love their mother and sister. But you boys are too young to know a mother's heart and I don't blame or hold it against you. A boy's best friend is his mother. He is never wise [to] tell others things he would not tell her, and I long for the full confidence and love of my two sons. I am trusting God and so bearing up under this thing which can't help being a strain. I am proud of both my boys and I love them with all my heart. I see your views and trust that as you say you will both come back well and strong. I love you with all my heart. Life to me would be blank without you.

Kiffin sent a letter to his old boss, Mr. Massengale, in Atlanta. He mentioned having an opportunity to transfer to the British Army, where he might have gotten a commission, but said he came overseas to fight for France and he was going to stick with them, even though he'd never rise above common soldier because he didn't speak French. He closed with

> The war will probably be over this fall, then no doubt I will go back and work and lead a quiet uneventful life for a year or so and then see some other fool stunt to do. . . . I often think of American cigarettes and tobacco but doubt if they would ever reach me even if you sent them, so let it go at that and wait and buy me a drink and a good all Havana cigar at the M&M Club the first day I am back in Atlanta.[17]

And so the cycle went on. Front lines, reserve trenches. Front lines, reserve trenches. Once Kiffin spent six days in an advance post, creeping so close to the German lines that he could hear them talking at night and then creeping back to the French trenches to sleep during the day.[18] He wrote to the Vicomte and Vicomtesse du Peloux, telling them about his daily routine and assuring them that he was in no danger. He also asked them for a beginning French grammar book, as he wanted to improve his French.

There was, however, a major problem that he did not tell anyone but Paul about. Surprisingly, it involved another American. Edward Morlae had served in the US Army in the Philippines, had sailed on many commercial ships, and "claimed to have been everywhere and have done everything."[19] Because of his prior service and his ability to speak French, he was promoted to corporal while they were at Camp de Mailly. That winter he was promoted to sergeant and put in charge of the section that included most of the Americans. Kiffin gave his views on Sergeant Morlae when he wrote to Paul on February 16:

> The Americans here are Cap [Capdevielle], Zinn, Dowd, Seeger, Trinkard, King, Phélizot and Chatkoff. Morlae is also here. He came back the first of the year, after studying a few weeks in a Corporal's school. He is now the Sergeant in Charge of this section and a bigger son-of-a-bitch than ever. He takes every opportunity to insult the Americans in front of superior officers, so as to try and curry favor with them. He and I are always at swords' point and I have told him that

someday we will both be back in America. The first thing I do when we are back there is to beat the shit out of him.[20]

Matters with Sergeant Morlae almost came to a head over Fred Zinn. Zinn's snoring was more than an annoyance; it was a medical problem that was seriously affecting his performance. His snoring not only kept everyone near him awake but also prevented him from getting a good night's sleep. This in turn left him exhausted and frequently sick.

This was not a condition Fred could hide. When he fell asleep on guard duty, which he often did, everyone nearby could hear him snore. If he was at a *petite poste* near the German lines, his snoring could give away his position—much to the dismay of everyone else who was at that post. Sergeant Morlae's solution was to place Fred under arrest for falling asleep on guard duty and assign him additional guard duty as a punishment. This decision only made the situation worse. Finally, Sergeant Morlae warned Fred that if he fell asleep one more time, he would put him up before a firing squad. This was not an idle threat. Falling asleep on guard duty was a serious offense because it put the rest of the unit at risk, and it could be punishable by death.

At that point, Kiffin and some of Fred's other buddies went over the head of Sergeant Morlae and appealed to their battalion commander, Commandant de Gallé. They convinced the commandant that Fred had a medical problem, not a discipline problem. He had Fred sent to a hospital, where they operated on his adenoids. Kiffin wrote to Paul, "Zinn was evacuated yesterday. We had been trying to get him out for the last two or three months. He was a nice lad but a nuisance as a soldier. He was sick most of the time and would fall to sleep on guard and snore loud as hell. They gave him prison sentences and work but finally became convinced that he was really sick so now have sent him back."[21] The surgery didn't completely cure Fred's snoring, but it reduced the problem to the point that he could function normally.[22]

The distrust between the new recruits and the veterans boiled over in early March. The battalion had been pulled back from the front to Cuiry for a few days of rest. The cooks had set up a coffee wagon in the middle of a courtyard where a large group of legionnaires huddled for warmth. Herman Chatkoff, an American from Brooklyn and the man who had claimed prior service with the Salvation Army, tried to get a second cup of coffee, saying he had not had any before. The cook, who was an Arabian veteran with years of service in Morocco, called Chatkoff a cheat and a liar. He was like all the other Americans, the cook shouted, and given one other veteran, he could make the entire American contingent eat the dunghills that littered the courtyard. He called to a friend of his, a veteran Arabian machine gunner, and asked him to back him up on this assertion. René Phélizot, the American big game hunter, laughed as he stepped up beside Chatkoff and suggested the four of them settle the issue. The cook and Chatkoff quickly backed off, and Phélizot squared off against the machine gunner.

Phélizot was known to sometimes carry a gun, and the veteran challenged him to prove he was unarmed. Phélizot stretched out his arms to show that he was holding nothing and had nothing on his belt. The gunner grabbed René's wrists and head butted him in the face. René went down with the gunner on top of him, but René quickly reversed this situation. The two fought in the center of a ring of cheering legionnaires, and René was gradually getting the better of the gunner. Seeing his friend was losing, a veteran Alsatian machine gunner jumped into the ring, swinging a two-liter metal canteen filled with wine on a long leather strap. He struck René in the side of the head with the canteen, and René dropped like a stone, unconscious. The Americans jumped to René's defense and a brawl erupted. It was finally broken up by a group of armed guards, but not before five Americans and six veterans were knocked unconscious and a number of others suffered lesser injuries.

When René Phélizot recovered, he complained of a splitting headache. He got very little sleep that night and the next morning he reported to sick call at the infirmary. The doctor gave him a cursory examination, announced there was nothing wrong with him, and sent him back to his unit. That night he marched to the front lines at Craonnelle with the rest of the legionnaires. He tried his best to perform his duties, but the pain in his head kept getting worse. On his second morning at the front, his sergeant ordered him back to the infirmary at Cuiry. He managed to stagger back to town, where the doctor took another quick look at him and angrily declared, "There is nothing wrong with you. You only want to be sent back to the rear. Get on up to the front line again!" Phélizot began trudging back down the road that led to Craonnelle.

Captain de la Villeon, commander of Phélizot's company, rode down the same road on a horse. He saw a soldier lying by the roadside, but assumed he was just a weary infantryman trying to get some rest. He rode by, not wanting to startle the soldier by letting him know an officer had caught him sleeping. Later that day, he rode back and noticed the soldier had not moved. This time he stopped to investigate. It was Phélizot, who groaned as the captain tried to wake him. He was partially paralyzed with lockjaw (tetanus).[23] He was rushed to the nearest hospital, where it was discovered that he had a fractured skull as well as tetanus. The doctors did what they could for him, but it was too late. On March 9, Phélizot struggled to unwrap the American flag from around his waist, where he had carried it since Camp de Mailly. He rose to a half-sitting position, held the flag in front of him, and said, "I am an American," through clenched teeth. Then he fell back dead.[24]

When the Americans returned from the front and learned of Phélizot's death, there was a near riot. Paul Rockwell wrote that the Alsatian who hit Phélizot with this canteen disappeared from the Legion and was sent to a penitentiary regiment in Africa.[25] Paul sometimes "shaded" his history to protect the reputation of the Americans and the Legion. David King, who had no such concern, wrote that Chatkoff, who began the incident by asking for a second cup of coffee, picked a fight with the Alsatian. "In two minutes it was general, but the Alsatian was a marked man. While we kept up a milling battle with the others, every one of us concentrated on the Alsatian. When he went down it was all over. It is surprising how quickly hob-nailed Army boots can reduce a man's head to pulp."[26]

The Americans' section was placed under what amounted to house arrest and they were not allowed to leave their barracks, "for their own protection," an officer later admitted.[27] Kiffin wrote to Paul that "we can't go out in the streets because it would mean a war. Phélizot died night before last as the result of foul play in a scrap between him and two Arabs of the M. section, which afterwards turned into a battle royal between the two sections." He promised to fill Paul in on all the details later.[28]

Within days Kiffin was transferred to the First Regiment of the Foreign Legion. Whether this was the result of Paul pulling strings, a response to René Phélizot's death, or just a routine approval of Kiffin's request for a transfer is unknown. In any event, Kiffin came back from a work detail and was told he had to leave in two hours to report to the First Regiment. After hurriedly packing, he was for once able to ride back to town on a wagon instead of marching. The next morning, he went to a headquarters where he was interviewed by a general and several other officers who treated him courteously—another nice change from the Second Regiment. From there he was given rides in a series of automobiles until he reached his new outfit. He marched into the trenches with them that night. He was pleased with the transfer and described the trip to his new outfit as "the most pleasant thing I have experienced since leaving the States."[29]

Kiffin was not sad to leave the Second Regiment. Most of the Americans he had trained with in that unit were already gone, whether through transfer, injury, disease, or death. He was now assigned to Company 2, Battalion B of the First Regiment, and he found the officers and discipline in this unit to be much better. There were a number of other Americans in his squad, including Lawrence Scanlan, Kenneth Weeks, and Paul Pavelka. Lawrence Scanlan had been studying electrical engineering in New Jersey when the war broke out.[30] He left school and worked his way to France taking care of horses on a cattle boat, a job that was both exhausting and disgusting. Thirty-three "cattlemen" were packed into a cabin designed for twelve seamen, which gives an indication of the high regard that the captain and his crew had for the cattlemen. Scanlan joined the Foreign Legion on November 24, 1914.[31] Kenneth Weeks was an MIT graduate and successful author who was studying architecture in Paris and enlisted at the beginning of the war.

Paul Pavelka had an unusual background, even for a member of the Foreign Legion. He was born to Hungarian immigrants in New York City.[32] He grew up in the Bronx, but when he was sixteen his father bought a farm in Madison, Connecticut, and the family moved there. Shortly after they moved, his mother Anna died when she "accidentally" fell on a pitchfork. There was some skepticism about her death at the time, and more doubts were raised a few months later when his father married a beautiful twenty-two-year-old woman from New York City. (The people of Madison still question the death of Paul's mother, and the "ghost" of Anna Pavelka is featured in the town's annual Historical Society Ghost Walk.)[33] Pavelka found himself uncomfortably attracted to his new stepmother and suspicious of his father. He left home and began working on farms in Vermont and New Hampshire.[34]

Pavelka discovered that he liked moving from place to place, picking up odd jobs here and there. To say that he had wanderlust would be like saying Lady Macbeth had "issues." He learned how to catch free rides on freight trains and headed out west, venturing into Canada along the way. He worked in lumber camps, cattle ranches, and sheep farms. In 1908, he spent some time shearing sheep in North Dakota before wandering to Montana.

many aëroplanes, Zeppelins, captive balloons, etc. There is quite a change in the civilians also. They are not so hysterical and excitable, and instead of crying, they give one a cheerful smile.[41]

However, Kiffin was not so excited about the upcoming attack that he could overlook what he considered unwarranted publicity about his adventures:

Paul wrote me that the Atlanta papers had been giving me quite a lot of publicity and that the Journal had published my letter to Agnes. Others also have written me, and all of you write and act as if you thought I came over here for notoriety and to try to be a hero. It has hurt me and made me mad also to think how few people there are who give me credit for any strength of character. Maybe the restless life I have led justifies all in their opinions. However, I am sorry that such is the case and it means to me that I will never try to live in the South.[42]

He expressed a similar sentiment in a letter to Paul a few days later when he said, "I am glad to hear that you are making a success with your writing but I don't want any publicity or fame so don't count [on me] to write for the journal or any papers. Was sorry to hear that my letter to Agnes had been published."[43] Throughout his experiences in the war, Kiffin would never be comfortable with publicity. No matter what he was doing, he could always point to others who were doing as much or more, and he didn't feel it was right that his efforts were publicized while theirs were not. This could be frustrating to his brother, as Paul was writing articles about the war for the *Chicago Daily News* and other newspapers and would soon be assigned to the French "Section de Information." Even Paul described that work as "propaganda."[44] His job was to present the French war effort, and especially the Americans contributing to that effort, in a favorable light. The United States was neutral, but American supplies of food and war materials were crucial to the Allied war effort and the French hoped the United States would eventually enter the war on their side. Paul was assigned to help make that happen. His brother Kiffin was making a very visible contribution to the French war effort, but Kiffin didn't want to be publicized.

Preparations for the attack intensified. French artillery bombarded German defenses for six days before the attack, with an especially heavy bombardment of the German front lines in the final hours. Kiffin, Kenneth

Weeks, and other legionnaires were detailed to crawl into no-man's-land and shovel dirt into small "walls" that men could dive behind for protection during the attack. They had to build these earthworks while lying on the ground, within eighty yards of the German trenches, with bullets whizzing overhead. Teams of riflemen on either side of them were supposed to protect them, but these men had to hug the earth for protection, too.[45]

Men discarded all extraneous items from their packs and loaded up with extra ammunition and grenades. Kiffin and the other men in his unit shaved off their beards for sanitary and morale purposes. Kiffin was no longer known as *le grand avec la barbe* (the tall fellow with the beard).[46] Kiffin's unit marched into attack trenches facing the German positions at La Targette, France.

The first wave left the trenches at 10:00 a.m. on May 9, 1915. Kiffin's unit was scheduled for the second wave, which would go over the top in seven minutes, so he watched the first wave attack. Today we look back at the infantry attacks of World War I and are appalled by the senseless waste of lives when young men charged across open fields while machine guns and artillery fire mowed them down. That's not necessarily how soldiers viewed it at the time. Like Kiffin, many grew up hearing tales of heroic attacks and magnificent courage in the face of the enemy. To them, this was how you won a war. If they succeeded in capturing the enemy's trenches, the attack was a success. Kiffin described the Artois attack to Paul as follows:

> At ten o'clock, I saw the finest sight I have ever seen. It was men from the Premier Étranger crawling out of our trenches, with their bayonets glittering against the sun, and advancing on the Boches. There was not a sign of hesitation. They were falling fast, but as fast as men fell, it seemed as if new men sprang up out of the ground to take their places. One second it looked as if an entire section had fallen by one sweep of a machine-gun. In a few moments, a second line of men crawled out of our trenches; and at seven minutes past ten, our captain called "*En avant*," and we went dashing down the trenches with the German artillery giving us hell as we went.[47]

Kiffin's excitement at watching the attack continued when he joined it. To him, the glorious part was not that men were falling but that other men leaped forward to take their places and continue the attack. His letter to Paul continued:

Just as we reached the first-line trenches, a shell burst near the captain, and left his face covered with blood. He brushed his hand across it, and I heard him say "*Cochons*" [swine], and that it was nothing. Then he called for everyone out of the trenches.

We scrambled out, and from then on it was nothing but a steady advance under rifle, machine-gun and artillery fire. We certainly had the Boches on the run, but at the same time they were pouring the lead at us. We would dash forward twenty-five or fifty meters, and then when the fire got too hot, would drop to the ground with our sacs in front of us, and lie there until we had our breath, and the bullets were not quite so thick. Then we would take our sacs in one hand as a kind of shield, and make another dash.

To think of fear or the horror of the thing was impossible. All I could think of was what a wonderful advance it was, and how everyone was going against that stream of lead as if he loved it. I kept that up for five hours. By then we had advanced three or four kilometers, but were badly cut up and also mixed up with men from other regiments, mostly Algerian tirailleurs [a different infantry unit]. Most of our officers had fallen, including the Colonel and three commandants. I understand that there only remain now four officers out of the whole regiment. We had taken most of a village and were taking the rest of it. My outfit was a little to the left, and we were being raked by fire from in front and from the end of the village still held by the Germans.

Skipper Pavelka and I were lying alongside the sous-lieutenant when a messenger came and told him that the captain and lieutenant had both fallen, and that he was in command of the company. The fire had been so heavy for the last half hour that we had been advancing one man at a time to the section. The sous-lieutenant gave us the direction to take, and told us to follow him, one at a time. He jumped and dashed forward. I turned to Skipper and told him we might as well get it over with at once, so I started with Skipper behind me.

I go about twenty meters when a bullet catches me in the thigh, through the fleshy part, without touching the bone. I continue for a few steps, and then topple over. Skipper sees me drop, so drops also in

65

order to bandage me up if necessary. But I told him I could do it myself and for him to go ahead.[48]

Kiffin was near the village of Neuville-Saint-Vaast when he was hit. He had advanced about two miles. A few men in that sector eventually made it past the village and captured a portion of Vimy Ridge. Portions of the village were still in German hands, though, and Kiffin was exposed to rifle and machine gun fire from the village. He crawled to a shell hole and bandaged his wound. Another wounded soldier was already in the same shell hole, one who had been shot through both hips and the stomach. Kiffin tried to bandage him, but he was too badly wounded for the bandages to do much good. The man pleaded for water, but Kiffin had no water to give him and there was no place to get water. Kiffin could hear wounded men in nearby shell holes calling for water. Kiffin stayed with the wounded man until he died, all the while under heavy German shelling. Three times Kiffin heard the scream of an incoming shell that sounded like it was headed straight for him. Each time he closed his eyes and braced himself for the impact, but all three were near misses, exploding less than thirty feet away. He was showered with dirt, but unhurt. After the third explosion Kiffin crawled to the forward troops, who hadn't moved since he'd been hit. The soldiers there told him to get back to the rear, as he couldn't help them move forward and he was liable to be captured if the Germans counterattacked. He then crawled about a half-mile back, keeping his belly pressed into the dirt to avoid the rifle and machine gun fire that was still sweeping the battlefield.

He found a number of wounded men huddled behind a haystack. By this time it had gotten dark, and the fire had slackened. He was able to sit up and reapply his bandage, which had slid off while he was crawling. A stretcher bearer came by and said there were so many seriously wounded men that it would be a day or longer before an ambulance could transport him to the rear. Kiffin found a stick to use as a crutch and managed to hobble a couple miles back to a farm where a number of wounded men had collected. He slept there, and the following day he hobbled and hitched rides until he got to a medical evacuation station. They put him on a train that night, and although he asked to go to a hospital in Paris, the train rolled through the city and took him to a hospital in Rennes, about two hundred miles west of Paris. His wound had gone untreated for four days, but for the first time in nine months Kiffin got to sleep between clean sheets.

5

Recovery

I had rather be fighting for France than doing anything else.

—Kiffin Rockwell

Kiffin was very lucky not to lose his leg after his injury. Penicillin wasn't discovered until 1928, and there were no antibiotics in 1915. Wounded soldiers were usually given a shot of anti-tetanus serum, but there were many other types of bacteria that could infect a wound. Gas gangrene was particularly dangerous during World War I.[1] If gas gangrene developed, amputation was the only way to save the soldier's life—particularly when overworked doctors had to treat thousands of wounded soldiers after a battle and had only a little time to spend on each one. Kiffin's wound had been untreated for four days when he arrived in the hospital, and he had dragged it through the mud when he crawled away from the battlefield. He wrote Paul that it had "festered a little,"[2] so they would have to open it up, but it was nothing bad and he would soon be all right.[3] Kiffin's prediction that he would soon be all right turned out to be true. There was severe muscle damage that would take a long time to heal, but no bone damage and no serious infection. (In 1916, before the introduction of the Thomas Splint, the death rate for soldiers with a fractured femur was 80 percent.)

Kiffin was also fortunate just to have survived the attack. The initial attack gained ground in some sectors, including the sector where Kiffin attacked, but German counterattacks soon took back most of the lost ground. Like far too many battles during that war, the fighting raged for weeks but left the lines virtually unchanged. Pushing the lines back and forth cost the French more than one hundred thousand casualties, one of whom was Kiffin. More than a third of those casualties were men killed in action. British casualties were close to thirty thousand, and the Germans who opposed them had more than seventy thousand men killed, wounded, or captured during this futile offensive. Kiffin's company sent 250 men into the battle. Fifty-five of those men were able to answer roll call when the unit was pulled out of the fray. The rest were killed, wounded, or missing.[4]

Paul Rockwell was on convalescent leave following his bout with bronchitis, and he obtained permission to travel to Rennes to visit Kiffin. Visiting hours were rigidly enforced, but he was able to spend most afternoons there. They undoubtedly discussed the sinking of the *Lusitania* during these visits, as a German submarine had torpedoed this civilian ocean liner just two days before Kiffin was injured. Nearly 1,200 people were killed when the liner sank, including 128 Americans. On May 10, while Kiffin was painfully hobbling back to an evacuation center with his wounded leg, President Wilson responded to the *Lusitania* sinking by declaring, "There is such a thing as a man being too proud to fight." The American volunteers were outraged by this statement. Kiffin wrote his mother, "We are all watching the U. S. now. If she wants to keep up her name as a nation and be respected by other nations, I don't see how she will keep from fighting."[5]

Kiffin obviously was not too proud to fight, and as he lay in his hospital bed, he was still excited about the ongoing Battle of Artois. The French Army exercised tight control over the information it provided to the press, and soldiers' letters home were censored. The French press also censored itself to help uphold the country's morale. Gains made by the attacking French troops were given much publicity, ground lost to German counterattacks was seldom mentioned, and casualty figures were sketchy at best. Estimates of German casualties were greatly exaggerated to make it appear that the French dominated every battle. Thus Kiffin was totally unaware of the fact that most of the ground his unit had captured had subsequently been lost, or that the Allies had lost nearly twice as many men as the Germans in this costly battle. He described his feelings about the soldiers who fell in a letter to the Vicomte du Peloux:

> I don't want you to think that I am cold-blooded, without feeling, but the horror of it all is overshadowed by the feeling of pride and admiration I have for them all. This life does not hold such great value in my eyes as it does in some people's, and I feel that those men who died that day, died having made a success of their lives in their own

little way, doing something for the world, for posterity, and that their characters are their souls which will forever live and be passed down from generation to generation. So, is not that success! And what more can a man ask for his life than success?[6]

On May 21, Kiffin wrote to his mother, saying that he expected to stay in the hospital at Rennes for six to eight weeks, after which he would probably get a week's convalescent leave in Paris. Then he broached a new topic.

Loula's early letters to Kiffin and Paul often blended a theme of self-pity with overtones of pleading and guilt. This was not what one would expect from a strong-willed, independent woman like Loula. It apparently was not what Paul and Kiffin were expecting, either. Kiffin even scrawled, "Please don't write such pitiful letters," on top of one of his letters to his mother.[7] When Paul visited Kiffin in the hospital, Kiffin learned that his mother had not just sent letters like that to the two of them. She had also written to the US ambassador and anyone else she could think of to try to get them sent back home. Kiffin addressed this subject directly in his May 21 letter:

Paul tells me that when he arrived in Paris he found we were quite well advertised, but not to our advantage, by a number of rather wild letters you had written to everyone you could think of. If you had understood a little more about war and diplomatic affairs, you would have known that the Ambassador could be of absolutely no assistance to us while we were in the army. Now I have often laughed to myself about the letter of advice you wrote me as to what to do in case I was taken a prisoner. I never entertained the idea of being taken a prisoner, but if I had been and had followed your advice, I would have been immediately put up against a tree and shot.[8] Now, we appreciate the fact that your efforts are out of love for us, but there are a lot of things you do not understand in regard to conditions over here and the war, and it is hard for a person to give advice on something they know nothing about. It is marvelous to me the way the women of France are doing their share and the courage and fortitude they show.[9]

What neither Paul nor Kiffin knew was that Loula had suffered what she described as a "nervous collapse" after they went to France.[10] She later told a newspaper reporter that when they left for France, she couldn't understand their motives. She thought it was a "wild adventure of youth." Kiffin had always sought her advice on important matters, and she didn't understand how the two of them could take such drastic action without first conferring with her. She told the reporter:

I guess I was selfish, but I did not understand. I could not see where my two boys meant anything to France, whereas they meant everything to me. Their life was mine. When my husband died, six years after our marriage, leaving me with three babies—for babies and books, he said, were all that preachers had in this world, my life became theirs. It was my purpose to train them for careers of scholarship, and my hope and inspiration in this task was that they would be my comfort and stay in old age. . . . Perhaps I was a silly mother, but I made every possible effort to have my boys taken out of the army and returned to this country. During the months following their departure I was almost frantic with grief, for I felt that I should never see them again. I wrote letters to the War Department, both at Washington and at Paris. I had reason to believe they would not be accepted in the French Army and it was only by chance that they were allowed to enlist even in the Foreign Legion from Africa, at a penny a day for their services.[11]

The newspaper reporters weren't the only ones Loula told about this episode. In 1917, she wrote to a Mr. Olds, "Remember that only through great suffering did I attain my present state of mind. That first awful winter of the war came near costing me my mind and my life."[12] And in 1920 she wrote to Mr. Robert B. House,[13] "I broke down in health because of overwork and strain of war."[14]

Loula's anguish is perhaps easier to understand in light of the fact that the United States was not yet involved in the war, and most people felt that it should not get involved. Even after the sinking of the *Lusitania*, there was a strong feeling that the war in Europe was none of America's business. Loula's sons had not been urged on by cheering crowds and patriotic music when they marched off to war. They left in silence, and there were many in the country who felt it was wrong for Americans to get involved in the war on either side. In 1915, the year of Loula's breakdown, one of the most popular songs in the country was "I Didn't Raise My Boy to Be a Soldier."

I didn't raise my boy to be a soldier,
I brought him up to be my pride and joy.
Who dares to place a musket on his shoulder,
To shoot some other mother's darling boy?
Let nations arbitrate their future troubles,
It's time to lay the sword and gun away.
There'd be no war today,
If mothers all would say,
"I didn't raise my boy to be a soldier."

The sheet music to that song sold more than 650,000 copies—a huge number for that time. There was no commercial radio in 1915, but dozens of artists recorded the song on popular records. Loula could not have avoided hearing it, and it would not have helped her mood.

Kiffin and Paul weren't the only things troubling Loula that winter. Her younger sister Mary's husband, Jacob Andrew Susong, wrote to Paul to express his concern. Andrew was the president of the First National Bank in Newport, Tennessee, and he helped Loula with her financial affairs. Her partnership with Dr. Meacham had broken up, and Dr. Meacham owed her money.

> Your mother was run down and spent about six weeks with us. She is badly run down in health. Her nervous condition is fearful. Dr. Meacham has annoyed her no little since they dissolved partnership.... As I see it, she made a very great mistake when she let Agnes go to Dallas. If she ever needed the help, comfort, and protection of her children, she certainly does need it now.... Dr. Meacham owes her some money. He has never taken up the mortgage he had given before she bought the house. He doesn't seem very anxious to do so. I have told your mother if she would turn the matter over to me, I would see that he settled it, and settled it at once. The matter has reached the point where your mother is almost afraid to stay in Asheville alone.[15]

The reference to Kiffin's sister Agnes going to Dallas stems from the fact that Agnes had gotten a job teaching at Southern Methodist University.

Surprisingly, the moment when Loula said she finally understood why her boys had gone to France came when she read a letter that Kiffin wrote after he was wounded. In the same interview in which she told a reporter about being frantic with grief, she said:

> It was while Kiffin was in the hospital at Rennes recovering from his wounds that he wrote me the letter that brought me to my senses.... I shall never forget that day. I was on my way to see a patient one morning when his letter was handed to me. I sat alone in my little car and there read his letter for the first time without shedding a tear. I saw then, for the first time, what impelled them to go to France, and saw it in the light that they saw it.[16]

She shared the letter with the reporter. It was the May 21 letter where Kiffin complained about the "wild letters" she had written trying to get him out of the Legion. She told the reporter, "It was this letter that brought me to myself. I realized that my sons were no longer boys to be dictated to, but men, and I felt the seriousness of their purpose. I was proud of their forefathers' fighting spirit that I saw in them, and I honored them for the vision of justice and right that they had caught."

Although Kiffin's letter may have been a turning point, it did not immediately resolve Loula's nervous strain. She still worried about her sons, and she still had to resolve her business problems with Dr. Meacham. She spent the winter of 1915–1916 at the lower altitude of Winston-Salem, North Carolina, for her health.[17] Kiffin's letter simply marked the beginning of her recovery. Her letters to Kiffin and Paul took on a cheerier note after Kiffin's hospitalization, filled more with family news and gossip than complaints. The interview with the newspaper reporter was given in 1918, by which time she was able to proudly declare, "If I had a dozen sons I should want them, too, to fight for France."

On May 30, Kiffin wrote his mother a much cheerier letter. He had heard good news from his regiment: The casualties weren't as bad as he initially thought. The five other Americans in his squad were unhurt, and two Americans in a different battalion were only slightly injured, so all eight of the Americans in the First Regiment made it through the attack. He described that as "a kind of a miracle."[18]

Kiffin also wrote to the Vicomte du Peloux to say that he was receiving excellent care and was working on his French. It was clear that even though he maintained his idealistic outlook, he was not immune to the horrors of war. "Sometimes, I nearly imagine that the whole war has been only a horrible nightmare," he wrote. "But it doesn't take me long to disillusion myself. The hospital has so many pitiful examples of the effects of the war—men crippled and terribly disfigured for life."[19]

Kiffin wrote to his mother again on June 15, assuring her that his wound was going to heal completely:

> In this war, if a rifle bullet doesn't kill one outright he can feel pretty sure of getting well, and in most cases have absolutely no bad effects. When a man gets hit by a rifle bullet he is considered lucky by everyone, himself included. It is only the pieces of shell and the poisonous gases that we are afraid of. The only rest one gets is when he is wounded; so it was really rather welcomed by me, although I am very tired of the hospital now and will be glad to leave it soon.[20]

The reference to "poisonous gasses" was prompted by the fact that the Germans used chlorine gas in an attack at Ypres on April 22, 1915, less than three weeks before Kiffin attacked at Artois. This was the first major use of a lethal gas during the war. Fortunately for the Allies, the German Army had little faith in the weapon, so they did not press the attack, and they did not have additional stocks of chlorine for follow-up assaults. The Allies quickly began improvising gas masks, many of which were made by civilian volunteers on the home front. It is doubtful that any of these masks reached the front before Kiffin's attack, however, so if the Germans had used gas at Artois, Kiffin would have been defenseless. The fact that Germany would use chemical weapons despite having signed an international agreement to ban them reinforced Kiffin's view that he was fighting for a greater cause. The letter in which he told his mother that the troops feared poison gas is also the first letter in which he said he was fighting for the cause of all humanity:

> So if I should be killed I think you ought to be proud in knowing that your son tried to be a man and was not afraid to die, and that he gave his life for a greater cause than most people do—the cause of all humanity. To me that doesn't appear a bad death at all. Otherwise, I may never do anything worthwhile, or any good to anyone after the war, and may live to regret that I wasn't killed in it. So whatever comes

I don't want you feeling sorrowful or worrying. And don't be afraid of my taking any foolish chances just to appear brave. I always take every precaution possible and have no desire to be killed by foolishness. Whatever is necessary to be done I try to do conscientiously, but that is all.[21]

He wrote to Paul on the same day, but not with the same cheery optimism: "I am damn tired of the hospital and either want to be where I can do as I please or back at the front." He had begun to hear from some of his friends in the Legion, and their letters didn't sound as though the big breakthrough he thought they had achieved was leading to a German collapse and the end of the war. Adding insult to injury, there had been several days of rainy weather, which was aggravating the rheumatism in his shoulder. His description of a woman who came to see him every day (Paul called her a "pretty blonde Alsatian") gives an indication of how low he was feeling: "The blonde comes down to see me every afternoon and I enjoy talking to her very much, as we have become quite friendly, but I'll be damned if women make much impression on me any longer."[22]

Paul Pavelka wrote to Kiffin on June 20 to let Kiffin know that he had been wounded during an attack. The Legion charged through a "most dreadful" hail of machine gun, rifle, and artillery fire only to leap into the first line of German trenches and find them empty. (This was not an unusual occurrence. During the intense bombardment before an Allied attack, the Germans frequently pulled men out of their front line trenches to reduce casualties.) The surviving legionnaires organized themselves into new squads in the trench and then attacked the second line. Pavelka's letter continued:

How many times I was compelled to lay down I could not say, but eventually I managed to reach that dear old second line of Germany. Say Rocks some surprise was in store for me you can bet. As I reached the edge of the trench I noticed the gray caps of the Bavarians, and almost instantly I felt a stinging pain shoot through my left leg. I got mine, and I dropped just in front of the trench. The next was a mix up of howling, and hurrahing, for tirailleurs, zouaves [Algerian light infantry units], and the Legion were all piling in on them. It was soon over, the Germans getting out and running for their lives, to the rear without any arms. Nobody stopped them. I got in the trench now and the rest went on. The blood ran freely from my wound as I put on the first aid package.

"Skipper" Pavelka had been bayoneted in his leg. Like Kiffin, he managed to hobble back to an evacuation station and was eventually transported to a hospital at Nogent-le-Rotrou. He concluded his letter to Kiffin by saying, "I got a horse on you though, for I had ten packages of tobacco in my sack where you only had six. Well you lost yours and so did I. But I should worry. I guess I'll get some tobacco and papers again some day in the near future. Well, Boy, keep up your courage, and get better so we can go down and pay them back in full. I will try my best not to die in the trenches."[23]

Kiffin forwarded the letter to his brother Paul, who quickly sent Pavelka some tobacco. Kiffin described Skipper and his correspondence to Paul:

Skipper evidently never received my letter in which I enclosed the "piece of change," so I am sending him five francs to-day to keep him in tobacco until I can send him more, and I want you to do anything you can for him from Paris. Skipper's family didn't amount to anything and he never had any education to speak of, and he has been on his own lookout ever since a child, rambling about the world, but he has the sentiments of a gentleman. He did not have to enlist for France, he could have gotten a boat away from Europe and continued as a sailor. But he is a good lad and brave. He has no way of getting money from home and no friends in France. Now I want you to find someone in Paris who appreciates that a chap like that is fighting for France, and who will take him when he gets his convalescence, so that he can enjoy it before returning to the front. You and I can keep him in spending money, and his wants are simple and few.[24]

Kiffin was relieved that Paul Pavelka had survived the attack, but a letter he had written to Kenneth Weeks had been returned, simply marked *retour à l'envoyeur* (return to sender). Kiffin attached a postscript to his letter to Paul, saying, "If you can locate Mrs. Weeks [Kenneth's mother, who was staying in Paris] you might see if you can find out anything about Kenneth." Paul did indeed locate Mrs. Weeks, who soon became an adopted member of their "family" in France.

Pavelka wrote to Kiffin a few days later, on June 24. His leg wound apparently was not as serious as Kiffin's, as he was already walking with the aid of a cane. The hospital where he was staying was in one wing of a girl's school, and Pavelka was asked to talk to a class where the girls were learning English. He did, and, much to his surprise, he was hired to tutor the girls for a few hours each day for as long as he remained in the hospital. He described his feelings to Kiffin:

Now what thinkest thou of thy boy Skipper? Some advancement from "soldat du deuxieme class" to "instituteur Anglais" [second-class soldier to English teacher]. Really dear Rocks. I can't see how it is, such funny adventures keep staring me in the face. Say boy after all I am beginning to like France. They are treating me different here, than those grouchy old non-coms in the Legion. . . . How K. W. [Kenneth Weeks] came out of it OK is more than I can see, for you know he was a grenadier and they armed him with a sack of bombs, besides a long knife with which to kill the German wounded who were left in the trenches after we had taken them, and then the bombists were ahead of us throwing their grenades. God, boy! He sure has nine lives like a cat. Some good luck for him too. All the Greeks had long knives given to them before the attack, and were ordered not to leave a living German behind them for on May 9, after we had crossed the German line many of them came out of their "caniacs" [dugouts] and opened fire on us from the rear. Not only these but also the wounded were shooting at us, causing us nearly double the loss. Damned skunks![25]

Pavelka was especially pleased that Paul Rockwell had written to him, even though they had never met, as he said that Paul and Kiffin were the only ones who had replied to any of his letters. Lying wounded in a foreign land, it meant a lot to him to hear from people who cared. Paul had commented in his letter that he expected the war to last another winter. "If that is the case," Pavelka replied, "I am going to propose to have the front removed to the south." He also said he was honored that the boys had nicknamed him "Skipper."[26]

On June 24, 1915, Kiffin was finally transferred to the convalescence hospital, *Hôpital Convalescence No. 83* in Rennes. There he learned, to his dismay, that although he was going to get thirty days' convalescent leave, he would have to spend those days at a troop depot because he had no proof that he had somewhere to stay in Paris. He sent a frantic postcard to Paul asking him to send a certificate of lodging, signed by the mayor, to prove he had a place to stay. Paul sent the certificate, and Kiffin was able to spend his leave in Paris. Before he left, he wrote a short note to his mother thanking her and Agnes for the letters they had sent him while he was in the hospital. It appears that in one of those letters his mother may have suggested that he had already done enough for France, as Kiffin replied:

In regard to what I have done for France—I had rather be fighting for France than doing anything else now. If one is going to fight, I don't see why the *country* should have as great an influence as the *principle*. I am just following out my old theory that we are a part of this whole scheme of affairs and that we can't successfully confine ourselves to one small district. Everyone over here is suffering but the people are growing calmer all the time.

6

Maman Légionnaire

The soldiers are not all at the front.

—ALICE WEEKS

MRS. ALICE WEEKS'S NAME DOES NOT SHOW UP ON ANY OFFICIAL ROSTER of the French Foreign Legion, but she was an important part of that unit just the same. She was the mother of Kenneth Weeks, a legionnaire in the First Regiment with Kiffin. Before the war, Kenneth graduated from the Massachusetts Institute of Technology (MIT), and in 1911 he went to France to study architecture. Life in France seems to have encouraged his literary talents more than his architectural skill, as by the time the war began he had published five books of plays, short stories, and essays. He enlisted in the Foreign Legion at the beginning of the war.

When the war began, Mrs. Weeks was living in Boston with her husband, a Harvard associate professor of zoology and entomology.[1] In January 1915, Kenneth wrote that his unit might be given thirty days *repose* (rest) soon, and if she wanted to take a trip to France, they could see each other. (She had spent considerable time in France before the war, so this was not an unusual suggestion.) He said he would send her a cable if he learned anything definite about the repose.[2]

Mrs. Weeks did not wait for the cable. She made arrangements to go to France, and by late February 1915 she had rented an apartment in Paris. Initially her focus was on Kenneth. In the months to come, however, she would meet many of her son's friends from the Legion. Most of the Americans serving in the Legion had no friends or family in France, so she began sending them letters and packages. In time she became known as *Maman*

Légionnaire, "mother" to the legionnaires. She didn't just help American legionnaires; Russian legionnaires, Belgian legionnaires, French legionnaires whose families were trapped behind enemy lines, and any other legionnaire who didn't have a family in France found an adopted mother in Mrs. Weeks. The grateful legionnaires in turn often stopped by to visit her when they were on leave. (Considering how rare it was to get leave, and how many other "entertainments" wartime Paris had to offer, the fact that they would use some of their precious leave time to visit Mrs. Weeks indicates that they held her in very high regard.)

Mrs. Weeks also got involved with many volunteer aid societies in Paris. They made clothing for the soldiers, prepared first aid packets, and sent food to the troops. When the Germans launched the first poison gas attack, Mrs. Weeks immediately organized an effort to make gas masks for the troops. The masks consisted of a cloth pad soaked in chemicals with an elastic strap so a soldier could wear the mask over his nose and mouth to neutralize the gas. They were primitive, but they would save a life. Mrs. Weeks described making these masks to her brother Fred in the United States:

> I have just turned out 150 gas masks and sent them to the front and have 200 more to do this week. There is a lot of work in them and they have to be made with great care as any carelessness would mean a life. They are shaped like a small mattress made of cheesecloth, dipped in coffee, to be as near as we can make them the color of the face. The chemicals are put between the cotton inside and the little mattresses are tufted and an elastic on either end goes about the head. They have to be soaked in water and worn wet. I do not leave the chemicals for anyone else to use as they have to be measured carefully and one must be sure a mask is not overlooked. On each I put a couple of safety pins.[3]

She would make hundreds of gas masks in the coming weeks, until mass production of a more sophisticated mask that protected the eyes as well as the lungs rendered the home-made masks obsolete.

Mrs. Weeks's involvement with her son's friends became more intense in May, as a result of the Battle of Artois. Her son Kenneth took part in the initial attack on May 9, the attack in which Kiffin was wounded. Kenneth was unhurt in that attack, and for several days he participated in the fighting around Neuville-Saint-Vaast. He wrote a letter to his mother on May 11, which he gave to a wounded soldier heading back to safety. The letter said they had captured the enemy trenches. He was all right, but he was still involved in heavy fighting. She shouldn't worry if she didn't hear from him for several days.[4]

In the short time she had been in France, Mrs. Weeks had made some influential friends. One afternoon she had lunch with Madame Jousselin, the American wife of a Paris councilor. Monsieur Jousselin worked closely with Monsieur Georges Leygues, president of the French government's Foreign Affairs Committee, and Monsieur de Sillac, a diplomat attached to the French Ministry of Foreign Affairs. Among other things, these men took an interest in French aviation. Monsieur Jousselin asked Mrs. Weeks whether her son Kenneth would like to transfer to the aviation service. That would get him out of the trenches, and he would spend an extended period training in the south of France. Mrs. Weeks wrote to Kenneth about this opportunity.[5]

In Kenneth's reply, he said that he wasn't interested in the aviation service. He was doing his best to get revenge for the *Lusitania*.[6] He followed up with several letters over the next few days. His unit was resting behind the lines and had finally received their tobacco issue, so things were going well, although he did say they were in a "wretched little village" where it was hard to even get an egg. A legionnaire on leave in Paris had told Mrs. Weeks that Kenneth was wounded, but Kenneth reassured her that he was unhurt. "A chap named Rockwell was shot in the knee," he wrote, "and X. [the soldier who told her Kenneth was wounded] mixed him up with me. If you see him [Rockwell], by the way, be kind to him."[7]

Relieved to know that Kenneth was alive and unhurt, Mrs. Weeks happened to run into the American ambassador to France at a social function. (The president of France, Raymond Poincaré, was also at this event. Mrs. Weeks was definitely traveling in elevated circles.) This was not Ambassador Herrick, the Taft appointee who had advised the Americans to join the Foreign Legion to preserve their citizenship. He had been replaced by a Wilson appointee, William C. Sharp, who strictly adhered to Wilson's neutrality policy. Mrs. Weeks wrote about their meeting to her brother, Fred:

> I had a talk with our Ambassador the other day, and he did not seem
> to understand what prompted the American boys to join the Foreign
> Legion. He said very emphatically, "You know our President has asked

the people to be neutral." This started me on a long harangue about our love of freedom and also our connection with France through Lafayette. I also added that those who had lived and loved France before the war should be willing to fight for her and I felt proud that our boys had the courage to do what they considered was right, which after all is what our country must depend on in time of trouble.

The ambassador was apparently impressed by her passion, and also with the circles she traveled in. He told her, "You know, I believe you have more power than I have over here."

"Of course," she replied. "Because I am a woman!"[8]

Her efforts to change America's attitude weren't confined to conversations with the ambassador. She also wrote to newspapers and to friends to let them know what was really happening in Europe. She told her son Allen, "We are doing all we can to correct the ridiculous letters and speeches in America." She was particularly upset about a letter published in the *New York Times*, supposedly from someone in Paris, saying the city lived in fear because of nightly bombing raids by German Zeppelins. The letter also said the city was filled with sad-eyed women. Mrs. Weeks thought this letter was absurd. On the rare occasions when Zeppelins did try to raid Paris, she said, everyone went outside to watch just as if it were a fireworks show. (The searchlights and anti-aircraft fire probably reminded many of fireworks.)[9] As for the sad-eyed women, she had never seen a tear in the street. Once in a while she would walk into a store and see a shop girl surrounded by her friends, consoling her because she had just received bad news, but the moment someone walked in, the girl would proudly straighten up and ask, "What will Madame have?" Mrs. Weeks concluded by saying, "The soldiers are not all at the front."[10]

Mrs. Weeks continued to exchange letters with her son Kenneth as the balmy May weather eased into unusually hot days in June. On May 27, Kenneth apparently had second thoughts about learning to fly, as he asked his mother to find out whether he could still get into Aviation. "Of course, I know nothing of aeroplanes," he wrote, "but I did once of motors, and I could study."[11] She sent him the information about how to request a transfer to Aviation, but the request would have to come from him. She sent him reminders to submit his request over the next several weeks. On June 14,

1915, he wrote to her that he was about to go into the trenches to prepare for another attack. "In view of this attack," he wrote, "I think I may as well wait until afterwards about my demand for the aviation."[12]

And then the letters stopped coming. Like any mother, Mrs. Weeks feared the worst but hoped for the best. His letters had been held up before. Wounded friends from the Legion (among them Kiffin and Paul Pavelka) wrote to their friends to try to find news of Kenneth. There were rumors that he was among a group of legionnaires that had been taken prisoner by the Germans. Perhaps he was being held in Belgium, where rumor had it prisoners were not allowed to write home.

A little over a month after she received her last letter from Kenneth, the government officially notified her that Kenneth was "missing." He might be dead, or he might be alive. They did not know. She contacted the American ambassador for help but was told that "this agency knows nothing about those Americans who have volunteered in the Foreign Legion ... and makes it a point to know nothing about them."[13] Finally, on New Year's Day 1916, Mrs. Weeks was notified by the French government that Kenneth had fallen on the Field of Honor on June 17, 1915.[14] Later she would learn that her son's body had actually been found and buried the previous November, but it took more than a month for her to receive the notification.[15]

Much to her credit, Mrs. Weeks realized that even though her son was gone, there were many other soldiers in France who needed her help. She continued to send letters and packages to Americans fighting in France and to soldiers from other nations who, for whatever reason, did not have a family to turn to. She rented a larger apartment, with several rooms, so her *filleuls* (godsons) would have a place to stay when they were on leave in Paris. When the United States finally entered the war in 1917, she organized a new charity, the "Home Service for United States Soldiers," to help take care of these men when they were in Paris. Eventually she worked herself into a state of exhaustion, and her doctor insisted she return to the United States a few months before the war ended. A grateful French nation made her a Chevalier de la Légion d'Honneur (Knight of the Legion of Honor).

It would be hard to overestimate how important Mrs. Weeks was to the soldiers she adopted. Young men, some of them away from home for the first time, serving in a foreign country where they might not speak the language, spending month after month in the mud and filth of the trenches, suddenly had a "mother" who would write to them and send packages. Sweets, warm clothing, tobacco—things they couldn't buy at the front and couldn't get from home. And when they finally got a few days' leave, they could show up at her doorstep and she would give them a place to stay. And it wasn't an army barracks, nor a threadbare hotel room—it was a home. With clean sheets. And home cooking. And a "mother" who looked after them and cared about their welfare. A *Maman Légionnaire.*

7

Back to the Legion

I am going to try to get Kiffin Rockwell into the aeroplane service.

—ALICE WEEKS

KIFFIN WAS FINALLY RELEASED FROM THE HOSPITAL AND GOT TO SPEND the month of July 1915 in Paris on convalescent leave. He and Paul called upon Mrs. Weeks early in the month, and they quickly became good friends. They saw her frequently during Kiffin's leave, and in fact Paul (who was himself still on convalescent leave but soon to be discharged) would begin sharing an apartment with Mrs. Weeks after Kiffin's leave was up.

Kiffin and Paul also visited the Vicomte and Vicomtesse du Peloux. Kiffin described them to his mother as "two of the finest people I ever knew." And, of course, Kiffin met Paul's fiancée Jeanne and her family. He described them as "awfully nice people, and very influential in France." He concluded his first letter to his mother after meeting Paul's fiancée by saying, "I think Paul will be married before many months, and he has certainly found a fine girl. Agnes will enjoy coming over to see them and the Vicomte & wife very much after the war."[1]

Paul and Kiffin had dinner with another old friend in Paris. Bill Thaw was there on a twenty-four-hour leave from his assignment flying French Caudron observation/bombing planes at the front. Bill encouraged Kiffin to request a transfer to Aviation, especially since Kiffin's leg was still bothering him and he didn't know whether he could manage the Legion's long marches. Kiffin agreed and submitted his request.[2]

Kiffin met with one other notable during his convalescent leave— Ambassador Sharp. Kiffin wrote his mother, "He was very nice to me, but I don't think much of him as an ambassador." The ambassador told Kiffin he had received a letter from Loula asking him to get Kiffin and Paul out of the army, but when he had gone to the War Department, they told him that was impossible. He then asked Kiffin whether there was anything else he could do for them. Kiffin asked him to go back to those same people and let them know that Kiffin regretted that such a request had ever been made. "I hope to get a few favors from the War Department now," he told his mother, "so I want to fix things up with them."[3] Presumably those "favors" included a transfer to Aviation.

Mrs. Weeks buried herself in war work to help keep her sanity, as at this point her son was still listed as "missing." Now she realized that Kiffin would soon return to the front. She wrote to her other son, Allen, "I have become very fond of Kiffin and Paul Rockwell, and Pavelka, and it is going to be hard to let them go back. I am going to try to get Kiffin Rockwell into the aeroplane service."[4]

Kiffin left on a train that night to return to the Foreign Legion. He wrote to Mrs. Weeks the next day, obviously feeling blue that his leave in Paris was over:

My dear good, sweet second mother,

I read your letter last night on the train and it did make me feel much better and happier. But I spent, I think, the saddest night in my life. I was not sad because I was going back to the war, but it was from thinking of the ones who stay behind. I was in a second-class coach and very comfortable but I could not sleep. I just thought and thought all night long and could not keep the tears out of my eyes. I want to live now more than I ever did in my life, but not from the selfish standpoint. This war has taught me many things, and now I want to live to do whatever good is possible. But if I am killed at any time during the war I will not be afraid to die, and you may know that I will die like a man should, feeling that it is the greatest death that a man can die. I will always take the greatest care of myself and not do foolish things, but will always try to do my duty to the utmost for what we are fighting for.[5]

His initial assignment was to a depot at Lyon. He described it to Paul:

Well, I arrived here all o. k. this morning and spent the morning getting settled. Conditions don't look very good. The place is filthy dirty
and they say rotten food, but tomorrow morning I am going to the
doctor and ask for electric treatment [probably an electrical stimula-
tion of his damaged leg muscles] . . . I only found one man here that I
know. He was in my squad and shot through the shoulder. Every time
I inquire after anyone they say "dead," except Kenneth Weeks and the
other boys. No one seems to know. But I was told that we lost ground
on June 16th.[6]

Paul Pavelka also returned to the Legion. He was sent to La Valbonne,
a training site about twenty-five miles from Kiffin's camp. Mrs. Weeks had
also convinced Pavelka to apply for a transfer to Aviation, but he couldn't
write French well enough to fill out the paperwork. Kiffin offered to help,
but the officers at La Valbonne wouldn't grant Pavelka leave to go visit Kiffin. Kiffin then tried to get transferred to La Valbonne. He was extremely
fed up with the unit at Lyon. He had absolutely nothing to do, was bored
out of his mind, and worried that all the best legionnaires were being
released and only a "rotten bunch" would remain. At one point he wrote to
Paul, "To hell with a commission. All I want now is to get out."[7]

Kiffin's frustrations at Lyon included not seeing eye to eye with the
corporal in charge of his squad. The corporal started to call Kiffin out at
drill, but the adjutant interceded and said he wished he had more men like
Kiffin in the company. While that saved Kiffin in the short term, it left the
corporal with a brooding dislike for him. In a letter to Mrs. Weeks, he commented on how the stress of this relationship bothered him. "I have a strong
constitution and for that reason physical hardships do not bother me," he
wrote, "whereas mental ones do very much."[8] He would encounter much
more mental stress when he began flying combat missions at the front.

On August 9, Kiffin finally managed to get transferred to La Valbonne,
so he was once again in the same unit as Pavelka. He helped Pavelka fill out
his application to transfer into Aviation, and Pavelka sent it to Mrs. Weeks
the next day. Surprisingly, they almost immediately got results. Kiffin wrote
to Mrs. Weeks:

Yesterday afternoon, I was to the point of not caring about anything or
what happened, when Pavelka came over to where I was. He had just

been called up about the aviation. In a few minutes they were around looking for me. I went to the bureau and found that an order had come in to transfer the two Legionnaires, Pavelka and Rockwell, to the aviation corps. We were so happy that last night we got several of the boys together and had a regular celebration. This morning, Pavelka and I were busy signing papers at the bureau and passing the medical visit to see if we were all right. Now we are just waiting for the order to move.[9]

Kiffin and Pavelka may have been happy, but they seemed to be the only ones. Kiffin described the bad attitudes he was seeing in a letter to Paul: "There is really not much hard work to do here, and plenty of cafes right in the camp, but it seems to be in the air for everyone to be completely demoralized and it is nothing but grumbling and yelling from morning to night. Prison sentences are handed out freely on the slightest pretext."[10]

A few days later, Kiffin was called to the Bureau (Camp HQ) and told to sign a *contre visite* (a reason for not going). Apparently paperwork had been received ordering Kiffin and Pavelka to leave that morning for flight training, but no one had told them about it. Now he was being asked to explain why he had not followed those orders. Kiffin was furious with "the stupidity of these fellows here in the Bureau."[11]

Adding to their frustration, they began a period of intense training on trench warfare, something Kiffin and most of the other soldiers had experienced for the past year. He wrote to his brother:

Just got in this morning from twenty-four hours of trench life. Yesterday morning, they took the company out at daybreak. It was awfully hot and the company worked all day long digging trenches. . . . twenty-four hours of steady work with three hours rest in the middle of the day and one hour at midnight, and then the regular hourly ten-minute repose. All to teach them how to make trenches and how to live in them, most of us knew more about it through experience than the officers did. This afternoon we go out for bayonet exercise and grenade throwing.[12]

The training was far from being the worst aspect of life at Valbonne. Paul Rockwell wrote, "The officers at the camp were as a rule not up to the standard of those who commanded the Legionnaires at the front. Many of them, by means of intrigue or influence, had been able to keep away from the firing line, and had little sympathy for either the recruits or the men who had been wounded." Kiffin gave a few examples of the problems he saw in his letters to Paul:

Two days ago the Commandant passed a review of the men proposed for the *reforme* [medical discharge]. Nearly all of them had been wounded, the only one not was Krogh, who is proposed owing to heart trouble. All of the men had been in the trenches all winter. Because these men were going to get out of it through the doctors, the Commandant was sore as hell. He lined them up, some of them could hardly walk, and cursed them out. He told them they were not worth a damn, that they disgraced the Legion, and that they only came here for *la gamelle* [the food bowl]. Now, we have heard that from sergeants and such all the time. But for a Commandant to tell men who have ruined themselves for life out of a love for France and the principles she is fighting for, I think it is going a little too far.

The same day, August 25th, Sergeant Bergeron, 2eme Cie. [2nd Battalion, Company C], went up to a Greek volunteer who could not speak French, and began to curse him about something or other. The Greek could not answer him but just stood at attention. The sergeant kept on talking, and finally hit the Greek twice in the face, knocking him down. The Greek got an interpreter and went to the bureau to réclame [file a complaint], but they only laughed at him.

My corporal is a Greek about twenty-one years old. He served through the Balkan wars, coming out a sergeant. He was wounded twice in them, once a revolver bullet, the other time a bayonet. He enlisted here at the outbreak of the war, was a 2ème classe [2nd Battalion soldier]. On May 9th he was in the first line of men out of the trenches. He was the only man in his squad that didn't fall May 9th, and was named Corporal a few days afterwards. On June 16th, he was wounded, but left the hospital as soon as possible, came here and asked to return at once to the front. They said he was not well enough, and kept him here. He sleeps next to me. Three nights ago he didn't sleep a wink, owing to a toothache. The following morning he reported sick. The doctor gave him consultation motive ["excused absence" for seeing the doctor], but didn't exempt him from exercise. To report sick he had to miss the morning exercise. They have a rule now that if you report sick and are not given exempt service you go to prison for eight days. This morning they read out eight days prison for the corporal. He took it badly, telling me that he had never before in his military career served a half-hour's prison sentence. He came back here, and I held his coat, while he cut his stripes off. On his way to the prison he carried the stripes and threw them on the floor at the bureau, and told them he wouldn't have them.[13]

Sadly, it wasn't only Kiffin who was encountering treatment like this, and it wasn't limited to the Legion. During this period, the French Army was infamous for its mistreatment of enlisted troops, infrequent and unfair granting of leave, and senseless bayonet attacks against fortified positions. In less than two years, it would lead to widespread mutiny. Troops refused to attack and only reluctantly manned defensive positions, baa'ing like sheep as they marched to the front to show that they were lambs being led to the slaughter. That mutiny was still in the future, however.

On September 1, 1915, Kiffin wrote to his brother:

Just came in this morning from another twenty-four hours of work and no sleep in the trenches. That is a better idea than the kind of drilling we had last fall [the bayonet rushes across empty fields at Toulouse], but I get tired of it, after having had seven months of the real thing. . . . There is not much doing here. I will leave sometime between now and the 15th for the front, not later than the 15th, if I am not transferred before then. I can't tell anything about what they are going to do, so don't know whether it will be for the Dardanelles or this front. If I go to the Dardanelles will go to Algeria first and spend one week at Sidi Bel-Abbès before going on.[14]

For some reason, Kiffin did not mail this letter the day he wrote it. Paul received it several days later, and tucked into the same envelope was an undated, jubilant note from Kiffin at Avord Aviation Training School. His transfer to Aviation had finally come through.

8

From Flying Birdcages
to War Machines

*Elijah was reputed to be the patron saint of aviators, but as he went
to Heaven in a chariot of fire, this was something we weren't too
keen about.*[1]

—KIFFIN ROCKWELL

AVIATION WAS STILL IN ITS INFANCY WHEN KIFFIN ENTERED FLIGHT
training, but it was growing up fast. Today it's hard to comprehend how
rapidly aircraft evolved during World War I. A new design might become
obsolete in a matter of months, overtaken by even newer and better designs.
The Wright brothers made the world's first airplane flight—a twelve-second
hop that covered 120 feet—in December 1903. Less than six years later
Louis Bleriot made the first flight across the English Channel, a distance
of thirty-one miles. Almost exactly five years after that, in August 1914,
the Royal Flying Corps (RFC) flew sixty aircraft across the channel to go
to war. This was roughly three-quarters of the entire British air force.[2] By
the end of the war, the RFC had become the RAF and boasted more than
twenty thousand aircraft.[3]

None of the sixty airplanes the RFC initially flew across the channel
were armed. The same was true of the eighty airplanes the French had when
the war began,[4] and the roughly two hundred airplanes the Germans had.[5]
While the pilots were certainly eager to fly and fight, the primary mission
of these early planes was reconnaissance and that did not require an armed

plane. Weapons and ammunition added weight, and the aircraft of 1914 had a tough enough time crawling into the air without weapons.

Early airplanes look almost comical by today's standards, but it's important to realize there was nothing funny about them at the time. They were the cutting edge of technology. The designers did the best they could with the materials and the knowledge they had. To keep the planes lightweight, they used wood, fabric, and tubular metal. Early engines produced very little power, so wings had to have a large surface area to produce lift at slow speeds. In 1914, this meant thin wings that required external bracing wires to keep them from bending or breaking. As the war progressed, designers developed ways to make stronger airframes and the need for external wires decreased, leading to faster and more streamlined aircraft. But in 1914 the planes had so many wires and braces they were sometimes called "flying bird cages."

Another critical factor that affected airplane design was power. Pioneer aviator/daredevil Lincoln Beachy is credited with originating the phrase "give me enough power and I'll fly a barn door."[6] There is some truth in that statement, but the source of power has to be light. Aircraft engines developed rapidly during World War I, and many airplanes were literally designed around an available engine. There were two basic engine types used during the war—inline engines and rotary engines.

Inline engines were similar to the engines used in most cars today. Cylinders were arranged in a line. This resulted in a long crankshaft and crankcase, which added weight. Aircraft engines couldn't afford to use the heavy flywheels that car engines used to dampen vibrations, so engine speed was limited. Most inline engines were water cooled and required a radiator, which added still more weight.

A clever solution to many of these problems was the rotary engine. The cylinders were arranged radially around a short crankshaft, like the radial engines used during World War II. In a radial engine, however, the engine stays still, and the crankshaft turns. Rotary engines worked the other way. The crankshaft was fastened to the airplane. This meant the crankshaft stayed still and the engine spun around the crankshaft. The propeller was bolted to the spinning engine.

This unusual design had several advantages. It was short and compact, which kept it lightweight. The spinning engine block acted as a flywheel. And because the finned cylinders were spinning through the air, the air kept the engine cool and it didn't need a radiator.

The design also had some disadvantages. In general, they ran at full throttle or not at all. To reduce speed for landings, the pilots used a "kill switch" on the control stick to "blip" the engine on and off. This produced a distinctive "Brrrrp . . . Brrrp . . . Brrrp" sound when landing. To keep the bearings lubricated, oil was continuously injected into the air intake. It was not unusual for a rotary engine to use six to eight quarts of oil per hour.[7] Unburnt oil spewed out the exhaust and splattered everything within reach, including the pilot's windscreen and goggles. Pilots carried a rag to wipe these clean. Also, the engines were lubricated with castor oil because it didn't turn to sludge at the cold temperatures encountered when flying at high altitudes. Castor oil has been used as a laxative for centuries, and castor oil fumes could make pilots very uncomfortable on long flights. (Fortunately, pilots seemed to develop a tolerance for this problem over time.)[8]

The gyroscopic forces generated by the spinning mass of the engine caused rotary engine planes to have unusual handling characteristics. When the pilot turned to the right, the gyroscopic forces pushed the nose of the plane down. Unless the pilot compensated, the plane would go into a spiraling dive. When climbing, the gyroscopic forces made the plane try to bank to the right.[9]

Despite these drawbacks, the high power-to-weight ratio and compact size of rotary engines made them an ideal choice for many planes in 1914, especially for small single-seat aircraft. Later in the war, engine manufacturers would develop inline engines with enough power to overcome their other drawbacks and make them the engines of choice, but rotary engines were popular early in the war.[10]

At the beginning of the war all the combatants had a mixture of different aircraft types. Single-seat and two-seat, monoplanes and biplanes, rotary engines and inline engines—all saw service in 1914. As the war progressed, however, aircraft began to be used for specialized missions, and different types of aircraft were developed for each type of mission.

One of the first, and perhaps most obvious, uses of military airplanes was for reconnaissance. Or at least, it was obvious to the pilots. They knew how easily they could spot things from the air, and they suspected they could fly over enemy lines with a fair chance of survival. Higher-ranking, non-flying officers who commanded the armies were skeptical. In 1910, Ferdinand Foch, who would eventually become the Allied commander in chief, said, "The airplane is all very well for sport, but useless for the army."[11]

Skepticism was even greater among cavalry officers, as reconnaissance was *their* mission. Before the war one British cavalry officer declared that airplanes could never replace the cavalry and complained that "the noise these damned things make will frighten our horses."[12]

Once the war started, the airplane quickly proved its worth for reconnaissance. French and British pilots reported on the enormous size of the German armies marching through Belgium, although at first the high command refused to believe the armies were really that large. Aerial reconnaissance also brought the first reports that the German right wing was turning short of Paris, exposing its flank to General Galliéni and the "Taxicab Army" that helped precipitate the Battle of the Marne.[13]

There were also some mistakes, caused mostly by the inexperience of the pilots. Early in the war, British pilots mistook gravestones for tents, and tar spots on a roadway for marching German soldiers.[14] French lieutenant Georges Thénault proved aircraft weren't invulnerable to ground fire, even when flying at what he thought was a safe altitude of 3,600 feet. He was brought down on August 7, 1914, while returning from a reconnaissance mission. Lieutenant Thénault believed he was the first pilot to be shot down during the war,[15] but although his engine was disabled by ground fire, he was able to glide back to French-held territory. He survived and later became the commander of the Lafayette Escadrille (and Kiffin Rockwell's commanding officer).

Bombing was another obvious use of aircraft. Since airplanes could fly over enemy troops, they could drop things on them. Early in the war the problem was that airplanes barely had enough power to lift a pilot into the air. While some planes could carry bombs, they had to be very small, little more than hand grenades. When used against vulnerable targets, these could be effective, provided they hit the target (which proved to be more difficult than pilots expected). On August 28, 1914, Lieutenant Louis A. Strange made what is believed to be the first successful aerial bomb run of the war. He dropped a homemade petrol bomb on a German truck near Mons, Belgium. The truck swerved off the road and caught fire, and the fire spread to a truck behind it.[16] (Lieutenant Strange took part in several history-making exploits during the war. More remarkably, he was one of the few prewar pilots who flew throughout the war and lived to see it end.)

Lieutenant Strange and Lieutenant Thénault both described another form of bombing: dropping steel *fléchettes* on enemy troops. Fléchettes were steel darts, about the size of a pencil. They could be deadly if they struck their target, but, again, aiming them was extremely difficult. Lieutenant Thénault fastened a case of fifty fléchettes to his airplane, rigged to drop all fifty at once when he pulled a cable.[17]

A third basic mission, and one that arguably was the most important during this war, was artillery spotting. Artillery was *the* dominant weapon during World War I. Troops huddled in trenches were well protected from rifle and machine gun fire. For the most part, those weapons were only a threat when the troops climbed out of their trenches to attack. Artillery could strike anywhere, at any time. It could kill troops huddled in a trench. It could pulverize enemy defenses before an attack. It could destroy targets of opportunity, like the kitchen that Kiffin's Foreign Legion unit brought too close to the lines. It could even hit targets up to twenty-five miles behind the lines, destroying marshalling areas, supply depots, and enemy artillery. But artillery couldn't hit anything unless someone could see the target and direct the fire. Balloon observers could direct artillery fire against targets in the enemy's front lines, but anything farther back required an airplane to help aim the guns. Someone had to fly over the target and tell the battery to aim farther to the left or right, or to increase or decrease the range. Airplanes sent Morse code signals to the battery by radio, or "wireless," as it was called at the time. This was a one-way communication. The equipment needed to receive radio signals was much too bulky and fragile to be carried in an airplane, and the noise of the airplane would have made it useless anyway.

Of course, the enemy was not content to sit back and watch the spotter plane circle overhead until the artillery hit its target. Artillery spotters had to contend with intense anti-aircraft fire. They could usually fly high enough to be out of range of rifle and small arms fire, and by changing course and altitude unpredictably they could often throw off the aim of anti-aircraft cannons. It was dangerous work, though, and very nerve-wracking. Sometimes the enemy jammed the radio signal or sent false signals to the receiving station. That was the dawn of Electronic Counter-Measures, or ECM.[18]

These early missions proved that aircraft could successfully conduct multiple types of missions, but they also showed the need to use different kinds of aircraft for different missions. Reconnaissance and artillery-spotting aircraft needed to fly high enough and fast enough to avoid getting shot down. Two-seat aircraft were generally preferred, as the pilot could fly the plane while the observer took notes on enemy activity, photographed points of interest, or tapped out Morse code signals to the artillery.

Ideally a bomber would also be fast and fly high, but it was more important that it be able to carry a large bomb load. In practice, this generally meant larger, heavier aircraft. That made them bigger targets, but able to do more damage when they reached their target.

Single-seat aircraft were occasionally used for reconnaissance, especially if there was a specific objective, such as "look for activity at the railhead." Being smaller and lighter, single-seat aircraft were generally faster and could get in, take a look, and get back with less chance of being hit by ground fire. Rarely were single-seat aircraft used for artillery spotting, because it was difficult to watch a target, signal the battery, and fly the airplane at the same time.[19] Most pilots enjoyed flying single-seat aircraft because they were fast and responsive, but early in the war there was little military use for this type.

Despite the danger posed by anti-aircraft fire, during the early part of the war reconnaissance missions and artillery-spotting missions were usually successful. An indication of how successful they were is given by the fact that in January 1915, Sir Douglas Haig, then the commander of the British First Army, called Colonel Hugh Trenchard, who commanded his aviation section, to his office and told him about plans for an upcoming offensive. Haig told Trenchard he was planning to attack in April but said, "If you can't fly because of the weather, I shall probably call off the attack."[20] In six months the airplane had gone from being a machine to frighten horses to an indispensable component of an upcoming offensive.

Because airplanes were an indispensable component of any military operation, it was imperative that commanders *not* let enemy airplanes operate freely over the battlefield. This was obvious to the men in the trenches, too. Just like Kiffin's unit and the field kitchen, troops learned that when enemy airplanes flew over, bad things happened. The artillery barrage might hit immediately or it might come later, but if enemy planes were allowed to fly unimpeded, troops on the ground would die. Enemy airplanes had to be shot down. This was a critical part of the military mission, and it was essential to maintain the morale of troops on the ground.[21]

Shooting down an enemy plane was harder than it looked. Ground gunners had to estimate the altitude and speed of the enemy plane and aim at the point where the plane would be when the bullet reached that altitude.

Pilots were usually able to avoid ground fire by flying high and taking evasive maneuvers. This made it harder for them to carry out their mission, but they did carry it out. Occasionally ground fire succeeded in shooting down airplanes, but it was not a dependable way to prevent the enemy from carrying out air missions. A more reliable way of shooting down enemy aircraft was needed, and the obvious solution was to use your airplanes to shoot down the enemy's airplanes.

This was not as easy as it sounded. Contrary to popular mythology, pilots and observers carried pistols, rifles, and shotguns to shoot at enemy planes from the earliest days of the war. There were a few instances where unarmed pilots waved at each other, but that was generally because neither one had expected to encounter an enemy plane during that flight. In most cases, the next time they took off, they carried a gun. This was a shooting war, and they were ready to shoot at the enemy. It was very difficult to hit an enemy plane with these weapons, however. The problems that ground troops had hitting a moving airplane were multiplied when the shooter was also in a moving airplane. Now the shooter had to take his own plane's speed, direction, and altitude into account as well as the speed, direction, altitude, and distance to the enemy plane. This was called "deflection" shooting because the relative movement of the planes made it appear as though the bullet was deflected into a curve.

Using a machine gun obviously improved one's chances of hitting the enemy machine. The ability to launch a spray of bullets would help compensate for the difficulty of aiming. Pilots tried using machine guns early in the war. The problem was weight. Machine guns of that era were heavy. Even a "lightweight" Lewis machine gun weighed nearly thirty pounds, plus roughly ten pounds per ammunition drum. This didn't mean an airplane couldn't carry a machine gun, but the extra weight definitely affected the plane's performance. During the first month of the war, the indomitable Lieutenant Strange mounted a Lewis machine gun on his Maurice Farman biplane. On August 22, 1914, a German Aviatik flew over his airfield at an altitude of 5,000 feet. Strange took off with a Lieutenant Gaskell as his observer/gunner to shoot it down. Unfortunately, with the added weight of the gun and the ammunition, Strange could not coax his plane to go above 3,500 feet. The German flew home unmolested, probably unaware that he had even been chased. When Strange landed, his commanding officer ordered him to remove the machine gun and stick to using a rifle.[22]

Engines and aircraft developed quickly during the war, and it wasn't long until it was possible to carry a machine gun aloft and still have acceptable performance. Two-seat airplanes were the first to be armed with machine guns. This made sense at the time because they were larger, with more powerful engines, and the extra weight did not affect them as much as it affected a small single-seat plane. Also, having a second person aboard allowed the pilot to concentrate on flying the plane while the observer/gunner kept his focus on aiming and firing the gun. And, of course, two-seat aircraft were the primary military airplane of the day, used for bombing, reconnaissance, and artillery spotting. They were more likely to come into contact with enemy aircraft, as single-seat "scouts" were just used for quick dashes over the lines.

While two-seat airplanes could and did shoot down enemy aircraft, arming an observer in the back seat proved not to be the ideal solution. While he had an excellent field of fire to the sides and above the plane, his field of fire to the rear was partially blocked by the tail and, more important, he could not fire forward without hitting the wings, the pilot, or the propeller. This meant that when chasing an enemy plane, the attacker would have to catch up and pull alongside the other plane before the observer could shoot. If the other plane had an armed observer, the attacking plane would come within his field of fire long before the attacking plane could fire back. Observers in the back were much better positioned for defense than for offense. And even if the attacking plane caught up and the two planes exchanged "broadsides," it was still difficult to shoot down a plane. Oswald Boelcke piloted an armed two-seat plane during the summer of 1915. He flew escort missions, protecting German reconnaissance planes, for three weeks before his observer was able to bring down an enemy airplane. (They chased away several enemy aircraft during those three weeks, which meant they were successful as escorts, but they had no aerial victories.) On July 4, 1915, Boelcke repeatedly brought his plane alongside a French airplane at a range of 100–300 feet. His observer fired 380 rounds during the twenty-minute battle. When they examined the downed plane afterward, they counted twenty-seven bullet holes. While Boelcke considered his observer an excellent shot, this meant that only one out of every fourteen bullets had struck the plane, and most of those simply poked holes in the wings or other nonvital areas.

Part of the problem was the difficulty of deflection shooting—that is, calculating how far ahead, above, or below the target you needed to aim when firing at a moving target from a moving target. One difficulty was stability. The wood and fabric planes of World War I had a lot of "give" to them. Even a machine gun that was bolted solidly to the fuselage vibrated when firing, and those vibrations caused the bullets to scatter around a target rather than repeatedly striking the aiming point. When the gun was mounted on a pole or some sort of swivel mount, the problem was magnified. And a problem with aerial battles at the beginning of the war was that the gunner couldn't see where the bullets were going. Tracer rounds, which glowed brightly and left a smoke trail, were developed by the British in 1915, but, like most innovations, it took a while to get them into mass production and make them widely available. British pilots began mentioning tracer rounds in late 1915.[23] Boelcke first mentions using them in June 1916.[24]

The engine and aircraft improvements that made it possible for two-seaters to carry machine guns also made it possible for single-seat scouts to carry them, but there was a major problem. Most single-seat scouts had the propeller in the front. This was called a "tractor" layout because the propeller pulled the plane through the air. With a tractor plane, the pilot couldn't shoot straight ahead without hitting the propeller. (Contrary to what you may have seen in cartoons, the pilots did *not* discover this by shooting off their own propeller. They were intelligent people.) Experiments with mounting guns to fire off to the side of the plane were unsuccessful, as it was virtually impossible for a pilot to calculate the deflection needed for a shot at this angle and aim the gun while still flying the airplane. What was needed was a way to shoot the gun straight ahead, so the pilot could aim the gun by aiming the plane.

The idea was not new. Even before the war, pilots and aircraft designers had foreseen the need for planes that could fire forward. Patents for forward-firing guns were issued to German and Swiss inventors, and the French designer Raymond Saulnier not only obtained a patent but also conducted tests on his invention in 1914. His design synchronized the firing of a gun with the propeller so the gun was only triggered when the propeller was not in the way. The tests were not successful, possibly because the gun and ammunition he used had a tendency to "hang fire"—that is, to not fire immediately when triggered but instead fire after a short delay.[25] This delay meant some bullets hit the propeller.

The first pilot to successfully fire a machine gun through a spinning propeller was a Frenchman named Roland Garros. Garros flew a

Morane-Saulnier Type L monoplane, and he worked with the Morane-Saulnier factory to develop a way to fire through the propeller. Since Saulnier's synchronization device hadn't worked properly, they tried a simpler solution—an armored propeller. They fastened triangular steel plates to the section of the propeller that the bullets would hit, with the point of the triangle facing the machine gun. Because the propeller was fairly narrow, while it was spinning most bullets would miss it completely. The few that did hit the propeller would hit the steel triangle and be deflected away from the propeller.

On April 1, 1915, Garros flew straight toward an unsuspecting German airplane, fired through the propeller, and shot down the plane. He repeated the technique on April 15, and again on April 18. His luck ran out on the third attempt, though, as he was forced to land behind German lines either because of ground fire or due to an engine failure. Garros tried to destroy his plane, but he was captured before he could set it on fire. The Germans now had his plane, and the propeller, and his secret was out.

The Germans rushed the propeller to Berlin and asked the talented aircraft designer Anthony Fokker to examine it. They gave Fokker a Parabellum machine gun and asked him to take it back to his factory and duplicate the Garros system.

Fokker quickly saw drawbacks to the Garros system. Bullets that hit the deflectors could ricochet in any direction, including back at the pilot who fired them. (Bystanders had been killed by deflected bullets during tests of the French deflector plates.)[26] Also, even though the steel plates protected the propeller, the impact of the bullets shook the engine violently and could cause problems. There is some speculation that Garros's engine failure was caused by these vibrations.[27] In his autobiography *The Flying Dutchman*, Fokker claimed that in a matter of days he developed a synchronization system that worked.[28] His tale of how he convinced skeptical German staff officers that his system worked makes for entertaining reading, but unfortunately the dates and events he cites contradict other written records.[29]

Fokker's tale of *how* he developed the synchronized machine gun may be suspect, but he (or his engineers) did indeed develop a successful synchronizer. Armed Fokker Eindekkers (monoplanes) soon began taking a toll on Allied aircraft. A British politician's complaint in Parliament that Allied pilots were mere "Fokker Fodder" was stretching things a bit, but by integrating a forward-firing gun into a single-seat aircraft, Fokker had produced the world's first successful plane that was specifically designed to shoot down other aircraft. At the time, it was called a "scout." Today we would call it a fighter.

It took the Allies several months to develop their own synchronization gear. In the meantime, both factory and field-improvised workarounds were used to arm existing airplanes. One of the most obvious solutions was to arm pusher aircraft. Pushers tended to be less aerodynamic and have poorer performance than airplanes with a propeller in front, but they gave the pilot and observer an unobstructed view. This made the design popular for reconnaissance aircraft before the air war turned deadly, and when machine guns were needed, a pusher was an ideal platform on which to mount a gun. The pilot or observer could have an unobstructed field of fire in front of the plane, as the propeller was behind them. The British FE-2 two-seat airplane and DH-2 single-seat airplane proved to be very effective when armed, as were Farmans, Voisins, and other French planes.

Another solution to the problem of firing a machine gun forward without interrupter gear was to mount the gun on the top wing, so it would fire over the propeller. The Lewis machine gun proved to be ideal for this purpose, as it was relatively lightweight, air cooled, and drum fed. In the early days of air fighting, this allowed pilots and mechanics at the front to improvise mounting for the Lewis, and soon afterward factory-made mounts were produced that could easily be fitted to a variety of airplanes.

Top-wing mounting had a number of disadvantages. One of the most significant was that the ammunition drums originally available for the Lewis held forty-seven rounds of ammunition. (Later in the war, ninety-seven-round drums were produced.) Since the Lewis fired at a rate of five hundred to six hundred rounds per minute, a pilot could empty the drum in less than six seconds. Firing in short bursts was obviously a good idea. But even with short bursts, the drum would soon be empty and the pilot would need to change it. This could be difficult, especially with early improvised mounts that had the gun rigidly fixed to the top wing. The ubiquitous Lieutenant Strange discovered this when he mounted a Lewis gun on the top of his Martynside. On May 10, 1915, he emptied a drum while attacking a German plane. He had to pull out of the fight, loosen his seat belt, and rise up from his seat to change the drum. He tried to hold the control stick between his knees as he did this, but his plane stalled, flipped over, and went into a spin with him dangling beneath the plane, hanging onto the drum for dear life. He eventually managed to swing his feet into the cockpit, smashing several instruments in the process. From there he was able to pull himself up farther, grab the joystick between his legs, and right the plane. He fell back into his seat, but the seat cushion had fallen out and he crashed through the bottom of the seat, pieces of which jammed the controls. Squatting with his feet on the rudder bar and his back pressed against the back rim of the cockpit, he cleared the controls and flew back to his airfield.[30] And he survived the war!

More sophisticated mounting brackets allowed the pilot to pull a release and pivot the gun back on its mount to change a drum, but it still was not easy. The pilot had to control the plane with his knees and change the drum in a one-hundred-miles-per-hour slipstream while wearing heavy gloves.[31] Even when the drum wasn't empty, firing the Lewis wasn't foolproof. British pilot "McScotch" (William MacLanachan) described his first attack while flying a Nieuport with a Lewis gun on the top wing. (This plane had a relatively sophisticated Aldis optical gunsight.)

> I was at about eight thousand feet with the enemy about two thousand below my level and, diving on him with the wind whistling through the wiring and the le Rhone engine purring away easily, I pressed my eye to the Aldis sight. The yellow shape came properly into the lines and circles that enabled us to make allowances for the relative positions and speed of the two machines and, breathlessly maneuvering my Nieuport so that there should be no doubt that my bullets would hit the enemy, I pressed the firing lever. Nothing happened, there was no clack-clacking of the gun; I had forgotten to "cock" it. Being then within two hundred yards of the enemy I had perforce to pull out of the dive. As the gun was on the top plane the cocking lever was attached to a wire which hung down inside the windscreen alongside the wire which liberated the front of the gun to allow it to be lowered for reloading. In my anxiety and haste I pulled the wrong one, and the heavy weight of the Lewis gun hit me a stunning blow on the top of the head. Possibly the thickness of my flying helmet prevented a complete "knock-out." As it was, I was blinded and almost senseless when the pop-pop-pop of several machine-guns sounded from above.[32]

MacLanachan was fortunate to escape this situation, and also to survive the war. It was not unusual for novice pilots to make mistakes during their first dogfight, but even experienced pilots had problems with Lewis guns mounted on the top wing. The wind that pushed MacLanachan's gun back when he accidentally unlatched it also tended to pull the ammunition drum away from the breech, which, combined with the vibrations and G-forces from maneuvering, frequently caused the gun to jam. The pole-mounted gun support was not as rigid as the cowl mount of a synchronized gun, causing the vibration "spray" when firing to be even more pronounced. And because the gun was mounted two or three feet above the pilot's head, the path of the bullets would be two or three feet above the pilot's natural line of sight. If the pilot aimed his plane directly at an enemy pilot, the bullets would sail harmlessly over the enemy's head. The pilot needed to put his plane into a slight dive and aim a few feet below the spot he actually wanted to hit. For all its drawbacks, though, a machine gun on the top wing was better than no machine gun at all. When a superb plane like the Nieuport was fitted with a machine gun on its top wing, it could hold its own against a mediocre plane like the Fokker Eindekker armed with a superb synchronized gun.

Once pilots began flying with the express purpose of shooting down enemy airplanes, it was perhaps inevitable that they would capture the imagination of the public. This was the newest, most high-tech form of warfare imaginable.[33] Pilots were regarded with the same kind of awe that was given to astronauts in the 1960s. It was also, at least when viewed from a distance, a clean, "gentlemanly" form of combat. One pilot against another, dueling to the death against a background of clear blue sky. Newspaper reporters stumbled over each other in a rush to report every victory. They compared pilots to the legendary (and largely mythical) medieval knights errant, jousting against their foes on the field of honor and obeying the rules of chivalry. Pilots began receiving "fan mail" from an adoring public. In a war where unbelievable horror, stomach-turning filth, and incomprehensible casualty numbers dominated the news, where the capture of a few hundred yards of mud was hailed as a major victory, the public needed heroes. Pilots filled that need, sometimes unwillingly.

In a competition between knights, there has to be a way to keep score. For fighter pilots, the score was the "confirmed victory." Aerial warfare was not always a one-on-one proposition, two planes facing off, with the victor able to leisurely circle above while watching his victim crash into the ground. There might be dozens of planes from both sides involved in a battle. A pilot might fire at one plane, take evasive action to avoid being shot by another, and then swerve violently to avoid a collision with a third. He might suspect he had hit the first plane but not have any idea what happened to it after he fired. Planes often dove or spun out of a dogfight looking like they'd been shot down, only to recover and fly back to their base. To count as a victory, someone had to "confirm" that the plane was destroyed—that is, it had crashed and had not recovered or made a forced landing on its own side of the lines. An enemy that made a forced landing on your side of the lines counted as a victory, because obviously neither that plane nor that pilot was going to fly in combat again. A forced landing on the other side of the lines didn't count as a victory.

In all the air forces, the "someone" who confirmed the plane was downed had to be someone other than the pilot who claimed the victory. Most countries allowed pilots from the same squadron to confirm each other's victories. The French imposed a stricter rule for confirmations. To count as a confirmed victory, the plane had to fall within the Allied lines or its destruction had to be witnessed by a ground observer or an air observer "other than the pilot himself or his squadron mates."[34] Since pilots normally flew with other pilots from their own squadron, this generally meant the victory had to be confirmed by a ground observer. Only on rare occasions would a pilot from another squadron chance to see a victory and confirm it. Even a pilot's own squadron commander could not confirm a victory. It had to be independently confirmed. This policy undoubtedly caused a lot of French victories to be unconfirmed. For most of the war, the German Army maintained a defensive posture on the Western Front, concentrating instead on knocking Russia out of the war on the Eastern Front. The German Air Force likewise opted for a defensive strategy, only flying into Allied territory when an upcoming offensive or some other specific mission required it. Most air battles therefore took place over the front or behind German lines. If a French pilot shot down a German plane behind the German lines, and it was so far behind the lines that a ground observer couldn't see the plane crash, it wouldn't be confirmed as a victory.

Aircraft design, engine design, and aircraft armament all developed very rapidly during the war. Surprisingly, one technology that did not develop was the design of parachutes. Balloonists had been making successful parachute jumps since the 1700s. During World War I, observers in captive balloons were equipped with parachutes from the beginning of the war, and they routinely parachuted to safety when their balloons were attacked. Airplane pilots and observers, however, did not have parachutes until the last few months of the war, and then only German aircrews had them. Many aircrews died because their airplane broke apart, or, worse still, caught fire in the air, and they had no way to save themselves. Pilots talked about their fear of having their plane catch fire, and many said they would rather jump to a quick death than be roasted alive during an agonizing descent to the ground. Some carried a pistol to use on themselves if their plane caught fire.

The parachutes used by balloon observers were bulky packages that hung over the side of the balloon until they were needed. They wouldn't fit in the cramped cockpit of an airplane. Someone needed to develop a way to fit them into a package that could be used by airplane pilots.[35] This was not a trivial task, and it was not something that could be improvised by pilots at the front, but it was essentially just a refinement of an existing technology. The fact that this was not done early in the war has traditionally been blamed on an insensitive command structure. Non-flying generals and colonels were said to be afraid that if pilots had parachutes, they might jump from an airplane that could otherwise be saved. Air Vice Marshal Arthur Gould Lee, who was himself a fighter pilot during the war, examined the British War Office files after the war and found no evidence to support that theory.[36] Instead, he found a combination of ignorance, insensitivity, and misinformation that caused the Air Staff to have no interest in developing parachutes. Early in the war, when many planes didn't even have enough power to carry a machine gun aloft, pilots were more interested in improving aircraft performance and armament than in developing parachutes. It should be noted that this was before pilots began shooting at each other, and aerial combat was rare. Pilots worried more about being forced to land behind enemy lines than about having their planes break apart or catch fire. The situation changed as the war progressed, but the Air Staff didn't. There was still a general feeling that "pilots don't want parachutes" coupled with a conviction that suitable parachutes couldn't be developed. Senior officers who had refused to divert resources to developing parachutes early in the war, when there was some justification for that decision, got upset if their decision was questioned later on. The French Air Staff presumably had similar attitudes, as it wasn't until Allied pilots began seeing German pilots parachute out of crippled airplanes that the cry for parachutes became too strong to ignore. In September 1918, the Air Staff finally placed an order for five hundred parachutes, but the war ended before they could be delivered to the front.

When you see a World War I airplane in a movie or a museum, the cockpit may look substantial, but it's really just fabric wrapped around a wooden frame. As far as providing protection from machine gun bullets is concerned, it's roughly the equivalent of sitting in a lawn chair and wrapping your body in a tarp. Considering the fact that pilots flew these machines without parachutes, using unreliable engines, and shot at each other with phosphorous bullets, just what was the life expectancy of a World War I pilot? There are many opinions on this question. "Two or three weeks at the front" is an often-quoted but unattributed statistic. Ted Parsons, an American pilot who joined the Lafayette Escadrille at the beginning of 1917, wrote that the average life expectancy of a French aviator was considerably less than fifteen hours over the lines.[37] The UK *Daily Mail* claimed that at the end of 1916 a British pilot's life expectancy was eighteen hours in the air or eleven days at the front.[38] Whatever the actual number was, it wasn't good. Another Lafayette Escadrille pilot, Carl Dolan, wrote, "There was no one in the Escadrille who expected to survive the air war. It was not a question of would you die, it was just when."[39] (As it turned out, Dolan survived the war and lived to the ripe old age of eighty-six.)

One thing everyone seemed to agree on was that new pilots were woefully unprepared for combat when they first arrived at the front. The reason the *average* life expectancy was so low was that many pilots were shot down on one of their first flights across the lines. As Ted Parsons put it, "No green pilot was worth his salt till he'd been on the front at least a month. If he survived that time, he had about a fifty-fifty chance of coming through. There was so much else to look out for that the neophyte rarely saw any Huns [German airplanes] for the first couple of weeks, although they might be under his very nose."[40]

The situation was made worse by the fact that many green pilots arrived at the front thinking they already were the world's greatest fighter pilot. One pilot who did not have that attitude, who in fact began worrying about his prowess before he even went to flight school, was Jim McConnell. McConnell was born in Chicago, grew up in New York, and earned a law degree from the University of Virginia. While at that university, he also earned a reputation, though not necessarily a good one, by teaching himself to play the bagpipes. He was elected "king" of the Hot Foot Society, an organization that specialized in beer drinking and practical jokes. One of McConnell's jokes nearly got him expelled. He placed a chamber pot over the head of a veiled statue of Thomas Jefferson the night before the unveiling ceremony. That ceremony was attended by President Taft and other dignitaries. School officials were not amused.[41]

Early in the war McConnell traveled to France and joined the American Ambulance Service, a volunteer group that transported wounded French soldiers from forward medical posts to hospitals in the rear. Although they were a noncombatant group, they were frequently exposed to shell fire. Jim met Paul Rockwell in Paris, and they soon became close friends. Eventually Jim felt he needed to take an active role in the war, and in late 1915 he volunteered to become a pilot. While waiting for his orders to flight training he witnessed a dogfight, which he described in a letter to Paul Rockwell:

A Boche machine had crossed the lines and was flying somewhat to the rear of us. The enemy fliers had been bothering us all day. Our anti-aircraft batteries began firing at the enemy plane. The bursts of shrapnel were so thick that they merged into a long cloud bank. Suddenly a fast French plane shot out of the clouds and swinging alongside though somewhat under the Boche, fired with a mitrailleuse [machine gun]. The enemy plane gave a sudden forward lurch, turned nose down and fell. A blue stream of smoke followed in its wake. It fell like a huge wounded bird, turning as it went, the sun glittering on its shiny surface as it tumbled like a fish which shines when upward. It was a jolting, dead drop. Down it came, the soldiers on the ground yelling in delight. The machine crashed into the forest and I said to Haviland "Well, there are two more good Boches." . . . The wreck was terrible. Nothing but splinters and torn cloth. The pilot had been cut in two. His legs had been thrown beyond the wreck. His face was flattened to about four inches and his liver was stuck on the motor front. He had been killed by the machine gun but imagine the feelings of the observer who lived during the fall. His hands were clenched as if he had died in agony. . . . Maybe I'll take a header like that someday.[42]

9

Learning to Fly

The Penguins

I take to it just like a duck to water.

—Kiffin Rockwell

Like aviation in general, flight training was evolving rapidly when Kiffin reported to the aviation school at Avord. When he arrived, the French had two different methods of training. The Farman method began by having the student fly with an instructor in a dual-control Farman. It was similar to modern flight training in that the instructor would show the student how to take off, land, and keep the airplane from falling out of the sky in between. When the student became proficient at basic piloting skills, the instructor would tell him it was time to solo. Then the instructor would get out of the plane and the student would take off, fly a circuit around the field, and land by himself.

The Bleriot method was different. The student never flew with an instructor. Training began in a single-seat Bleriot XI. This was the same model that Louis Bleriot had flown across the English Channel in 1909, except that on the training planes the wings were "clipped" (shortened) and it had a smaller propeller so the plane could not fly. The planes were nicknamed "Penguins" as a result. They had a three-cylinder engine that produced enough power to lift the tail off the ground and propel the students across the grass field at twenty or thirty miles per hour. The student's job was to keep the plane in a straight line. This was more difficult than it sounds, and new students invariably zigzagged drunkenly across the field or spun madly around in a ground loop. Ted Parsons, a Lafayette Escadrille pilot who began his flight training about six months after Kiffin, described Penguin training as follows:

> Start two at opposite ends of the field with practically the entire width of the field between them, and somehow they'd run together in a horrible collision in the center of the field. That is, it always sounded horrible, but usually repairs could be effected by the phlegmatic, betel-chewing Annamite [Vietnamese] mechanics within a very few minutes. Then there was the bugbear of ground loops, or *chevaux de bois* (wooden horses on the merry-go-round) as the French so aptly named them. Once the Penguins started to turn in a ground loop, nothing could stop them except coming to a full stop with completely retarded motor. They'd whirl round and round like a dog chasing his tail. Then the red-faced, cursing neophyte would have to climb out, point his nose in the way he wanted to go and start all over again.[1]

Steering while taxiing was especially difficult during World War I because the planes had fixed tail skids instead of the steerable tail wheels used by more modern planes. Once the students learned to keep the Penguins in a straight line, they would be given a Bleriot with slightly longer wings. It couldn't fly far, but it could make short hops so students could practice taking off and landing. Describing the landings, Parsons wrote, "The sound was the general effect of an earthquake in a hardware store, but the miracle was that the ship seemed to suffer no particular ill-effects."[2] When the student mastered take-offs and landings with these machines, he would be entrusted with a machine that had longer wings and could sustain flight. The student's first flight was also his first solo.

Both the Farman and the Bleriot methods included classroom training on the theory of flight, the parts of an airplane, flight control, aircraft engines, and so on. When the student passed all the written tests and the instructor felt he had mastered basic flying skills, he would take a series of flying tests. If the student pilot passed all these tests, he was given his *brevet militaire* (military pilot's license) and considered a full-fledged pilot. This basic instruction remained fairly standard throughout the war. It was followed by training on the combat aircraft the pilot would fly at the front and, as the war progressed and flight training evolved, the student would also attend schools for gunnery, combat aerobatics, aerial photography, and other skills, depending on the aircraft and missions he would be flying.

Later in the war, the French decided the Farman method was the best way to train pilots for two-seat observation and bombing planes, while the Bleriot method was the best way to train pilots for single-seat fighters. Kiffin began his flight training before they made that distinction, as the whole concept of a fighter plane was still evolving. Kiffin described his arrival at the school:

This is a big camp and is about two kilometers from the station. There were two small hotels there and I tried to get a room for the night, but they were full. So I came out to the camp and spent the night at the *Poste de Police* [police station]. Then reported to the bureau this morning. Everything was fine. The Captain shook hands with me and was exceptionally pleasant. He asked me what machine I would like to fly. I didn't know much difference, but he told me that the Maurice Farman was one of the best and easy to learn. So I said all right. I have been getting located this morning and begin work this afternoon, when the Chief Pilot will take me up for a look around. . . . This is such a relief to be out of the Legion that I can hardly believe it. I think that if I had had to stay at La Valbonne for a month or so longer I would have gone completely "nutty."[3]

A week later, he described his training to his mother:

I am transferred to the aviation as a student-pilot. That is a jump from the lowest branch of the military service to the highest. It is the most interesting thing I have ever done, and is the life of a gentleman, and I am surrounded by gentlemen. I have been here only this week but I fly each morning and afternoon with an instructor sitting behind me, directing my movements. It is very easy to fly but I must get the habit of the movements, and understand the air currents.[4]

Kiffin turned out to have a gift for flying. He wrote to his brother:

I take to it just like a duck to water. My instructor is a marvel and an exceedingly nice fellow. . . . I think he will turn me loose this afternoon and let me fly alone. I am now on a 1913 model Maurice Farman, after

I am turned loose will stay on it for four or five days practice and then change to the 1914 model. Will stay on it two or three weeks and then hope to pass my *brevet militaire*, which will entitle me to go to the front. However, afterwards, I think I will ask to change to a Caudron, the same machine that Thaw flies.[5]

Most of the *élèves* [students] are lieutenants and sous-lieutenants. There is nothing *militaire* about the life and all the aviators are treated the same. The only difference is the officers wear stripes on their uniforms and are paid more. We all go out on the field at four-forty in the morning and assist in moving the machines out of the hangars. Then we see that the motors, etc., are in good condition. Then we go out on the field and take turns flying with the instructors. At seven o'clock we come in for a little breakfast. At eight, we have a lecture on flying, then go out and put the machines back in the hangars. We are free until nine-thirty. At eleven, we have *déjeuner* [lunch]. Then we usually sleep until three-thirty, when we go back on the field. We are out there then until after dark. Don't have dinner until eight or after. That is the day's routine. They are all a quiet bunch, little foolishness going on, and all intent on learning to fly as quickly as possible.[6]

The reason for the break in the middle of the day was that the winds were usually calm in the morning and the evening. Students had a difficult enough job learning to fly without having to cope with wind gusts, too.

Kiffin wrote to his brother a week and a half later to say that he was going to buy a new uniform.[7] It was common for student pilots to buy a new uniform after they'd earned their *brevet*, but Kiffin needed to buy one sooner because almost everything he had at La Valbonne had been stolen.[8] Because he received his orders at the last minute, many of his clothes were in the camp laundry. They were supposed to have been forwarded to him, but that didn't happen. Even his toothbrush, toothpaste, and comb were stolen.[9]

Kiffin's letter describes the uniform he was ordering as black with broad red artillery stripes, and a black kepi with a red stripe. It was, in fact, the uniform of an artilleryman. There was no standard uniform for French aviators. Officers generally wore uniforms from their previous assignment, but that didn't work well for legionnaires or other enlisted troops. A long greatcoat, hobnail boots, and a sash did not make a good outfit for flying.

So, aviators were allowed to essentially pick whatever kind of uniform they wanted. Pictures of the Lafayette Escadrille seldom show two pilots wearing identical uniforms. Kiffin, in fact, would eventually acquire several different uniforms—black, tan, and blue—as suited his fancy when he bought them.

Kiffin needed to pass several flying tests to earn his *brevet*. These tests included climbing to sixty-five hundred feet or higher and staying at that altitude for an hour, making a triangular cross-country flight and landing at two different airfields about fifty miles apart, shutting off the engine at an altitude of sixteen hundred feet and gliding to a "dead-stick" [10] landing, and flying one hundred miles to the city of Chartres.[11]

Curiously, Kiffin made no mention in his letters of his first solo flight, which is a memorable event for most pilots. Maybe flying came so naturally to him that he didn't consider his solo noteworthy. In a September 10, 1915, letter to Paul, he said that he thought his instructor might turn him loose that afternoon, and five days later he mentioned that he was now flying alone.[12] He also didn't write about the beauty of the clouds, how small things on the ground beneath him looked, or the marvelous sense of freedom he experienced while flying solo. Other student pilots described these sensations in depth, especially in these early days of flight when their first flight experiences took place in an open cockpit. Kiffin's letters focused on his progress toward earning his *brevet*. He undoubtedly did experience the joy of flight, but to him that was secondary. His goal was to become a pilot so he could fight the enemy. Kiffin did, however, describe his first attempt to fly a 1914 Farman in a letter to his "Aunt" Alice Weeks because it didn't end well. He flew some familiarization flights with an instructor, standard practice when switching to a new type of airplane, and then he had to wait until a plane was available for him to fly:

Yesterday, there were altogether nine machines smashed. I was unlucky enough to be one of the nine. Monday morning I went on the double command 1914 model and made three short tours lasting in all fifteen minutes. My instructor told me I was very good and there was no need of my continuing under the double command. I was well pleased as I had expected to spend two days under it, as that is the average. I immediately began to count on making my one hour at two thousand meters [sixty-five hundred feet] to-day and finishing my *brevet* by next Monday or Tuesday. Instead, I went in and asked for a machine, but was informed that there were so many broken I would have to wait for one to be repaired. I did nothing Monday afternoon or yesterday until 4:30. The mechanics had been working all day on a machine whose wheels were not good and whose motor did not work well. I was anxious to get started so they told me I could take it out and try it if I wished, but to be careful. I barely got started on the ground when it began to turn with me. I tried to straighten it but could not and saw that it was going to break if I didn't do something, so I tried to get off the ground. The motor, was not working strong enough, so it only made matters worse and threw it completely around, breaking it up pretty badly. It made me awfully mad. Although it was not my fault it does not help my record any and also delays me for several days, as I must now wait for another machine.[13]

Apparently, even a "natural" pilot can't take off if the airplane's wheels are forcing it to turn in a circle.

The fact that there were nine machines smashed in one day is perhaps unusual, but not astounding. Student pilots crashed frequently. If the plane was on or near the ground when they lost control, they could often walk away unharmed, as Kiffin did. Their underpowered training planes flew slowly, which meant they crashed slowly. The wood and fabric construction had a lot of "give" to it, which meant it crumpled and absorbed much of the impact. The pilots weren't always lucky, however. The following week, Kiffin would write his brother that three men had died and one had been seriously injured in a single morning. Two of the deaths were an instructor and a student who crashed when a gust of wind hit their plane on take-off. They were trapped in the wreckage and burned to death in front of the other students.[14] When Jim McConnell was in flight training, he wrote of seven crashes and two deaths in one day.[15] Flight training could be a deadly business.

Flight training wasn't the only dangerous business. On September 25, Kiffin's old Foreign Legion unit took part in what was known as the Second Battle of Champagne. Paul Pavelka's orders to Aviation still hadn't come through, so he was sent to the Champagne sector with his unit. Like the Battle of Artois, the French managed to capture some ground on a narrow front, advancing 2.5 miles in a few places, but the Germans recaptured much of that ground in counterattacks. The French halted the main attack after twelve days and stopped the "mopping up" activities a month later.

During that battle the French suffered 145,000 casualties, and the Germans lost 72,500 men.

Fortunately, Paul Pavelka was not one of the casualties. On October 3, he was able to scribble a note to Mrs. Weeks to let her know he was all right. A shell had burst about six feet in front of him, denting his helmet, demolishing his rifle, and tearing his overcoat to pieces, but he was unhurt. Another soldier who escaped unharmed was Sergeant Morlae, the man Kiffin had called a "son of a bitch." Morlae was crouching in a shallow trench when a large shell exploded nearby and buried him alive. Fred Zinn, David King, and a few other legionnaires left their shelter and braved the German fire to rescue him. At one time or another each of these men had sworn to kill Morlae, but they risked their lives to dig him out and revive him.[16] He repaid their efforts shortly after the battle when he deserted and fled to the United States. Their initial reaction was "Good riddance!" In a few months, however, they wished he was a little closer to them—say, within the length of a bayonet—as he published articles in the *Atlantic Monthly* describing his heroic struggles in the Foreign Legion. He described the Legion itself as a "conglomeration of outcasts, rascals, murderers, and thieves."[17]

The Battle of Champagne also marked the debut of a new American recruit to the Foreign Legion, a man who was colorful even by Legion standards. Daniel William Thorin was called "Billy" by most of his friends, but in the Legion he earned the nickname "Nuts." He was born on a farm in South Dakota but left home at the age of fourteen because there was "too damn much religion in the family." He became a cabin boy on a tramp sailing vessel and spent the next fourteen years at sea. For a while he enlisted as a marine on a Chinese gunboat and fought pirates and opium runners. He joined an army of American soldiers of fortune fighting in the Mexican Revolution, during which he was shot and almost killed. He traveled to Australia but had to leave that continent after he became engaged to two different women. (Apparently that was frowned upon by the local authorities as well as by the women involved.) When the war started, he decided to go to France to join in the action, but he was "shanghaied"; the captain of a ship bound for South America got Billy drunk, and when he woke up they were already at sea. When the ship stopped at a port in Africa, Billy beat up the captain and jumped ship. He worked for a while as a bouncer in a brothel until he was able to catch a ship to France, where he joined the Foreign Legion.[18]

Billy Thorin joined the unit at La Valbonne shortly before Kiffin left for Aviation. Paul Pavelka described Billy's participation in the Battle of Champagne: "Early in the attack Billy Thorin was struck in the head by a piece of shrapnel. He refused to go to the rear, but kept on. A few minutes later he was again hit, and toppled over. I knelt and looked at him, and he was stone dead." Except he wasn't dead. He regained consciousness a little while later and crawled back to a medical post, with a hole in his shoulder and a piece of his scalp missing.[19] Kiffin and Paul Rockwell would have several "adventures" with Billy Thorin in the months to come.

Kiffin met another legionnaire that September, one who came from a background that was quite different from Billy Thorin's. Victor Emmanuel Chapman was born in New York City in 1890. His father was a lawyer and noted essayist, and his mother came from a well-to-do Boston family. Victor earned an AB degree from Harvard in 1913 and went to France to study architecture and painting.[20] Tall, thin, and invariably cheerful, Victor had the soul of an artist. His outward cheerfulness masked two terrible childhood tragedies that impacted him deeply. When he was six, his mother died. She had taken him everywhere, and they had rarely been apart. His father said her death left Victor "suspended in an unknown universe, with his grief and his visions."[21] After her death, Victor and his younger brother Jay became extremely close. When Victor was twelve, he and Jay were playing beside a river in Austria. Victor left his ten-year-old brother alone for a moment and returned just in time to see Jay fall into the river. Neither boy could swim, and Victor helplessly watched his brother drown.[22]

Like Kiffin, Victor viewed the war as a crusade. He was at least as idealistic as Kiffin. He enlisted in the Foreign Legion in September 1914, and served as a machine gunner. He served in a quiet sector—too quiet for Victor's taste. In a letter to his stepmother, he complained that in the Legion, "I have thrown away ten months of my life, neither helped the French nor injured the Germans."[23] A week later, he wrote that he was looking forward to transferring to Aviation.[24] Describing Victor as a child, his father wrote, "Victor never really felt that he was alive except when he was in danger."[25] Considering the dangers of flying and the fighter pilot's image as a "knight errant," perhaps it's not surprising that he also said, "I do not think he was ever completely happy in his life till the day he got his flying papers."[26]

Victor arrived at Camp d'Avord while Kiffin was flying the 1914 Farman and working on his *brevet* tests. Kiffin mentioned meeting Victor in a letter to his brother: "An American named Chapman, from the 3eme de Marche [Third Marching Regiment] arrived here this morning and seems to be a very fine fellow indeed."[27] Victor was more effusive when he wrote to his father about Kiffin, and perhaps a bit envious that Kiffin had taken part in an attack while he had not:

> I find a compatriot I am proud to own here. A tall, lanky Kentuckian [*sic*] called Rockwell. He got his transfer about a month ago from the Legion. He was wounded on the ninth of May, like Kisling. In fact one-half of the 2eme de Marche [Second Marching Regiment], 2300, were wounded that day, not counting the killed and missing. He gives much the best account I have heard. . . . "There is nothing like it, you float across the field, you drop, you rise again. The sack, the 325 extra rounds, the gun—have no weight. And a ball in the head and it is all over,—no pain." Having charged with the third battalion and being wounded in the leg on the last *bouck* [rush or movement], he crawled back across the entire field in the afternoon.[28]

Obviously Kiffin had found a kindred spirit. The two would soon become close friends and roommates.

Meeting Victor was the one piece of good news that Kiffin mentioned in his letters from this period. The weather had been terrible, and he had been able to do very little flying. The few times the weather had been suitable, he had had trouble finding a plane to fly because most of the school's Farmans were broken. Out of forty-four planes, only sixteen were operational. One day he was on the field at daybreak and managed to get a plane, but the engine wouldn't start. The mechanics worked on it for two hours before they got it to run, but it stopped shortly after he took off and he had to make an emergency landing. Still, he was luckier than a friend who was at about the same point in his training. That student took off on his straight-line flight to Chartres and disappeared. They found his body in the crumpled wreck of his machine about twelve miles from the training field. That wreck convinced Kiffin not to rush so much to pass his *brevet*, as this was the fifth student who had been killed in a few days. Kiffin realized that flight training was more than just an obstacle to get through as quickly as possible so he could begin flying at the front. Flight training was an opportunity to practice flying and gain experience, experience that might save his life. "At the front one thinks little of a death because there is always more or less glory in it, and we feel that it is necessary there," he wrote. "Here, there is no glory in it, and it seems so unnecessary."[29]

Kiffin was also worried about his friends in the Legion. He read about the Champagne attack in the newspapers and he knew the Legion was in the thick of it, but he had not heard from any of his friends and apparently the only word his brother Paul had heard was that Billy Thorin had been wounded. They had not yet heard that "Skipper" (Paul Pavelka) was all right. Kiffin wrote to Paul about both of his friends:

> I am afraid that it has gone badly with Skipper, for otherwise I would think he would have written by now. Thorin is a fine boy. He is a little rough, as he has done nothing but knock around over the world, but he has a good heart and one could not find a better comrade in a fight. He was shot through both legs, jaws and his hand cut open while fighting in Mexico. I found him with Skipper at La Valbonne, anxious to get to the front. I liked him, and when he left for the front gave him a little money. As soon as he writes, send him some money, and also send me his letter so I can write him.[30]

Kiffin was not the only one who was worried about Billy Thorin's injury. It was a cause for concern by Kiffin's mother as well, but in a totally unexpected way. On October 6, the front page of the *Asheville Gazette* carried a story titled "Asheville Boy Shot in Battle. Kiffin Rockwell Is Wounded in Desperate Fighting in Champagne District."

> "Had Lately Joined Aeroplane Service. Recently Wrote His Mother That He Enjoyed Operating Flying Machines." "Kiffin Rockwell, younger son of Dr. Loula A. Rockwell of Asheville, was wounded in the back and head during the attack made by the French Foreign Legion on the German trenches in the Champagne district on September 25, according to a Paris dispatch to the New York Sun dated October 2."[31]

The article went on to quote at length from a letter "Kiffin" wrote describing his injuries. The article said the letter had been addressed to "D. W. Thorin of Canton, S.D." Apparently the Paris press bureau had somehow confused

Billy Thorin with Kiffin and combined the story of Billy's injury with information they had on file about Kiffin. Loula knew that Kiffin had left the Legion and was in flight training. She had indeed been getting letters from him at Camp d'Avord, so she suspected the newspaper article was wrong, but it was still an unsettling experience.

Back at Camp d'Avord, time dragged on for Kiffin. Bad weather and broken machines prevented him from doing much flying. He complained to Paul that he had only been able to fly on seven days over a three-week period, and on most of those seven days he had only been able to fly for a few minutes. When he did get an opportunity to fly, though, he was happy. He would climb to five or six thousand feet and then spiral back to the earth, in complete control of the airplane. In a letter to Alice Weeks, he devoted an entire sentence to saying the view of the surrounding countryside was spectacular, and clouds were beautiful.[32]

On October 15, Kiffin finally got a chance to attempt the triangular cross-country trip that was required to earn his *brevet militaire*. This flight was intended to test a student's navigation and map-reading skills as well as his flying abilities. It also frequently tested a student's ability to make emergency landings, diagnose and fix mechanical problems, and generally cope with unexpected situations. There's an old saying that "Good decisions come from experience, and a lot of that comes from bad decisions." Kiffin gained experience on this flight. In fact, it was almost his last flight.

He took off from Camp d'Avord at 2:30 in the afternoon headed for Châteauroux, a town about fifty miles to the southwest. When he started, the cloud ceiling was at twenty-six hundred feet and he flew underneath them. The clouds got lower and lower, and within ten minutes the ceiling had dropped below a thousand feet. At that point he climbed through the clouds and was able to find clear skies above them. Since he could no longer see the ground, he navigated by "dead reckoning"—that is, using his compass to fly in a direction that should lead him to his destination while using his watch to time the flight and determine when he had arrived. That method works as long as the calculations are correct, the instruments are accurate, and there are no unexpected winds. When Kiffin calculated that he was over Châteauroux, he descended through the clouds. This could have been dangerous because he didn't know how high the cloud ceiling was. In dense fog the clouds extend all the way to the ground, and Kiffin could have hit a tree or some other obstruction before he even saw the ground. In this case, he was lucky. He broke out of the clouds and discovered that he was indeed over Châteauroux. He found the airfield, landed, and had an official sign his flight log to prove he had completed that leg of the triangle.

The next leg of his flight was to Romorantin, a town about forty miles to the north. There was another student at Châteauroux, a student who had started on his triangular course before Kiffin but damaged his airplane in the landing and was stranded at the airfield. He advised Kiffin not to try flying the next leg, as it was getting too foggy. Kiffin, relying on the vast experience he had gained during the fourteen hours of flight time he had accumulated, replied that since he had found Châteauroux, it would be even easier to find Romorantin.

Kiffin took off for Romorantin. Dense fog rolled in, the wind picked up, and Kiffin was totally lost. He wrote Paul, "For two hours I hunted for Romorantin, but could not see a damned thing."[33] He finally found a place to land and learned that he was less than ten minutes from his destination. It was getting dark, but he figured it wouldn't get much darker in the ten minutes it would take him to fly to Romorantin, so he asked for directions and took off. As the minutes ticked by and he saw no sign of the town, he realized that he was lost again. Only now it was completely dark. He searched for half an hour with no luck. He had run out of light, and now he was running out of oil and gasoline. He finally did see the lights of a town, so he flew to it. He made low passes over the roofs of the houses, hoping someone would realize he was in trouble and would signal him or set up a light to show him where it would be safe to land, but no one did. So he was forced to pick a spot with no lights that looked like it *might* be an open field and land. When his instinct told him he was nearly down, he cut his engine and eased back on the control stick to lose speed. The plane settled onto the ground. He had made a perfect landing in the dark, with the horizon hidden by fog, something he later admitted wouldn't happen one time out of a hundred under similar circumstances.

Kiffin had landed near the city of Vierzon, about eighteen miles southeast of Romorantin. It seemed to him that the entire town turned out to greet him. They had heard him fly over but knew nothing about airplanes and had no idea what he wanted. They were thrilled to have an aviator in their town, and an American volunteer to boot. They provided a guard for his plane and promised to get oil and gasoline. The next day was too foggy even for Kiffin to take off, so he spent the day in the town and wrote to Paul from the *Café du Commerce*:

> I have the pick of the town for everything I want, girls included. I am followed by two or three hundred people everywhere I go. My machine is covered with flowers, also names of girls. People meet me in the streets with bouquets, and in all I am *bien content*. I have not gotten drunk yet but it is not the fault of the inhabitants. Well, I must close now, as someone is waiting for me to go to dinner.[34]

The fog kept Kiffin grounded at Vierzon for three days. The people treated him royally during that time and covered his plane with phrases like *"Vive l'aviateur américain engagé volontaire pour la France"* (Long live the American aviator who volunteered for France) and *"J'adore l' aviateur"* (I love the aviator).[35] On Sunday, the visibility cleared enough that he could make a demonstration flight for the benefit of his hosts, but it didn't clear enough for him to return to Camp d'Avord until Monday. Even then, it was so foggy that the flight instructors were surprised he was able to make it back. The bad weather continued for several more days. Finally the weather cleared, and Kiffin quickly completed the remaining flights needed to earn his pilot's license. On October 21, 1915, he wrote his sister Agnes from Chartres, "This is the finishing thing for my *brevet militaire* and I am no longer a student pilot but a full-fledged aviator."[36] He returned to Camp d'Avord the following day and was awarded his *brevet*. Then he left for Paris on the eight-day leave that was traditionally awarded to new pilots. Like all wartime leaves, the time passed very quickly. Kiffin stayed with Paul and Mrs. Weeks. Kiffin wrote his mother that they made him feel at home in their apartment and that Mrs. Weeks was doing a little sewing on his uniform.[37] She was probably sewing on his aviation insignia. Now that he had earned his *brevet*, he was entitled to wear a winged star on his collar. Jim McConnell, who had finally gotten orders to transfer from the Ambulance Service to Aviation, wrote, "Afraid I won't have any chance at 148 Bis [Jim's girlfriend's address] after Kiffin appears in his flossy get up before the button loving young lady."[38]

Kiffin shopped for warm clothes in Paris, as he knew the upcoming winter weather would be brutal in an open cockpit. He returned to Camp d'Avord to find things in an uproar. The previous commander had been fired. A Captain Boucher replaced him, and he was making sweeping changes. He was reported to be a very strict disciplinarian, and the men Kiffin talked to worried that things would soon get much worse. Kiffin thought he saw a way out. The French Army was asking for volunteers to fly Farmans in Serbia. Austria had just invaded that country and the Serbian Army was forced to retreat. The Allies were scrambling to create an army in northern Greece (Salonika) that could come to Serbia's aid. To Kiffin, this must have seemed an almost irresistible opportunity. The Serbs were the underdogs, and they badly needed help. He could go to the front and make a difference in the war, only this time it would be as an aviator. He was already qualified on the Farman airplane. And to entice airmen to volunteer for this mission, the French paid enlisted aviators in Serbia 600 francs a month versus 100 francs on the Western Front.

Kiffin went to see Captain Boucher the following day. He was surprised by how friendly the captain was. When he told the captain he wanted to volunteer for Serbia, it took Boucher "off his feet." The captain praised his flying abilities and said he was proud to have an American volunteer at his school who was willing to make such an offer. He then told Kiffin that unless he was absolutely certain he wanted to go to Serbia, he would prefer to have Kiffin stay in France and fly on the Western Front. He told Kiffin he could have any plane he wanted if he stayed. Kiffin asked for a Nieuport, which was the newest and best fighter in the French Air Force. Captain Boucher immediately promised to put Kiffin in Nieuport training. Later, as Kiffin was at the school office filling out paperwork to apply for this new training, a clerk showed him the fitness report his instructors had written about his flying. Kiffin was astounded at the praise they heaped upon him. He wrote Alice Weeks that there never was a better report sent in on an aviator.[39]

While Kiffin was amazed to be given the choice of which airplane he wanted to fly, his good fortune seems to have been purely based upon his flying skill. In a few months the French would decide to form an *escadrille* (squadron) composed entirely of American volunteers flying Nieuport fighters. Once that decision was made, they automatically assigned all American volunteer aviators to the Bleriot school followed by Nieuport training. That wouldn't happen for another month or two, though. At the time Captain Boucher agreed to assign Kiffin to Nieuport training, the proposal to create an American escadrille was still mired in bureaucracy. Kiffin turned out to be an excellent Nieuport pilot, and he fully justified Captain Boucher's faith in him. Chances are that Kiffin would have been extremely disappointed had he actually been posted to Salonika. There was only a small amount of flying on that front, and for most of the war the Allies had thousands of troops doing nothing in Salonika. Senior German officials joked that Salonika was their largest internment camp.

Before Kiffin could fly a Nieuport, however, he had to essentially start flight training all over at the Bleriot school to get a feel for the more sensitive controls of a single-seat plane.[40] That meant starting with the "Penguins," taxiing back and forth across the field in a straight line in a plane that could not fly. Some pilots found it difficult to master a single-seat plane after having flown the larger, slower two-seaters. One wrote that it took him several days just to be able to make the required six straight runs in a Penguin.[41] Kiffin did it in a matter of hours. Other students had problems because the strange handling characteristics of rotary engines were much more pronounced in a small single-seat plane. One student complained that flying a Nieuport was like "trying to fly a gyroscope."[42] Kiffin had no problems mastering small planes with rotary engines. His biggest problem was that winter weather had set in and students were not allowed to fly for days on end. During the first ten days of November, Kiffin was only allowed to train four times, for roughly ten minutes each time.[43] During the next eight days the weather improved somewhat and he was able to fly for ten hours, which was long enough to complete the entire course of single-seat training and be ready to fly a Nieuport. They had Nieuports at the school, but no Nieuport instructors. So Kiffin had to content himself with flying a Morane Parasol monoplane, an aircraft that the instructors said was more difficult to fly than any other plane the French had.[44] The instructors also told Kiffin that it took most students from six weeks to three months to progress as far as he had come in three weeks.[45] Their only concern was that he did not have enough hours in the air. They assigned an airplane specifically to him, and he was free to fly it as much as he wanted. He and Victor Chapman rented a little house near the flying field and devoted themselves to flying.

Meanwhile, Paul Pavelka was still cheating death in the Legion. Mrs. Weeks got a letter from him in early November, telling how the Legion was trying to make life easier on the soldiers:

To make life here a little more agreeable the Government has commenced to issue a ration of charcoal to each one of us. This consists of 250 grammes [a half pound] daily. Not only does it help us to keep warm, but we can warm our food and also make a piece of toast.... To pay for the charcoal they have reduced the ration of wine to one cup a day. They have also ceased to give rum in the morning. I suppose all this is to make ends meet.[46]

Pavelka then went back into battle, and she heard nothing from him for close to three weeks. She had just about given him up for dead when he showed up on her doorstep. He was covered with mud and his coat was nearly shot to pieces, but he was still alive.[47] After spending a short leave in Paris, he returned to the Legion and found that his orders to Aviation had finally come through. (When he arrived at flight school, he learned that his orders had actually been issued long ago and everyone wondered what had taken him so long.)[48]

The immortal Billy Thorin, the sailor/roustabout/general roughneck who was left for dead on the Champagne battlefield, was another frequent visitor at Mrs. Weeks's apartment. He was given convalescent leave in Paris and he frequently stopped to see Mrs. Weeks for dinner. People noticed that when he was there, her maid, a middle-aged Belgian woman, "served very badly and gazed continually at the Legionnaire." Billy had dinner with Mrs. Weeks the night before he left to go back to the Legion, and the maid offered to make a box lunch for him to take with him. She slipped a note into the box declaring her ardent love for him. Billy responded in kind, and afterward he got regular parcels containing cigarettes, chocolates, and other comforts from the maid.[49]

Apparently the maid wasn't the only woman Billy saw during his convalescent leave. In late November, he wrote a letter to Kiffin:

Just to let you know I am alive & still kicking. I can't say that I am all right because it is hell here.... Helen wrote me a letter yesterday and asked me for your address & damned if I know [what] she can see in a long hay rick like you, never mind kid, if you make me your best man it is all right, if not, the devil shall take you when I get a hold of you.... Well, so long for this time my honey. I hope you will write me an answer to this, and don't be too damn slow.[50]

It's not clear who "Helen" was. Kiffin received two letters from a Helen (last name illegible) who gave him her phone number and told him to call.[51] A few weeks later, she wrote again and complained that she saw him in a crowd at the Ritz but he wouldn't even look at her. She invited him to come for lunch or tea someday, *any* day, he was in Paris (her emphasis).[52] There are no additional letters from Helen, so it would appear that, perhaps not surprisingly, Kiffin's taste in women was somewhat different from Billy's.

Kiffin's main focus was on learning to fly the Nieuport so he could go to the front and take on the German Air Force. He said, "I feel that I have many scores to settle, and there is going to be more than one 'Boche' aviator to settle them, or I will not live to tell the tale. As the French say, I am *vraiment un as* [really an ace][53] when in the air, and I am going to take advantage of it."[54] He also commented about how cold it was flying during the winter weather. Cold winters were a problem for all flyers during the war. Ted Parsons, who would go through pilot training and join the Lafayette Escadrille several months after Kiffin, described winter flying as follows:

> When the weather on the ground was so freezing cold that motor oil had to be heated over an open fire, poured hurriedly into the reservoir and the motor started immediately to keep it from freezing up again, then it was cold. On top of that, take a ship up to fifteen thousand feet, sit there for two hours immovable, and mere words are difficult to describe the pure agony of mind and body. The subzero temperature penetrated the very marrow of your bones. Despite three or four pairs of gloves, fingers coiled around the stick would be paralyzed in five minutes. Then they would have to be forced open and pushed away from the stick with the other hand and the paralyzed hand beaten against the side of the fuselage to restore circulation. A few minutes later the process would have to be reversed. Feet were twin lumps of ice, rigid and unfeeling; shooting pains throughout the entire body, eyeballs and teeth smarting and burning, icy scalp contracting till it felt as if the skull must burst through and explode in a shower of bones, heart pumping half-congealed ice water instead of warm blood—thus it can be easily understood why liquor was a necessity. Without it, a man might easily come to earth a frozen corpse.[55]

While many pilots complained about flying in cold weather, Parsons's candid admission that he carried a flask of brandy aloft to ward off the effects of the cold is unique. If other pilots did this, they didn't admit it. Of course, Parsons was also one of the few pilots who freely admitted that he was terrified during aerial combat, and he used his flask to steady his nerves for that condition, too. (He was a highly decorated pilot who shot down eight enemy planes during the war, so he was no stranger to combat.) Kiffin never mentioned carrying a flask aloft, but during the winter he did wear a heavy fur coat given to him by Alice Weeks.

In mid-December, Kiffin completed his Nieuport training at Camp d'Avord, graduating at the top of his class.[56] He was assigned to the General Reserve of the Aviation at Camp Le Bourget, just outside Paris.[57] This was a standard assignment for pilots who were waiting for assignment to an *escadrille* (squadron) at the front. Kiffin spent his time at Le Bourget honing his skills on a Nieuport. Pilots were allowed to do as they wished when they weren't flying, and Kiffin spent most nights in Paris with Paul and Mrs. Weeks. Kiffin wrote his mother that there was little activity and he was taking things easy, but that didn't mean every day was uneventful. Mrs. Weeks wrote her brother Fred that Kiffin nearly killed himself one morning because his motor stopped while he was coming in for a landing. He just barely cleared a house but ran into a pole which sheared the wings off his airplane.[58] Kiffin wisely chose not to mention that incident in his letters to his mother.

Since Kiffin had finished his "formal" pilot's training and was awaiting orders to the front, it is interesting to consider what was *not* included in his training. He had not received any detailed training in aerobatics or combat maneuvers, although he had been encouraged to try some "stunts." He had not been given any gunnery training. Indeed, he had never fired a gun in the air or flown an armed aircraft. He also had not received any training on formation flying, or on how to fly and fight as a unit. Basically, Kiffin had received the equivalent of civilian flight training. His instructors probably had combat experience because it was standard practice to rotate front-line pilots into instructor positions to give them a rest, and Kiffin may have received some advice on combat flying from them. There was not yet any formal training on how to survive and succeed as a fighter pilot because the whole concept of a fighter pilot was brand new. That was rapidly changing, and classes to teach this new form of combat would soon follow.

Kiffin spent a quiet Christmas in Paris with Mrs. Weeks and his brother, definitely an improvement over his previous Christmas. Billy Thorin spent his Christmas in jail, but he didn't seem to mind. He described the incident which landed him there:

The other night we went to a cafe called "L'Univers." Two Spaniards told us the U.S.A. was no good and that the Americans could not fight. So just to show them that there was no ill feeling and that none of us American guys was afraid to fight, I cracked one between the eyes. That started it. We were four and they were five, but it didn't make no odds to us. We went through them in good old style; they got assistance from two civilians, but they were no good with their dukes, so we laid them low as well. They sent for patrols, but we had just warmed up then, and, as the gendarmes said, "Nothing but a seventy-five [a 75 mm cannon] could have stopped those four Americans." We smashed up a few things, like chairs and windows, etc. Well, they got too many for us at last, but the gendarmes were good sports and told us they would help us right as much as they possibly could. Their word was good. When we were taken up in front of the four-striper [commandant], the gendarmes told him that the other fellows started the trouble and that if we each paid fifteen francs the cafe would let it go at that. We have paid ten francs each already, but, believe me, I wouldn't have missed that fight for a fifty-dollar bill. I will be sitting in a cell over Christmas, but what of it?[59]

An American Escadrille

Well boys, one day a lot of us will be flying up there too. It'll be a bunch of Americans flying.

—Bill Thaw

The year 1916 began on a sad note. On New Year's Day, Mrs. Weeks received official notification that her son had been killed in combat.[1] Of the forty-three Americans who had enlisted in the Foreign Legion in August 1914, 95 percent had been killed or wounded by the end of 1915.[2] Many of the wounded, like Kiffin, had recovered and were still serving.

"Skipper" Paul Pavelka had recovered from his wounds and was happily beginning his flight training at Pau, a training school in southern France. He was joined there by Jim McConnell, who had finally managed to leave the Ambulance Service and enter Aviation. To avoid losing his American citizenship, McConnell enlisted in the Foreign Legion and was detailed to Aviation. This was the path that Raoul Lufbery blazed in 1914, and it would be followed by many American volunteers in the years to come. McConnell was excited to finally be able to take an active role in the war, but he wasn't thrilled about military life. He wrote to Paul Rockwell, complaining that every morning they woke the students with a bugle, at night they stood around and saluted the flag, and "all that sort of bunk like a prep school."[3]

The hazards of his new life were brought home to Jim when the school required him to make "final arrangements." The sense of humor that had gotten him elected King of the Hotfoot Society was evident in his arrangements. When asked whether he wanted to be buried as a Catholic or a Protestant, he replied, "Whichever one gives the best send-off."[4] He had to make out a will, but since his family disapproved of his going to war, he elected to have all his things sent to Paul Rockwell. He sent a letter to Paul asking him to give his clothes to the poor and to throw a party with any small sums of money he might have. He also left tender instructions on how to break the news to Marcelle, a girl he was dating, whom he called "Bright Eyes." "Tell Bright Eyes I croaked muttering her name," he told Paul. Then he added, "Tell Betty the same thing."[5]

Meanwhile, Kiffin was still marking time in Paris, flying when the weather permitted, and anxiously awaiting orders to a flying unit at the front. He wrote his mother:

> The weather is nearly always bad, so it means little activity in the aviation and less demand for more pilots for the front. I am still taking things very easy. When we do have a day fairly good I fly a little and the rest of the time I stay in Paris. I seldom go around, however, in Paris and dread it every time I have an invitation out to dinner. Paul, Mrs. Weeks and I stay very quietly at home and I usually go off to bed as soon as we have finished dinner.[6]

Apparently Kiffin didn't always stay quietly at home. Billy Thorin finished his jail sentence at La Valbonne and managed to obtain leave to visit Paris, where he saw Kiffin and Paul. Billy, at least, spent a night on the town, and it would appear that Kiffin joined him for at least the first part of that night. Paul later drove Billy back to La Valbonne, and along the way Billy mentioned that he had overstayed his leave by twenty-four hours and would be sentenced to eight days in jail as a result. He thought he might be able to "fix things up" with his corporal if he just had ten francs, but he was broke. Paul gave him ten francs, but he was surprised to find Billy in jail the next day.

"What's the matter?" Paul asked. "Couldn't you 'fix' the corporal?"

Billy candidly replied, "Well, I got to thinking it over, and decided I'd rather do the eight days and keep the ten francs myself."[7]

Billy then wrote Kiffin from jail to say that, despite the jail sentence, he had a good time in Paris, so he was satisfied. The years he had spent at sea were apparent in the wording of his letter.

> Say, have you seen that lady love of my life that you bought me that night? She was not a bad old craft, but she ought to be taken in to dry

dock & overhauled. Otherwise I don't think she will pass the board of trade. The other little peach, she was old and battle worn, but she was seaworthy all right. I pumped her out four times that night & she was perfectly dry when I took her to her moorings in the morning.[8]

One of the reasons Kiffin was languishing in Paris instead of flying at the front was that the French were finally starting to create an all-American flying squadron. They didn't want to assign Kiffin to a French escadrille only to reassign him to the American escadrille. The creation of this unit was taking longer than anyone expected, and Kiffin grew increasingly frustrated with the delays as rumors and counter-rumors circulated. The delays and changes in plans also affected Americans in training, as the training schools tried to second-guess when the American escadrille would be formed and what plane they would fly. Jim McConnell described how these changes affected several American student-pilots:

> This damned Aviation bunch in Paris has gone wild. First they put Rumsey on Voisin, then send him back here to Caudron and they put Skip [Pavelka] there too. Then they move both to Morane to pass to Nieuport along with Hill. Then they order them all off. In three days Rumsey, who had done well on Morane, was sent to G.R. [General Reserve] on Caudron. Skip back to Morane and Hill to Caudron at this school.[9]

The question of who originated the idea of an American flying squadron has generated much debate over the years, but it appears that several people had the idea independently and worked along different paths to make it happen. Bill Thaw and Norman Prince were the two most prominent advocates of this idea, with Thaw working to bring Americans into French Aviation and create a de facto American escadrille while Prince worked from the outside, lobbying the French government to create an official American escadrille. Eventually the two met and worked together to create what would in time become known as the Lafayette Escadrille.

Early in the war, the French were not interested in recruiting foreigners to be pilots. For one thing, they already had enough trained military pilots for the planes they had. They also had a large number of cavalry officers who were already trained to scout enemy positions. It quickly became apparent that these officers were not going to gallop horses behind enemy lines to reconnoiter, so they were ideal candidates to become airmen.[10] The French also had a reason to be suspicious of foreign volunteers. An American bicycle racer named F. C. Hild somehow talked his way into the French Service Aéronautique during the first month of the war. They sent him to the training school at Pau, but after a few weeks he deserted and returned to America. He gave several interviews to American newspapers, detailing sensational (and false) stories about how bad the French equipment and training was. The French also suspected him of selling their aviation secrets to German agents.[11]

So, when Bill Thaw offered his services as a pilot in August 1914, the French were not interested and he joined the Foreign Legion instead. Four months later, when he hiked to a French airfield and asked his prewar flying associate Lieutenant Brocard to help him transfer to Aviation, things had changed. For one thing, the French needed pilots. Early losses coupled with the need for a rapid expansion of the Aviation corps had shown that it was much easier to build additional airplanes than it was to train new pilots. The other factor in Thaw's favor was that the French had already admitted a couple of Americans into their Aviation corps, where they were doing excellent work. Both were at least as much French as they were American, which is probably why they were allowed in. One was Raoul Lufbery, who was serving as Marc Pourpe's mechanic. Pourpe was subsequently killed in a flying accident, a death that Raoul blamed on the Germans, and Raoul became a pilot so he could avenge Pourpe's death. The other American was Didier Masson. Like Lufbery, he was born in France and grew up there. He learned to fly in 1909 and then moved to the United States. He spent several years giving flying exhibitions and test-flying new aircraft for various manufacturers. He also traveled to Mexico during the Mexican Revolution, where he joined the rebel forces and flew some of the world's first bombing missions, dropping improvised bombs on Federal gunboats. When World War I broke out, he returned to France, briefly served in an infantry unit, and then transferred to Aviation.[12]

Since the French needed pilots and these two Americans had done well in Aviation, they approved Bill Thaw's transfer. They also approved the requests of two of his legionnaire buddies, Bert Hall and Jimmy Bach, who had submitted their requests with Bill's. Like Bill, they swore they were experienced pilots. In Bill's case, this was true. The other two had never even seen an airplane up close. Ironically, their requests were approved before Bill's was.

Bert Hall was sent directly to a French flying school. Since he had claimed he already knew how to fly, they asked him to make a demonstration flight. He tried to carry through with his bluff. He climbed into an airplane, had the mechanics start the engine, and zigzagged across the field like a jackrabbit on steroids, lurching first one way and then the other as he tried to figure out the controls. He actually managed to get the machine off the ground for a moment—before he crashed into the wall of a hangar. The plane was a total loss, but Bert emerged with only a scratched knee and a bruised ego. The French officer in charge demanded to know what had gone wrong. When Bert said he didn't know, the officer shouted, "Haven't you ever been in a plane before?" Bert admitted that he hadn't. When asked why in God's name he hadn't told them that, he replied, "Well, I thought I *might* be able to fly." His honesty, even if a bit late, seems to have taken the edge off the officer's anger. "You have guts. That much I will say for you" was the officer's reply.[13] They allowed Bert to stay at the school and enrolled him as a beginner. He earned his pilot's license and spent the next year flying at the front and serving as an instructor.

Jimmy Bach followed a more traditional path and earned his pilot's license in July 1915. He flew at the front and, according to one account, was the first American to shoot down an enemy aircraft.[14] He then came to grief in an experiment that proved *not* to be an appropriate mission for aircraft. He and a French pilot were ordered to fly two saboteurs behind the German lines, land them in a field near a railroad line the saboteurs were to blow up, and then fly back to their base. (The saboteurs were expected to find their own way back to the Allied lines.) Both pilots successfully landed in the field, which proved to be very rough, with stumps hidden in tall grass. After the saboteurs got out, Jimmy Bach managed to take off again. His fellow pilot was not so lucky and wrecked his plane. Jimmy turned around and landed a second time to pick up the other pilot. This time he smashed his plane while trying to take off. Both pilots were soon captured by the Germans. Jimmy was the first American aviator taken prisoner, and he was charged with being a mercenary. Conviction on this charge would lead to a firing squad, but when Bach was put on trial, he proved to the judge that he had enlisted in the Foreign Legion, a recognized military unit, and he was cleared of the charges. He spent the rest of the war in a POW camp, but he ensured that future American volunteers would not be treated as merce-naries.[15] (Bach's capture also demonstrated the bond that existed between aviators during the war. The day after he was captured, a German plane flew over a French airfield and dropped a note stating that the two pilots had been captured and were unhurt. The next day Bert Hall flew over a German airfield and dropped a "thank you" reply.)[16]

Bill Thaw was finally transferred to Aviation on Christmas Eve 1914. He was assigned to Escadrille D6, which flew two-seat Deperdussin airplanes. Bill flew as an observer while waiting for a vacancy in a flight training school.[17] If it bothered him that Hall and Bach had gone directly into flight training, apparently filling the last two vacancies, he never men-tioned it. He was delighted to be out of the infantry and into Aviation. On February 1, 1915, he began taking flight training. With his previous flying experience, he passed rapidly through the course and received his *brevet militaire* on March 15.[18] He was sent to the front flying bombing and recon-naissance missions in a Caudron G-4 aircraft, and he continued working to bring other Americans (including Kiffin) into Aviation. Before the year was out, he would become the first American to be commissioned as an officer in the French Army.[19]

On the other side of the Atlantic, an American named Norman Prince also conceived the idea of an all-American flying squadron. The scion of one of the wealthiest families in New England, Norman was born in Pride's Crossing, Massachusetts, and grew up both in the family home in America and on the family hunting estate near Pau, France. When he was eleven, he grew dissatisfied with his Latin tutor and replaced him, after first timing the new tutor to make certain he could translate more than ten lines of Virgil a minute. At fifteen his father gave him an opportunity to spend a year study-ing abroad, but Norman was concerned that he still needed another year of prep school at Groton before he could go to Harvard. At his insistence, he was allowed to test out of the final year at Groton and take the entrance exam for Harvard, which he passed, before going abroad.[20] He graduated cum laude from Harvard in 1908 and earned his bachelor of law degree from the same school in 1911.

Norman learned to fly in 1912. When World War I broke out, he wanted to offer his services to France, the country where he had spent much time as a child, but he didn't want to serve in the infantry. He wanted to fly for France. He went to Paris in January 1915 and began lobbying for an American flying squadron. He made very little headway. At the time, the French didn't see any reason to form an American unit. Norman was soon joined by Frazier Curtis, an old friend and fellow pilot who tried to fly for the British until he learned that would cost him his American citizenship. Curtis worked with Norman to try to convince the French to create an American squadron. When that effort stalled, the two enlisted in the Foreign Legion and were sent to a French flying school. Curtis suffered a couple of bad accidents and was sent back to Paris on convalescent leave. Eventually his injuries led to a medical discharge, but while he was in Paris he resumed his lobbying efforts. There he met an influential American, Dr. Edmund L. Gros, who had previously helped form the American Ambulance Field Service. Dr. Gros helped Curtis promote the idea of an American squadron and introduced him to important people within the French government.

Even with Dr. Gros's help, things moved slowly. It wasn't that the Ministry of War opposed the idea. It just wasn't a priority for them. They were, after all, in the middle of a war for national survival, and they didn't see how creating a special unit for millionaire playboys from America would help that effort.

In the meantime, Norman Prince completed his flight training and was sent to the front where he quickly proved that, like Bill Thaw, he was more than just a millionaire playboy. He was initially sent to Escadrille VB108, flying bombing missions in a two-seat Voisin pusher biplane. Ever optimistic, he wrote his father that he would just be flying with this unit until the American Escadrille was formed.[21] Temporary or not, it was definitely a combat tour. At that point in the air war the primary threat was from ground-based anti-aircraft fire, and within a few weeks he would write his brother that since he arrived the unit had lost two out of its six pilots to the "vertical guns" of the Boche.[22] An American named Elliot Cowdin, who had served in the American Ambulance Field Service before transferring to Aviation, joined Prince in this squadron.

The idea of forming an all-American flying unit was progressing through French Ministry of War channels with glacial slowness, but that didn't stop Prince, Thaw, and Dr. Gros from trying to recruit Americans to fly in the unit. In September 1915, Norman wrote to his grandmother:

There are ten American pilots with us in the French service and twelve others in training with their number constantly increasing. Some day soon we will all be united in one escadrille—an Escadrille Améric-ain—that is my fondest ambition. I am devoting all my spare energies to organizing it and all the American pilots here are giving me every encouragement and assistance in the work of preliminary organization. As I have had so much to do in originating and pushing the plan along, perhaps I shall be second in command.[23]

Kiffin was one of the American pilots in training at the time Norman wrote that letter. It's not clear that Kiffin knew of the plan to create an American squadron at the time. When Kiffin did learn about it, he expressed more concern than excitement. His overriding goal was to fight the Germans, and he was afraid the formation of this special unit would delay his arrival at the front.

Despite Norman Prince's optimism, the proposal for an all-American unit didn't make much headway in September. Or October. Or November. It wasn't until late December 1915 that the French Ministry of War began to get enthused about the idea. The event that caught their attention was a trip by three American pilots back to the United States. There was an established program in the French Army to give soldiers eight days paid leave at their home. Travel time to and from their home did not count against this leave, and the army paid for the travel.[24] Thaw, Prince, and Cowdin applied for Christmas leave under this provision and their request was granted. Neither the three Americans nor the French government had any idea that this would turn out to be a major press event.

Newspapers had been following the exploits of the American pilots with even more enthusiasm than they'd followed the exploits of Americans in the Foreign Legion because aviation was a brand new and exciting technology. For both infantry and aviation, however, coverage had primarily consisted of press releases from Paris news bureaus, with an occasional photograph. Now there were three veteran pilots, fresh from the hostile skies over the Western Front, in the United States, available for interviews and photographs. Their arrival and daily activities made headlines across the country.

Not surprisingly, their visit was not welcomed by supporters of Germany. When Bill Thaw arrived in New York, he visited a barbershop and had the misfortune to be seated next to the German ambassador to the United States, Herr Johann Heinrich von Bernstorf.[25] The two men knew each other from prewar diplomatic functions. Their conversation remained civil, but Bernstorf made it clear that he thought the three aviators' visit was a breach of America's neutrality, and he suggested that they should voluntarily intern themselves. On December 24, the day after the three men arrived in the United States, the editor of the *Fatherland* newspaper publicly called upon the US secretary of state to order the immediate internment of the three aviators.[26]

The calls for internment and subsequent articles by eminent lawyers debating the legality of such a move only added interest and press coverage to the visit. Claims that the three should be interned were based in part on the belief that they had forfeited their American citizenship when they joined the French Army.[27] To add spice to the controversy, Bill Thaw was called upon to testify in a libel case against a New York newspaper that had confused him with one of his cousins. They printed an article that claimed Bill was married and was famous for drunken escapades. When questioned about his drinking, Bill replied that he did not consider himself a teetotaler, but "one can't drink in the aviation business."[28] (This last remark probably would have been a surprise to many pilots in France, particularly those who knew Bill Thaw.) He also explained the process of enlisting in the Foreign Legion to prove he was still an American citizen and not a French combatant. While it did not appear that the United States was seriously considering internment, the three airmen quietly slipped aboard a French ship and headed back to France a few days before their leave was up to forestall any difficulties.

Although their departure was quiet, their visit had shown the French government that the American people had an intense interest in American aviators. Both France and England were heavily dependent on the United States for war supplies, and the credit with which to buy those supplies, so France had a vested interest in maintaining good American press. France also hoped to convince the United States to declare war on Germany and take an active military role in the conflict, an action that would require the support of the American public. French officials realized that publicizing the role American volunteers were playing in the defense of France could generate support among the American public. The publicity given to the three pilots over Christmas clearly demonstrated that aviators attracted more attention than infantrymen, and it was reasonable to assume that an all-American flying squadron would attract even more attention. Suddenly the idea of an *Escadrille Américain* was more than just something to keep a few millionaire playboys happy. It was a move that could significantly benefit France. Paperwork started flying through bureaucratic channels. Bill Thaw's squadron commander, Captain Georges Thénault, happened to be on leave in Paris when the three pilots returned from the United States. He introduced them to some influential journalists, who promised to promote the idea of an American squadron. Captain Thénault then took them to meet with the French air minister, who listened to them with great interest.

The air minister approved the creation of the squadron in principle, and American pilots began receiving orders to report to a pilot pool at Le Plessis-Belleville, a town about twenty-five miles northwest of Paris. Kiffin, Bill Thaw, and Victor Chapman arrived at the end of January and they reserved four rooms at the only hotel in town. (They were expecting Norman Prince to arrive the following day.) Kiffin described the place as "rather God-Forsaken country."[29] Kiffin wrote very few letters from Plessis-Belleville. It was close enough to Paris that he could visit Paul and Mrs. Weeks regularly, so there was little reason for him to write to them. More important, there was very little to write about. The weather was atrocious, and Kiffin was seldom able to fly. Plessis-Belleville was much like the pilot pool at Le Bourget that Kiffin had just left. Pilots were encouraged to hone their flying skills while they waited. Sometimes this was their first opportunity to fly front-line aircraft, but when the weather was bad, there was nothing to do. Kiffin was not good at doing nothing. He was excited when he first went to Plessis-Belleville because it was the last stop before being sent to the front, but week after week went by with no American escadrille, and no orders to the front.

On February 21, 1916, an event occurred that further delayed the creation of an American escadrille: the Germans launched a major offensive at Verdun. This turned out to be the longest battle of the war. It was also the most intense and futile battle of the war, a war that was characterized by intense, futile battles. The planning for this insanity began in December 1915 when General Eric von Falkenhayn, chief of the German General Staff, reviewed the current situation and developed his strategy for the coming year. Russia was reeling from the defeats Germany had inflicted on her. She was still in the war but did not pose an immediate threat. France and England had suffered heavily in their disastrous attacks of 1915—especially France. Falkenhayn felt that England still posed a major threat, but he thought France was on the verge of collapse. If Germany could knock

France out of the war, England would be forced to stand alone on the Western Front or to withdraw completely. Germany couldn't afford to weaken her forces opposing Russia or England, so Falkenhayn ruled out the possibility of a major breakthrough against the French. Instead, he envisioned an intense attack on a narrow front. He wrote to Kaiser Wilhelm, describing his plan to defeat France:

> To achieve that objective, the uncertain method of a mass breakthrough, in any case beyond our means, is unnecessary. We can probably do enough for our purposes with limited resources. Within our reach behind the French sector of the western front there are objectives for the retention of which the French General Staff would be compelled to throw in every man they have. If they do so the force of France will bleed to death—as there can be no question of a voluntary withdrawal—whether we reach our goal or not. If they do not do so and we reach our objectives, the moral effect on France will be enormous. For an operation limited to a narrow front, Germany will not be compelled to spend herself so completely.[30]

He went on to explain why Verdun, one of the most heavily fortified regions in France, was the ideal target for this attack. To put this plan into effect, Falkenhayn massed the greatest concentration of artillery the world had ever seen around Verdun and literally pulverized the French defenses. Long-range artillery destroyed rail lines and almost all roads leading into Verdun. Only a single, tortuous road remained open. The French depended upon that one road to bring in supplies and evacuate wounded soldiers. An unending stream of supply wagons, trucks, ambulances, and marching troops filled this road day and night. The road became known as *Voie Sacrée* (the Sacred Way). Falkenhayn also transferred a large number of aircraft to the battle in one of the first attempts ever made to achieve air supremacy. Aircraft were assigned to patrol at specific areas and altitudes on a rotating basis so that, in theory, the entire battlefield would be denied to all French aircraft throughout the daylight hours. They referred to this tactic as an "aerial barrage."[31] Artillery was going to dominate this battle, and the Germans were determined to have the only eyes in the sky directing it. When the Germans thought their bombardment had obliterated all French defenders, they sent their attacking force forward, in small numbers, to occupy the devastated landscape. When they ran into opposition, they stopped and called upon their artillery to destroy the resistance they had discovered.

Since the entire battle was built around the inhuman concept of bleeding the French Army to death, it is perhaps fitting that the biggest flaw in Falkenhayn's plan was that he ignored human nature. He didn't tell the attacking troops that their primary role was to draw more French soldiers into the killing zone and that it really didn't matter whether they captured their objective. Falkenhayn kept the "limited resources" part of his plan to himself. The German troops fully expected to achieve the breakthrough that Falkenhayn thought was beyond his means. During the opening days of the battle they made remarkable gains, even capturing the major French strong point in the region, Fort Douaumont. The German commanders underneath Falkenhayn also believed their objective was to achieve a breakthrough, and they began screaming for more troops to exploit the initial gains. Meanwhile, French reinforcements poured into the battle along the *Voie Sacrée*, and the French massed artillery along the flanks of Falkenhayn's intentionally narrow front. Now the battlefield became a killing zone for German troops.

The "logical" response, in keeping with Falkenhayn's original plan, would have been to abandon the gained ground, pull the German troops back to their starting positions, and let the French move back into the killing zone. That was politically impossible. The German public had been overjoyed by the initial gains and they expected a final breakthrough any day. The kaiser was jubilant over the success of the battle and pushed Falkenhayn to finish the job. Too much blood had already been shed, and too many expectations had been raised, to abandon the captured ground. And so Falkenhayn was sucked into his own trap. He had to capture Verdun, even if it bled the German Army to death. But the front was too narrow to allow the Germans to capture Verdun. French artillery on the surrounding hills prevented a breakthrough. Those hills had to be captured. And so the battle dragged on. German attacks gained ground that was then lost to French counterattacks. French attacks gained ground that was lost to German counterattacks. The phrase "*Ils ne passeront pas!*" (They shall not pass!) became a symbol of French determination and resistance. Officially the battle lasted ten months, until December 1916, but fierce fighting continued into 1917 and 1918. In the 1960s, it was estimated that the total casualties for both sides were 420,000 dead and 800,000 wounded,[32] but that figure is incomplete. Human bones are still being found on the battlefield today.

It's impossible to imagine the horrors that the troops on both sides experienced at Verdun. Estimates are that more than sixty million shells were fired into the battlefield, which means on the average every square foot of ground was hit by at least fifteen shells.[33] Entire villages in the battle area were reduced to dust. One disputed hill was labeled *Cote 304* (Hill 304) because before the battle it was 304 meters high. By the time the Germans captured it, it was only 300 meters high. The top 4 meters (13 feet) of soil had been blasted away. The first thing the Germans did after they captured that hill was to request double tobacco rations, to mask the stench of decaying bodies.[34] An American in the Foreign Legion, Eugene Bullard, fought at Verdun. He would go on to become the world's first black fighter pilot, but in 1916 he was a machine gunner in the French Army. Machine guns worked in pairs during attacks. One gun would fire until it got dangerously hot, and then the other gun would fire while the first gun cooled. Eugene was sickened by what he saw at Verdun. When the other gun was firing, he could see the Germans he'd shot writhing on the ground "like worms in a bait box."[35] French troops called Verdun "The Inferno" and "The Sausage Grinder."

The "aerial barrage" tactic tried by the Germans also did not succeed. Initially it was effective at blocking French reconnaissance. Essentially, though, the aerial barrage was a defensive strategy that ignored the basic airpower tenets of flexibility and concentration of force. It did not take the French long to realize that since the Germans had spread their aircraft evenly across the front and across the time span of all flyable hours, the French could concentrate a number of planes at the time and place of their choosing and punch through the German defenses. They began using the newly emerging fighter planes to escort reconnaissance and bomber missions. They created the first *escadrille du chasse*, a fighter squadron created solely to shoot down enemy planes.[36] The Germans in turn soon abandoned their aerial barrage and began to fly in similar formations. They also stationed fighters at airfields near the front lines, connected to anti-aircraft posts by a network of telephone lines, so they could "scramble" to intercept any French aircraft that were spotted crossing the lines. The net result was that the air war got much deadlier for both sides, and each moved more and more aircraft into the Verdun area.

With all this going on, it's perhaps not surprising that the French Air Ministry did not focus all its energy on creating an American escadrille. Captain Thénault was sent to Verdun at the beginning of the battle. He was instrumental in getting Elliot Cowdin transferred to escadrille N65 at Verdun in late February, and Bill Thaw was sent to the same escadrille when he completed Nieuport training in March. On April 4, 1916, Elliot Cowdin was credited with attacking twelve enemy aircraft and shooting down one of them, an LVG two-seater.[37] This made him arguably the first American fighter pilot in history to shoot down an enemy plane.

Meanwhile, Kiffin and Victor Chapman sat at Plessis-Belleville and waited for orders. (Captain Thénault probably did not send for them because he realized Verdun was not a good place to break in novice pilots.) Norman Prince was in Plessis-Belleville too, but he was busy learning how to fly a Nieuport. He began pushing to have a famous prewar sportsman and a personal friend of his, Captain Saint-Sauveur, named as the commanding officer.[38] However, Bill Thaw lobbied to have Thénault put in charge of the unit, and his choice ultimately prevailed.[39]

As the Battle of Verdun raged on, Kiffin grew more and more frustrated. France was engaged in the biggest battle in history—a battle for her very survival. The air war was crucial to winning that battle, and to win the air war, France needed fighter pilots. Kiffin had completed his flight training the previous year and had trained on Nieuport fighters, but he was sitting on the sidelines while the war was being won or lost at Verdun. On March 14, 1916, the director of French military aeronautics raised Kiffin's hopes when he announced plans to organize an *Escadrille Américain*. Two days later, he released a roster of American pilots for this squadron: Victor Chapman, Elliot Cowdin, Bert Hall, James McConnell, Norman Prince, Kiffin Rockwell, and Bill Thaw.[40] The squadron was to have a French commander and second-in-command, but specific individuals were not identified for these positions.

After this exciting announcement, several weeks went by with no further action. Kiffin chafed at the delays. He wrote to his friend the Vicomte du Peloux on April 6. His tone was formal, as it always was in his letters to the vicomte, but his frustration was obvious:

> I suppose you have been wondering why I have not written before this, but I really have not had anything to write. The fact is I have been more

or less demoralized by never doing anything and waiting each day to go to the front. I ask each week to be attached to a regular French escadrille, but they continue to keep us all back, waiting until the Escadrille Américain is formed. Why they don't form it, I don't know. We have enough men ready, the material ready, we know who will be the captain, that we are to go to Belfort, and that our number is "N124." Yet we are not sent out. In the meantime, I fly a little and spend much time in Paris. I have now written a captain at Verdun to please ask for me to be attached to his escadrille if he has a vacancy.[41]

The captain at Verdun whom Kiffin had written to was Captain Saint-Sauveur, the man Norman Prince wanted to lead the American escadrille. Saint-Sauveur was then leading N67, a Nieuport squadron fighting at Verdun. Lieutenant Jean Navarre, France's leading ace at the time and a man who had gained a reputation as "The Sentinel of Verdun," was a member of N67. Kiffin had presumably discussed his letter with Norman Prince and Victor Chapman, as he volunteered their services as well as his own. Saint-Sauveur's reply to Kiffin is interesting because it points out how desperate the French were for front-line fighters at the time, and it helps explain why it was taking so long to form an American escadrille:

I should be very pleased to have in my escadrille for some time my personal friend Norman Prince, Chapman, and you, but I am afraid it is impossible to obtain. The situation is this: we are ten pilots having only eight airplanes. Every day we break one or two on the awful landing field of this country. The company Nieuport produce, they say, 3 airplanes a day. All the production is for the aviation around Verdun; they give me all the airplanes they can, and I never can have more than eight available. You will understand easily that under those conditions I am unable to ask what you wish.[42]

The squadron designation of N124 indicated it would be flying Nieuport airplanes. (The first letter or letters of a French squadron indicated the type of aircraft flown by that unit. "N" stood for "Nieuport." Later in the war the squadron would be equipped with Spad airplanes, and the designation would change to SPA124.) The squadron would primarily be equipped with the Nieuport 11, often called the "*Bébé*" or "Baby" Nieuport because of its small size. This was a first-rate fighter that had only been in service for a few months. It was nineteen feet long with a twenty-four-foot wingspan. Its design was sometimes referred to as a "sesquiplane" or "1½ wing" because the lower wing was much narrower than the upper wing. This gave the pilot a better view downward than a conventional biplane provided, as well as a better top speed. It also provided better climb and maneuverability than contemporary monoplanes, but with more drag than a monoplane, which gave it a lower top speed. The Nieuport 11 was powered by an 80-horsepower Le Rhône rotary engine and had a top speed of 97 miles per hour and a ceiling of 15,000 feet. It was armed with a drum-fed Lewis machine gun on the top wing, firing over the propeller.

Victor Chapman described flying a Nieuport 11:

> The *Bébé* is the smallest and latest model. . . . It is a most delightful machine and responds so quickly and precisely. . . . Monday I went out for the fifth time on it, and climbing to 1000 meters [3,300 feet] I looped the loop a couple of times. . . . It is a beautifully balanced machine and it responds in a twinkling to the commands. Besides one has a great feeling of security and strength in its robust form and powerful motor. My! It is heavy for its size. To land well one must let it fall from about a yard and a half, taking care that the tail is well down at the time. . . . The first time I put my hand over for direction . . . it came over so fast that I wanted to climb on the upper side of the fuselage.[43]

Captain Thénault said simply, "They excited the jealousy of other pilots with slower and more bulky airplanes. They were mere lambs; we were wolves. In war it is better to be a wolf."[44]

Officially the unit was simply known as N124, but unofficially it was called the *Escadrille Américain*. That name was used widely in press stories, and, inevitably, the German government protested to the US government that this was a violation of neutrality. The United States in turn pressured the French government, and on November 16, 1916, the French issued a statement that said if anyone used a name to refer to N124, the name to use was *Escadrille des Volontaires*. Nobody liked that name, however, and it was soon changed to *Escadrille Lafayette*—the Lafayette Escadrille. It was a name that resonated with the pilots and with the public.[45] It honored the Marquis de Lafayette, a volunteer who came to the aid of the United

States during the Revolutionary War, when the young country badly needed France's help. It highlighted the fact that these American pilots were doing their part to repay the debt owed to France. And despite the fact that the name unmistakably linked the unit to the United States, it was a French name that satisfied the US concern over using the word *Américain* in the title.[46]

Despite the critical need for fighters at Verdun, the new unit would be assigned to the relatively quiet Vosges sector of the front, near the town of Luxeuil-les-Bains on the southern end of the Western Front. This was undoubtedly a wise decision on the part of the French government, as throwing a new squadron filled with green pilots into the inferno at Verdun would be tantamount to murder. Assigning the unit to a quiet sector would give Captain Thénault time to mold this diverse group of individuals into a cohesive unit, teach them to work together, and give them the skills they needed to survive in combat. He would need to use diplomacy to do this, as the Foreign Office had given him written orders not to impose the same strict standard of discipline that would be applied to a normal French escadrille.[47] They did not want the adverse publicity that would result if, say, a pilot were sentenced to jail time for overstaying a weekend leave in Paris. While it's unlikely the pilots knew about this restriction, they would frequently test the limits of Captain Thénault's patience in the months to come.

Pilots finally received their orders to report to the new squadron on April 16, 1916.[48] The following night, Sergeant Norman Prince gave a dinner at Ciro's in Paris. Bill Thaw, Victor Chapman, Jim McConnell, and Kiffin joined him in this celebration. The party was also attended by several American pilots in training who would soon be assigned to the Lafayette Escadrille: Clyde Balsley, Chouteau Johnson, and Laurence Rumsey. Paul Rockwell and Michel Plaa-Porte, a family friend of Norman Prince's who served as Norman's mechanic, also attended. Later that night, Kiffin caught a train that would take him to the front. His dream had finally come true.

Victor Chapman after being wounded on June 17. Note the shattered windscreen and the bullet holes (ripped fabric) immediately behind the cockpit. The aileron control rod that he held together with his hand was either the vertical rod just visible above his left shoulder or the corresponding rod on the other side of the windscreen. *Courtesy of the State Archives of North Carolina*

Kiffin in August 1916. A typed note on the back of this photograph, presumably from Paul Rockwell, comments on how Kiffin appears to have aged several years since April. Kiffin was twenty-three years old when this picture was taken. *Washington and Lee University*

"Senator Smart." Kiffin, age fourteen, in front of the Asheville house. *Courtesy of the State Archives of North Carolina*

Kiffin at Washington and Lee. *Courtesy of Sybil Robb*

Kiffin on the Behonne airfield after a flight over Verdun, looking older than his twenty-three years. The heavy flight suit shows how cold it was at high altitudes, even in the middle of the summer. *Courtesy of the State Archives of North Carolina*

A Bleriot "Penguin" training plane. The shortened wings and small propeller prevented students from actually taking off, but they could get a feel for the controls as they *tried* to taxi in a straight line. *Hall and Nordhoff, The Lafayette Flying Corps*

Kiffin poses for a newsreel photographer in front of his Nieuport 11. A note from his mother on the reverse notes that one tooth was chipped "in the trenches." It's more likely that it was chipped in the brawl that erupted after René Phélizot's death. *Author's Collection*

Kiffin (left), Agnes, and Paul, c. 1899. *Courtesy of the State Archives of North Carolina*

Pusher aircraft like this British FE-2 had an unlimited field of fire forward, but defending against an attack from behind could be a precarious endeavor. *Wikimedia Commons*

Norman Prince examining Le Prieur rockets on a Nieuport. *Washington and Lee University*

A Fokker Eindekker (monoplane) with machine gun. *Wikimedia Commons*

Jim McConnell (left) plays pool with Kiffin Rockwell (right) in Luxeuil. Victor Chapman talks to Madame Voge in the background. *Courtesy of the Virginia Military Institute Archives*

Kiffin Rockwell has what appears to be a difficult conversation with Captain Thénault shortly after Kiffin returned from Paris. (It may have been about the fact that Kiffin had no airplane.) Clyde Balsley, in a beret, is entering from the left while Raoul Lufbery waits patiently on the right. *Washington and Lee University*

Kiffin in his new uniform—with wings on his collar. *Courtesy of the State Archives of North Carolina*

The "founding members" of the Lafayette Escadrille at Luxeuil. Left to right are Victor Chapman, Elliot Cowdin, Bert Hall, Bill Thaw, Captain Thénault, Lieutenant de Laage, Norman Prince, Kiffin Rockwell, and Jim McConnell. Note that no two uniforms are identical. Captain Thénault's German shepherd "Fram" is front and center, along with two other squadron dogs. *University of Virginia Archives.*

An American volunteer wearing an early gas mask like the ones Mrs. Weeks made. *Courtesy of the State Archives of North Carolina*

Jim McConnell (left) with Paul Rockwell. Jim is wearing the uniform of the American Ambulance Service. Paul is wearing his Foreign Legion uniform and is on convalescent leave. His posture looks like he's still suffering from rheumatism. *University of Virginia Archives*

The beginnings of the Lafayette Escadrille. Left to right: Jim McConnell, Kiffin Rockwell, Captain Thénault, Norman Prince, and Victor Chapman stand in front of an unarmed Nieuport 10. This is sometimes called "The Tragic Photograph" because only one of these five men would survive the coming year. *Washington and Lee University*

A World War I inline engine. Note that the engine is long and uses a cooling radiator. *Wikimedia Commons*

A World War I rotary engine. When running, the cylinders spun around the central crankshaft. *Wikimedia Commons*

Luxeuil Luxury

Well, we're off to the races.[1]

—KIFFIN ROCKWELL

LUXEUIL-LES-BAINS IS A PICTURESQUE TOWN IN EASTERN FRANCE, ABOUT thirty-five miles from the Swiss border. Located at the edge of the Vosges Mountains, the scenic slopes of those mountains must have reminded Kiffin of his childhood in Tennessee and North Carolina. The Western Front ran through the Vosges, about thirty miles from the town. This was a relatively quiet sector. The town itself was largely untouched by the war, except that most of the military age men were at the front.

Les Bains, meaning "the baths," had been famous since Roman times for its natural mineral water. In peacetime, Luxeuil-les-Bains was a spa town, where over the centuries a succession of French kings, queens, and their consorts had frolicked in elaborate baths built around the warm spring. Early in the war the French built an airfield southwest of the town, which Captain Thénault described as "the largest and most beautiful of the Army Zone. It was over two miles long, perfectly flat, and surrounded by a circuit of high hills."[2] Its proximity to German industrial centers along the Rhine River made it an ideal place to station bombers. French bombing squadrons occupied one end of the airfield, while British, Canadian, Australian, and South African airmen occupied the other end.

Kiffin's career as a combat pilot began with a bureaucratic snafu. He was traveling with Jim McConnell, Victor Chapman, and Norman Prince, and their orders indicated they were to report to Rosnay. After riding all night in a train from Paris, they arrived in Rosnay only to discover that nobody had a clue as to why they were there. Rosnay was nearly 150 miles northwest of Luxeuil. Eventually the commandant at Rosnay discovered the mistake in their orders. He provided them with a car that took them to Épernay, where they could catch a series of trains to Luxeuil. The car ride interested Kiffin, as he motored effortlessly over much of the route he'd walked during his grueling thirty-five-mile march in the Legion. Jim McConnell sent a postcard to Paul Rockwell, telling him about the change in destinations. He told Paul they were "riding around in tractors as if we were somebody, but Prince has so much stuff we need a freight car."[3] The next day, trains took them close to Luxeuil, and Captain Thénault drove them the rest of the way in a squadron car. Jim McConnell said the captain's cheerful greeting was "Sixty-two pilots were killed last month."[4] Later in the war, Kiffin would have harsh words to say about Thénault, but at this point he described him as "a pearl of a fellow."[5]

Escadrille N124 was officially activated the following day, on April 20, 1916. Lieutenant Alfred de Laage de Meux was the second-in-command.[6] He started the war as a cavalry officer, charging German cavalry with a lance. He quickly realized the days of cavalry charges were over, so he became an observer in a Caudron and shot down a German aircraft. He taught himself to fly while serving as an observer and became one of the few pilots to earn his *brevet* without going to a training school. He was later trained to fly Nieuports and flew combat missions over Verdun. In addition to his impressive combat record, he spoke excellent English. He proved to be very well liked by the American pilots. He, in turn, liked and respected the Americans. His straightforward personality was summed up in the instructions he gave to each new pilot who reported to the squadron: "I only ask that you fly well, that you fight hard, and that you act as a man. I demand that you obey, explicitly and without hesitation, any orders I give when I am leading combat patrols. . . . Accept your share of the responsibility for upholding the good name of the squadron, and we shall get along quite well."[7]

The pilots ate together at *L'Hôtel Lion Vert* (The Green Lion Hotel), a small family-run hotel that served excellent food.[8] Captain Thénault set up a mess fund which everyone paid into. In addition to enjoying great food, the Americans used these meals to improve their fluency with the French language:

Conversation was never lacking at meals. In the morning we talked French; at night we used English. A mistake of a single word brought a penalty of a ten-sous [ten-cent] fine to the pool. The result was that some hard-headed fellows endeavored to maintain unbroken silence, as if they had been Trappist monks. But they could not stand the joking of their friends, who teased them until they answered. After trying a conversation with fingers and deaf and dumb signs, they broke into a weird French-American gibberish which would have made the fortune of a circus clown.[9]

Most of the pilots were quartered in a villa that had been requisitioned for them about a hundred yards from the baths, most likely the *Villa du Chatigny*. Every morning the pilots would go down to the baths to enjoy a leisurely soak. Kiffin said, "We live like princes." Jim McConnell wrote, "I thought of the luxury we were enjoying, our comfortable beds, baths, and motor cars, and then I recalled the ancient custom of giving a man selected for the sacrifice a royal time of it before the appointed day."[10]

It should be noted that not all French escadrilles lived in luxury like this. Carrol Dana Winslow, an American volunteer who flew with a French reconnaissance squadron on the Verdun front, described his living conditions thus:

The pilots of each escadrille shared two large tents, and in addition each group had a large mess-tent. Inside each sleeping-tent each one of us had a little alcove. Our cots were raised on wooden platforms. At one end we fitted up a shower-bath, for which purpose a gasoline tank punctured with holes proved ideal. Of course, every time you wanted a bath someone had to empty pails of water into the "tank" above you.[11]

As the war progressed, the American squadron would move frequently, going wherever the French needed fighter pilots in the ever-shifting air war. They would sleep in tents, unheated hangars, and slit trenches. But for their first assignment, the French were definitely giving them royal treatment.

The pilots were amazed to discover how much support was required to keep a flying squadron in the air. Their squadron was equipped with brand new FIAT trucks, spare parts, workshops, a telephone switchboard, an office tent, and a rest tent for pilots on alert at the airfield.[12] They also had seventy ground crewmen including mechanics, armorers, stretcher bearers, telephone operators, clerks, orderlies, and drivers.[13] The only thing they did not have was aircraft. Verdun was devouring all the airplanes Nieuport could build, so the new squadron had no planes. Captain Thénault sent telegram after telegram trying to obtain planes, but with no luck. His entire squadron was grounded.

One of the first things Thénault did at Luxeuil was introduce his pilots to the reason they were sent to this luxury spa. A French bombardment squadron badly needed their protection. The squadron was commanded by Captain Fèlix Happe, an exceedingly daring pilot who flew an ancient Maurice Farman biplane. With its huge wings and rat's nest of bracing wires, it could barely reach fifty miles per hour, but it could carry a one-hundred-pound bomb load and stay in the air for four hours. Nicknamed "Le Corsaire Rouge" (The Red Pirate) because of his reckless daring and his flaming red beard, Captain Happe had flown solo bombing raids against the Zeppelin factory at Friedrichschafen four times. His slow plane was subject to intense anti-aircraft fire and repeated attacks by German planes during the three-hundred-mile round trip flight on each raid, but although his plane was riddled, he and his observer came through unscathed. Based on his success, the French organized a squadron of similar planes for him to lead. His luck didn't transfer to the men under his command. When Thénault and the American pilots entered his office, he was arranging eight small boxes on his desk. "These boxes contain the eight 'Croix de Guerre' [Cross of War, roughly equivalent to a US Bronze Star] I am sending to the families of the eight pilots who were brought down by the Germans the last time we bombed Habsheim Arsenal," he explained. "Hurry up, and get ready as quick as you can, so that we may do some good work together."[14] This meeting made a deep impression on the Americans. Kiffin described it as "enough to drive fear in the hearts of some men. You never have to talk with him a minute to know that he is a man absolutely without fear and at the same time a regular ogre for other people's lives."[15]

The other task Captain Thénault could perform without airplanes was to orient his pilots to the surrounding countryside. There were very few places to make an emergency landing in the Vosges Mountains. Thénault and his pilots piled into an open touring car and drove through the mountains, while the captain pointed out the few places where a pilot could land a disabled plane without killing himself. There were a few French airfields closer to the front than Luxeuil, and they stopped at these airfields to learn about local obstructions and the best approaches. In addition to the natural obstructions of trees and hills, many airfields had power lines running nearby. The captain pointed out prominent landmarks that would help the pilots find these airfields, and also landmarks that would help them stay clear of the nearby Swiss border. (The Swiss were not amused when military aircraft of any belligerent accidentally crossed their border.) While on these drives they enjoyed the beautiful scenery, trees, waterfalls, and wildflowers of a Vosges spring. They stopped for lunch at fine Alsatian inns, washing down their meal with local white wines topped off by a small glass of kirschwasser. Sometimes they stopped to chat with the guard at a Swiss border post, where they could count on his looking the other way as they smuggled Swiss cigars into their car.[16]

On April 24, Thénault managed to borrow a well-worn two-seat Nieuport 10 reconnaissance plane from a nearby airfield. It was unarmed, but in some respects it was similar to the Nieuport *Bébé* fighters they were to receive. This plane let the pilots maintain their flying skills while familiarizing themselves with the area around Luxeuil. Or at least it did for one day. The following day Norman Prince crashed the plane into a hangar door. He was unhurt, but the plane was a total loss. Since they no longer had any planes to fly, Norman decided this would be a good time to go on leave to Paris. Jim McConnell wrote to Paul Rockwell, "Prince can't stand the horrors of our warlike existence and is beating it back to Paris to stay until our planes arrive. Kiffin and I are disgusted."[17]

Bill Thaw, Elliot Cowdin, and Bert Hall finally broke free from their previous assignments and arrived on April 29. The squadron was now complete, counting Norman Prince (who was on leave), but they still had no aircraft. To add insult to the injury, German reconnaissance planes routinely flew over their aerodrome. "Great big slow things," Kiffin complained to his brother. "One good man with a *Bébé* could have gotten all three of them before they could have gotten back to their lines."[18]

The men tried to keep busy as the days dragged on. Kiffin wrote his mother that most of the men had gone trout fishing but he stayed back to catch up on his correspondence. His mother had recently begun working in Winston-Salem. Kiffin named a couple of girls he knew in that city and asked whether they were still unmarried.[19] The *New York World* ran an article about how Elliot Cowdin joined the escadrille and promptly brought down his third Boche.[20] (Like the other pilots, Cowdin did not have a plane to fly.) For once it was Paul Rockwell instead of Kiffin who complained about the publicity. "The publicity hogs give me a pain," he wrote, "and they are mighty plentiful."[21] Jim McConnell commented that Prince was three days late on the twenty-four-hour leave Captain Thénault had given him, but nobody seemed upset. "This seems more of a social than military organization."[22] Such were the horrors of war at Luxeuil.

Thénault described one other aspect of waiting for planes that was more social than military:

Perhaps also, during the forced inactivity, there were some love adventures or sentimental affairs. They were young; a soldier's life was not very safe. My men had a fair chance to die within the next few months. So being only human, they needed the comfort given by the love of a sweetheart, and I hope that some day a poet will sing the praise of all the women who, without afterthought, gave the best of themselves with pure devotion to those who were protecting them.[23]

Jim McConnell was a little more specific when he wrote to Paul Rockwell:

Paul, this berg has Paris looking like a city designed after the heart of the late Anthony Comstock [a US postal inspector famous for promoting strict Victorian morality]. Why it's an effort to avoid being raped. I've obliged a couple but have settled down to occupy myself with a very interesting looking young lady of Italian birth. She is quite nice and not on the boards. Rosa is her name, and believe me Rosa is endowed with a beautiful form, graced with many charms and shows more animation than any I've seen in a long time. They're not used to soldiers here so things flow our way.[24]

The issue of publicity raised its ugly head again. Paul Rockwell, whose job included publicizing the Lafayette Escadrille, wrote to Kiffin and asked him to take some pictures of the pilots and their planes. Kiffin replied, "In regard to photographs, every single fellow seems to be trying to beat the others in sending news to the newspapers, so there is going to be a damn sight too much publicity as it is, and every time the least thing happens, four or five will be sending telegrams to the papers. So I had rather not bother with any of it."[25]

Kiffin apparently calmed down a bit on this subject, as a few days later he wrote Paul, "I will take your pictures the first good day that I am not too busy, but would really prefer that you lay off the stuff about us. Any time that one of us brings down a Boche will write you about it, but outside of that I hate to see anything at all come out about us."[26]

Things changed abruptly as the month of April came to an end. German planes bombed the airfield, killing one driver and wounding five others.[27] The pilots stood by helplessly, as they had no planes. Finally, on the first of May, the first planes arrived. There were three Nieuport 11s and three Nieuport 16s.[28] The Nieuport 11 was the "Baby" Nieuport, which they had been expecting, with an 80-horsepower Le Rhône rotary engine. These were assigned to Kiffin, Chapman, and McConnell. The Nieuport 16 was essentially the same plane, but with a larger 110-horsepower engine. These were assigned to the officers—Thénault, de Laage, and Thaw. Cowdin received his *Médaille Militaire* at a parade ceremony and then left on an eight-day leave to Paris. Prince briefly returned to the squadron and then was sent back to Paris to pick up another Nieuport 11. The Nieuports that were shipped to Luxeuil arrived disassembled, and it would take time to assemble, adjust, and test them before the squadron would be ready to make its first patrol.

The pilots worked with the mechanics and with specialists who came from the Nieuport factory to get the planes ready for flight and to adjust them to suit each pilot's preferences. Kiffin's plane was one of the first to be ready to fly. He took it for a test flight on May 5,[29] a flight that nearly ended in disaster. There were dark clouds on the horizon that afternoon, but it was clear and sunny on the airfield when Kiffin took off. He climbed to 6,500 feet and everything seemed to be working fine. As he was coming back down to land, the airfield was suddenly struck by gale force winds. Thénault described the storm:

> The canvas hangars, unsheltered from the wind, were upset like mere houses of cards. Any machines that were out on the field were swept away like straws, borne hundreds of yards on the tempest, and battered to pieces as they fell. . . . The dark line across the horizon . . . seemed to rush upon him [Kiffin] in a few moments at terrific speed. It was a

cloud of dust raised by the cyclone. The sun was hidden immediately, but from the ground we could witness Rockwell's struggle with the tempest. His Nieuport was thrown up and down like a dead leaf, but the pilot kept his head. He started descending head straight to the wind, with his motor full on and joystick right forward. The force of the wind was so great that he didn't go forward at all, but came down gradually. Our mechanics gauged the spot where this new-fangled helicopter was going to land. They ran to meet it. Rockwell landed right in their midst and immediately a score of vigorous hands gripped his fragile machine by the wheels, the wings, the supports or the fuselage—anywhere so as to prevent it from being whirled away. Rockwell got out safe and sound and his machine was uninjured. It was a splendid piece of work.[30]

Kiffin was safe and he had saved his precious Nieuport, but others weren't so fortunate. The storm ripped all the French observation balloons along the front line from their moorings. The observers jumped from the baskets as their balloons sailed away in the storm, but when they reached the ground the winds dragged twelve of these men to their deaths before they could release their parachutes.[31]

Kiffin finally had a plane, but it was unarmed. The squadron had to procure the Lewis machine guns and mount them on the top wing. So Kiffin, along with the rest of the pilots, had to wait a bit longer to challenge the Germans.[32] In the meantime, there was still much work to be done to get the rest of the planes airworthy and to make final adjustments to Kiffin's plane. The pilots put personal identification markings on their planes, so they could readily identify each other in the air. Initially they simply used initials. Kiffin had an "R" painted on the side of his plane, Bert Hall had an "H," and Jim McConnell had "MAC" on the side of his plane.

Later some of the pilots got more imaginative. Hall changed his markings after a dinner in Paris during which the French ace Charles Nungesser introduced him to the famous exotic dancer (and later convicted spy) Mata Hari. Nungesser told Mata Hari that Bert was a famous American millionaire and that back in the States he wore suits with dollar bills on them.[33] When Bert got back to the squadron, he had his plane decorated with dollar signs. Jim McConnell soon decided to commemorate his time as president of the "Hotfoot Society" at the University of Virginia and had that society's footprint logo painted on his plane, a mark that Thénault described as "cabalistic."[34]

Fortunately, it didn't take long for the guns to arrive. That cheered Kiffin up tremendously. He wrote to his mother on May 8, and told her he had his plane sorted out, with its machine gun mounted and regulated.[35] He would have made a patrol that afternoon, but the weather turned bad. He was beginning a routine where he would get up at 3:00 a.m. to make a patrol at daybreak, take naps during the day as his machine was made ready for another patrol, and fly as late into the evening as the summer sun would allow. He was obviously in excellent spirits: "I am feeling pretty good now in every respect. Am in good health, in a fine location for the front, have as good an aeroplane as there is, a fine Captain, and so nothing to kick about."[36]

Kiffin's plans for dawn-to-dusk patrols were frustrated by bad weather, although he and Victor Chapman did manage to make a few flights over the lines.[37] It wasn't until May 13 that the squadron was ready for its first "official" patrol. Kiffin led the V-formation of Nieuports, followed by Chapman and McConnell. Captain Thénault and Lieutenant Thaw flew at the rear of the formation so they could keep an eye on the new pilots and intervene if anything went wrong. This proved to be a wise decision. McConnell had never flown in formation before, and he decided it would be easier to keep the others in sight if he climbed above them. When the formation climbed through cloud layer, McConnell was the first to emerge and, not being able to see the others, he wandered off on his own. By the time Thénault climbed above the clouds, McConnell was a tiny spec in the distance, headed for Switzerland. Fortunately, Thénault's Nieuport 16 had a bigger engine than McConnell's Nieuport 11. Leaving Thaw in charge of the others, Thénault caught up with McConnell before he crossed the Swiss border.

By the time Thénault was able to turn McConnell around, the other planes could not be seen. It was easy to tell where they were, though, as black puffs of smoke from German anti-aircraft fire were blossoming in one area of the sky. When the captain got there, he discovered that Kiffin and Chapman were twisting and turning, deliberately flying through the puffs of smoke where a shell had just exploded. McConnell immediately joined them. Most pilots tried to avoid areas with heavy anti-aircraft fire, and if they couldn't avoid it, they changed direction and altitude frequently to throw off the gunners' aim. By flying through the puffs of smoke, the Americans were staying in the same area and at the same altitude as the previous shots. They may, in fact, have been deliberately taunting the gunners. This was probably their way of "thumbing their nose" at the unseen artillerymen far below. Ironically, the only pilot whose plane was damaged by this fire was Bill Thaw. He had not joined in this frolicking but was flying above the others to keep an eye on things. His plane received minor damage in the tail section.

Disappointed that no German aircraft had been attracted by the shell bursts, Kiffin next led the patrol over a German airfield at Habsheim. He dove over the aerodrome and put on an acrobatic display, challenging the Germans to come up and fight, but no planes rose to meet them. Thénault later speculated that the Germans must have been far away on another mission, as the pilots at that airfield never hesitated to fight when given an opportunity.[38] Kiffin eventually abandoned his efforts to entice the Germans into the air and led the flight back to Luxeuil. This first patrol may have been uneventful from the pilots' viewpoint, but it definitely garnered the kind of publicity the French hoped for. American newspapers ran headlines like "Aviators from America Soar over Lines of German Troops" and promised that more "Franco-American flotillas" would be formed in the future.[39]

This first patrol was also an eye-opener for Captain Thénault in that it pointed out how little training and experience his new pilots had. In addition to getting lost, Jim McConnell admitted that he'd never flown higher than seven thousand feet before. This patrol took him to thirteen thousand feet. He found it bitterly cold, even in his fur-lined leather flying suit, and he had trouble breathing the rarified air at that altitude. Jim also admitted that he had never fired a machine gun in the air, and there's no indication that Kiffin or Chapman had done so, either. There were no ranges nearby where they could fire their guns, but Thénault insisted his three novice airmen spend the afternoon flying over the Luxeuil airfield while they practiced changing ammunition drums in flight. It wasn't easy to do this while wearing thick gloves and fighting to accurately fit the drum onto the gun in a one-hundred-miles-per-hour slipstream while holding the joystick between their knees, but if the pilots were going to survive in combat, they needed to be able to do this quickly. Thénault also resolved to spend more time teaching them how to fly in formation.[40]

Later that afternoon Norman Prince and Elliot Cowdin returned from Paris, bringing a United Press reporter and a newsreel cameraman from the Triangle Company with them. The following day was overcast, with the cloud ceiling below one thousand feet, but with enough light for photography. The cameraman filmed the individual pilots, a preflight meeting with Thénault, the Maurice Farman bombers taking off, and the "escorting" Lafayette Escadrille pilots taking off and making low-level passes. The newspaper reporter who interviewed the pilots was excited because this was the first time he'd ever been to "the Front," although Chapman pointed out that the front was more than forty miles away. The film footage shows the pilots smiling, bashful, and uncertain of what to do with their hands. It was probably the first time many of them had ever posed before a movie camera.[41] Chapman wrote that several pilots were privately upset, as "none of us liked to maneuver so close together with the *plafond* [ceiling] at 300 meters." Kiffin and Bert Hall were particularly upset, although for different reasons. Kiffin was embarrassed about the publicity that was being given to the squadron when they hadn't yet done anything to earn it. He looked at the French pilots who were fighting and dying every day over Verdun, as well as the *poilu* who were fighting on the ground, and he felt they were the ones who should be getting publicity. Bert, however, was upset because he was risking his neck so that some newsreel producer in the States could make money, and he wasn't going to get any of it. "Think of the honor," Victor said to Bert. "Oh no," Bert replied. "Give me the cash."[42]

The discontent over the newsreel publicity, plus various comments in Jim McConnell's and Kiffin's letters, illustrate the fact that the pilots didn't fully bond into a cohesive team at Luxeuil. There were significant differences in the backgrounds of the seven "founding members" of the Lafayette Escadrille. Five were the sons of millionaires. Kiffin was the son of a Baptist minister, and Bert was the son of a Missouri farmer. Five grew up in states that were undisputedly "Union" during the Civil War. (Jim McConnell went to school in the South, but he was born and raised in Chicago.) Kiffin and Bert both had fathers or father figures who fought for the South and were "unreconstructed" Confederates. Six had at least attended college, and several had degrees from prestigious universities. It's not clear that Bert Hall ever finished high school. Bert was also the only one of the pilots who was married. He was actually married to his third wife, Suzanne Tatien, at the time. She moved to Luxeuil with Bert, but for reasons that only seem to have made sense to Bert, he kept their marriage and her presence a secret from his squadron mates. They assumed he was spending his nights at a brothel, which did not enhance his reputation with the "gentlemen" of the squadron.[43]

The differences in backgrounds didn't seem to cause significant problems, although they may have contributed to the fact that several pilots didn't get along with Bert Hall. Kiffin and Bill Thaw got along fine with "Bertie," though, and Kiffin's best friend was the northeastern, Ivy League graduate, millionaire's son Victor Chapman. A more serious problem seems to be that Norman Prince and Elliot Cowdin spent most of the squadron's formative days on leave in Paris. The fact that they showed up with the film crew and went back to Paris when the film crew left only added to the perception that they were in this for fame and glory. This had to be particularly galling to Kiffin, given his feelings about publicity. However, Norman Prince had worked for more than a year to create this all-American escadrille, and he wanted to publicize its existence to entice more Americans to support the French cause. Kiffin didn't particularly care whether he flew in a French squadron or an American squadron: he wanted to shoot down Germans, and he didn't feel the squadron deserved any publicity until they did that. He and Bert Hall discussed their feelings after the film crew left. Bert described that discussion:

> That night Kiffin Rockwell and I held a little conference of war. We had been in the Squadron long enough to find out that we didn't like all the members. Strange to say, we agreed on our dislikes. Thereupon, Kiffin and I decided to do each other a favor. If I was killed first, Kiffin would tell certain members of the outfit to go to hell and certain other things not usually reproduced on the printed page. If he was killed first, I would do the same thing for him.[44]

In fairness to Prince and Cowdin, it should be pointed out that they had been flying combat missions for the past year, most recently in the frenzied skies over Verdun. Then they were assigned to a squadron that didn't have planes, in a resort town, in a sleepy backwater of the Western Front. They could stay with the other pilots and wait for the planes to arrive, or they could take advantage of the liberal leave opportunities and spend what might be their final days in the enticing atmosphere of wartime Paris. They were veteran combat pilots. They saw no need to prove themselves to the neophytes at Luxeuil.

Bert Hall also had experience as a combat pilot, but his most recent assignment had been as an instructor at the French training school at Avord. Although he made at least one trip to Paris to pick up a Nieuport, during which he had his claimed encounter with Mata Hari, he seems to have spent most of his time at Luxeuil. He didn't have to purge fresh memories of the hell at Verdun from his memory. Bill Thaw had come directly from Verdun, but he didn't seem to need a break, apparently just because he was Bill Thaw. Seemingly unflappable, Thaw was the rock that anchored the escadrille. As the senior ranking American pilot, he was in unofficial command of the pilots. Captain Thénault was the squadron commander, but he didn't have the close personal connection with the individual pilots that Bill Thaw had. Ted Parsons would later write that "his word was law, not because he was our superior officer, but because he was Bill."[45] He described Thaw's role in the squadron thus:

> Most of the time he was in practical, if not nominal, command and handled with unfailing tact and good humor one of the toughest jobs ever thrown on the shoulders of one man. . . . It is reasonable to suppose . . . that he could have gotten along without the Escadrille. But most certainly the Escadrille could never have gotten along without Bill. . . . He made a brilliant success of a job where most men would have gone mad.[46]

The morning after the film crew left, Kiffin got down to business. He pulled "guard duty" that morning, waiting by his airplane in case a German plane was spotted over the lines, because he was the only one on the airfield who had a serviceable airplane. He wrote to Alice Weeks that he was planning to fly a solo patrol over the lines that afternoon.[47] Other pilots similarly flew solo patrols, but there are no references to any more formation flights over the lines. The Germans often bombed the airfield at night, shortly before dawn. (Night flying was in its infancy then, and they undoubtedly timed their raids so they could land at daybreak and not have to touch down in the dark.) Bill Thaw made it a "reckless" practice, in Thénault's words, to get ready for a patrol before daybreak and take off as soon as anyone reported hearing airplanes flying overhead. His plan was to fly toward the

German airfield and intercept the bombers on their way home, as soon as it grew light.[48] On May 17, he fired on a two-seater and saw it plunge straight down.[49] French ground observers reported that it recovered and landed under apparent control, so Bill was not given credit for a victory.[50]

On the following day, May 18, 1916, the squadron scored its first confirmed victory. Kiffin described it in a letter to his brother:

> Well, at last I have a little news for you. This morning I went out over the lines to make a little tour. I was a little the other side of the lines, when my motor began to miss a bit. I turned around to go to a camp near the lines. Just as I started to head for there, I saw a Boche machine about seven hundred meters under me and a little inside our lines. I immediately reduced my motor, and dived for him. He saw me at the same time, and began to dive towards his lines. It was a machine with a pilot and mitrailleur [gunner], with two mitrailleuses [machine guns], one facing the front and one the rear that turned on a pivot, so he (the gunner) could fire in any direction. He immediately opened fire on me and my machine was hit, but I didn't pay any attention to that and kept going straight for him, until I got within twenty-five or thirty meters of him. Then, just as I was afraid of running into him, I fired four or five shots, then swerved my machine to the right to keep from running into him. As I did that, I saw the mitrailleur fall back dead on the pilot, the mitrailleuse fall from its position and point straight up in the air, the pilot fall to one side of the machine as if he was done for also. The machine itself first fell to one side, then dived vertically towards the ground with a lot of smoke coming out of the rear. I circled around, and three or four minutes later saw a lot of smoke coming up from the ground just beyond the German trenches. I had hoped that he would fall in our lines, as it is hard to prove when they fall in the German lines. The post of observation signaled seeing the machine, and the smoke but losing sight of it before it reached the ground so they couldn't say how he landed.[51]

Apparently the column of smoke was enough to convince the French ground observers that the plane had in fact crashed, as they confirmed the victory.[52] Suddenly Kiffin was a hero.[53] Newspapers all over the world carried the story of his victory, although many misspelled his name as "Kiffen." He was toasted by his fellow pilots. Jim McConnell commented that "all

Luxeuil smiled upon him—particularly the girls."[54] Jim also sent a telegram to Paul Rockwell to tell him the good news: "Kiffin a descendu un Boche. Il a tiré à trente mètres, tué mitrailleur et pilote tombé en flammes sur les tranchées boches. Médaille Militaire proposé. [Kiffin has brought down a Boche. He fired at thirty meters. Killed the gunner and the pilot, who fell with the machine in flames into the German trenches. Has been proposed for the military medal.]"[55]

Paul excitedly wrote to congratulate Kiffin:

I don't know how to tell you the joy that Jim's telegram gave me yester-day morning, I was just starting to take a bath when it came, and I did a sort of barefoot war dance about the room. I knew that you would lay the boches low when you came in contact with one, and I am proud of you and your feat.... Mrs. Weeks looks about the most pleased person I ever saw, it has done her a world of good. She gave the Herald a little interview about you which I suppose will come out tomorrow, tho if that asinine sheet gets anything straight I will be surprised.[56]

In addition to the telegram, Paul sent Kiffin a bottle of Kentucky bourbon, something that was difficult to find in wartime Paris. Kiffin was going to share this prize with the other pilots, but somebody (tradition says Victor Chapman)[57] came up with the idea of only allowing pilots who had just shot down an enemy plane to take a drink from the bottle. Shoot down a plane, take a slug of bourbon. This became a squadron tradition, and the bottle became known as the "Bottle of Death."[58]

Congratulation notes poured in from all over. Old friends from the Legion, Americans in pilot training, and Kiffin's former boss in Atlanta congratulated him. Several notes came from French women who were strangers to Kiffin. One of the nurses who had taken care of him after he was wounded at Artois "scolded" him for not writing her about his victory. "Oh! The naughty little Rockwell who knocks down Boche Aviatiks and does not condescend to inform me of his high feat in the heights," she wrote. She also said she would put an inscription commemorating the event over his hospital bed, "but if you do not shortly give me news I shall add to the placard the most indolent and forgetful of airmen."[59]

Kiffin's celebration was short lived. That day the squadron received orders to move to the Verdun front. They packed up and prepared to leave on the morning of May 20. The Germans bombed the airfield that night, killing five support troops and destroying three trucks, but the rest of the squadron was able to leave on schedule.[60] Most of the pilots flew to Verdun. Elliot Cowdin was still in Paris and would join them at Verdun. Norman Prince crashed on take-off and had to travel by land, and Jim McConnell was left behind. He had broken two longerons (longitudinal braces) making a bad landing a few days before and was waiting for replacements so he could fly his plane to Verdun.[61] Adding to his frustration, they had received spare longerons with their original supply of spare parts, but those spares had been destroyed by an earlier German bombing raid.

As a closing note on the squadron's time in Luxeuil, it should be noted that while Kiffin demonstrated great skill and bravery in earning his first victory, he also had a fair bit of luck. Many new combat pilots had trouble spotting other aircraft on their first patrols, but Kiffin spotted his target almost half a mile away. (Eddie Rickenbacker confidently announced there were no other planes in the sky after his first patrol, only to have his flight leader Raoul Lufbery list all the planes that had passed less than five hundred meters from them.)[62] Kiffin also didn't make the common novice error of firing too soon and exhausting his ammunition before coming within range, something that was especially easy to do with the jam-prone forty-seven-round ammunition drums in the Nieuport. And, of course, shooting down a plane with four bullets shows exceptional marksmanship.

Kiffin's bravery was apparent in the way he ignored the fire coming from the gunner in the rear of the enemy plane, even though one bullet struck a main spar in his wing. It was also exceedingly brave (or foolish) to enter a dogfight with an engine that wasn't running right. The speed and maneuverability advantages a fighter had over a two-seater disappeared if the engine was missing, and of course it could have quit completely and left Kiffin in a very bad situation. And even with his engine missing, he was probably traveling at close to one hundred miles per hour when he dived on the enemy plane. The enemy was diving too, but since Kiffin withheld his fire until he was within twenty-five or thirty meters of the enemy, he was within a second or two of colliding with the other plane before he turned away. That takes courage. It's no wonder that he only had time to fire four shots.

Kiffin also benefited from a great deal of luck. By diving directly down on an enemy two-seater, he was giving the enemy at least as much of a chance of shooting him down as he had of shooting them down. More cautious fighter pilots attacked two-seaters from behind and below, sneaking up on the plane if possible and maneuvering to keep the tail of the enemy plane blocking the gunner's field of fire. In Kiffin's case, he gave the enemy a better than fifty-fifty chance of shooting him down because the enemy gunner had more bullets and wasn't firing a gun that was prone to jamming. If Kiffin had missed with his shots, the enemy also would have had a chance to shoot him from behind after he passed the two-seater, when Kiffin could no longer fire back.

Kiffin's attack style was probably influenced more by his Foreign Legion training on the "spirit of the offensive" and bayonet attacks than by any lectures on aerial combat he may have received. Charging directly into machine gun fire is exactly what Colonel de Grandmaison preached—and what resulted in millions of infantry casualties in 1914. In Kiffin's defense, there is no indication that he ever received any training in aerial combat. He was taught to fly, and he attacked with the spirit he learned in the infantry. He, and the rest of the squadron, would have to learn new tactics quickly. At Verdun they would face intense combat with some of Germany's best pilots. Pilots such as Oswald Boelcke. On the same day that Kiffin shot down his first German plane, Boelcke shot down his sixteenth Allied plane. Three days later, Boelcke shot down two planes in one day, including a Nieuport.[63]

12

Into the Furnace

This is a regular hell around here in the way of excitement and the world going crazy.

—Kiffin Rockwell

The Battle of Verdun had been raging for three months when the Lafayette Escadrille arrived, and the madness would continue for another seven months. The initial attack had caught the French by surprise, thanks in part to the German "aerial barrage" that prevented French reconnaissance aircraft from spotting the buildup of troops and artillery. The French quickly sent two hundred additional airmen and aircraft to Verdun, a huge concentration at that point in the war. Within a month, seventy French pilots had been killed.[1] Verdun arguably became the first major air campaign in history, and it was the first to employ the newly developed fighter planes. Basic fighter squadron tactics had to be developed during this battle, and the furious pace of activity was unlike anything the pilots had seen before.

While the additional French planes helped, they weren't a cure-all. The Germans started the battle with 168 aircraft on the Verdun front, but only 21 of these were single-seat fighters.[2] At the urging of German ace Oswald Boelcke, these fighters were soon detached from flying barrage patrols and were stationed at forward airfields with telephone connections to German anti-aircraft batteries so they could quickly intercept any French airplanes that crossed the lines. On March 14, General Philippe Pétain, commander of all French forces at Verdun, told his chief of air operations, Major

Charles de Tricornot de Rose, "De Rose, I am blind, sweep the skies for me."[3] De Rose quickly organized his fighter aircraft, primarily Nieuports, to make offensive patrols, seeking out and destroying German aircraft. Many of these patrols ranged far behind the German lines, which caused consternation among the French ground troops. They complained that they seldom saw any French planes overhead and they felt unprotected from the German planes, which they did see. By the time the Lafayette Escadrille arrived, French fighters were again being scheduled to fly patrols over the lines but pilots were also encouraged to fly voluntary offensive missions on their own.[4]

The Lafayette Escadrille was stationed at an airfield called Behonne, near the town of Bar-le-Duc. Captain Thénault described it as an airfield that "was dreaded for its difficulties, being surrounded on three sides by deep ravines and frequently swept by strong cross winds."[5] The pilots were once again fortunate to be quartered in a villa. Bert Hall described it as "about half way between our flying field and the town. It was situated up on a little hill, not very high. There was a winding stone stairway running up to the door with flower beds all around. It was really a lovely spot."[6] The villa proved to be the only lovely thing about their new assignment. There would be no drives through the countryside, no trout fishing, and no soaking in historic baths at Verdun. The battle raged day and night, and the pilots flew multiple missions over this cauldron every day that the weather permitted. The *Voie Sacrée*, the sacred highway that led to Verdun, wound through the town of Bar-le-Duc carrying an endless stream of men and supplies into the battle. An equally steady stream of ambulances and exhausted survivors plodded back from the battle, trying to come to grips with the fact that they were still alive and were likely to remain so, at least until it was time to march back into the battle.

The pilots arrived at Behonne on May 20, and flew their first patrol on the twenty-first. Thénault described flying over the battlefield:

There were three stages for patrols (later on there were as many as six): the lower patrol at one thousand feet; the middle at six thousand; the higher at twelve thousand. [High patrols would soon be flown at fifteen thousand feet or higher, often at the maximum ceiling of the planes involved.] At twelve thousand feet you cannot possibly see the heavy air-fighting which goes on near the ground; your friends may be destroyed without your knowing anything about it, and vice-versa. In the latter case, it is quite impossible to take part even if you should so desire, because of the long time required to attain the altitude; on the contrary, it does not take long to dive down several thousand feet. During our flight we heard the roar of the nine-inch shells; sometimes we even saw them in the form of a passing flash. In aviation slang, we called them *"les gros rats noirs"*—the big black rats. The smaller ones were not seen but there was no little danger of being caught on the trajectory of any of them. Occasionally a plane would burst literally into fragments, which meant that a big shell had hit it in full flight. It is really surprising that accidents of this nature did not happen more often, especially in the case of low patrols, which were always in the zone where these trajectories were the thickest. On account of this ever-present menace over one's head, it is easy to understand why the low patrol was not the most popular.[7]

On this occasion, the squadron was flying a high patrol and Bert Hall spotted a formation of six German planes beneath them. Thénault dipped his plane in the direction of the German formation, possibly to point them out to the novice pilots who were not yet adept at spotting enemy planes in the air. Bert misinterpreted the captain's maneuver as a signal to attack. He dove toward the Germans and picked out the plane he would attack first, not realizing the rest of the squadron was not following him. He soon found himself in the midst of a swirling mass of enemy planes, all intent on shooting him down. It didn't take him long to empty the drum on his Lewis gun. This was not a good time to fly straight and level while changing a drum, so he threw his plane into a spin and spun down to fifteen hundred feet, acting as though he'd been hit. Two planes followed him most of the way down, but when they pulled off Bert immediately leveled out and made a beeline back to Behonne. He landed safely with a plane that was riddled with bullet holes. Bert was unhurt, but his mechanic, Leon Barracq, was dismayed at the condition of Bert's airplane. Leon had to work all night to get it ready for the next day's sorties. When he finished patching it up, he painted a small dollar sign on each patch over a bullet hole, making the plane look like it had some sort of a pox.[8]

The next day, May 22, 1916, was a busy one for the squadron. Bill Thaw was promoted to full lieutenant that day, but there wasn't time for celebrating. General Nivelle, replacing Pétain in charge of the French forces at Verdun, launched an attack that morning to recapture Fort Douaumont. Planning for this attack had begun on May 13. Within forty-eight hours the Germans knew every detail of the plan and were ready for it.[9] The Lafayette Escadrille's role in the attack was to provide air cover over the battlefield. On the first sortie of the morning, Bert Hall singlehandedly took on three German Aviatik two-seaters. He failed to bring any of them down, but they didn't bring him down, either. Simply surviving a three-against-one battle was no small accomplishment. Later that day, Kiffin, Bill Thaw, and Victor Chapman were escorting low-level observation planes while Bert provided top cover. Bert spotted a German Aviatik slightly below on the French side of the lines and immediately dove to attack. The German dove toward the lines and the observer hit Bert's plane several times during the running fight that ensued. Bert finally succeeded in diving under the Aviatik and raking it with machine gun fire from underneath. The plane crashed just inside the German lines, and its destruction was confirmed by French ground observers.[10] Bert Hall had scored the second official victory for the Lafayette Escadrille. That night Kiffin described the fight to his brother:

> I have only time for a line, as it is nearly supper time, and I must sleep as soon as I finish eating and get up at three a.m. Bertie Hall attacked a Boche this afternoon at 4,000 meters high, brought him down. . . . This is a regular hell around here in the way of excitement and the world going crazy. Impossible to express with words one's impressions. I am badly played out for lack of sleep.[11]

Kiffin added a postscript, "Give Bertie some Publicity."

Presumably Bert got his swig from the Bottle of Death that night, but with pilots getting up at 3:00 a.m. there probably wasn't much celebrating. The French *poilu* (infantry) in the trenches certainly weren't celebrating. Although a few French troops succeeded in capturing some ground on top of the fort, they couldn't break into the fort and German artillery pulverized all attempted reinforcements. It took a few days for the Germans to mop up the last of the French positions on top of the fort, but the attack failed with heavy casualties. A young French lieutenant who had eagerly joined the assault on the day of the attack wrote in his diary the following day, "Humanity is mad! It must be mad to do what it is doing. What a massacre!

What scenes of horror and carnage! I cannot find words to translate my impressions. Hell cannot be so terrible. Men are mad!"[12]

Norman Prince and Elliot Cowdin arrived at Verdun on May 23, but they had no planes.[13] That situation was corrected the following day, but not in a manner that anyone wanted. The day started out well. Kiffin and Bill Thaw got up at 3:00 a.m. to fly a voluntary dawn patrol, and they came across an Aviatik protected by a Fokker. Kiffin attacked the Aviatik while Thaw shot down the Fokker. "No credit to me," Thaw said afterward. "It was plain murder. He never even saw me."[14] The Aviatik managed to escape Kiffin's attack. Kiffin and Bill flew back to Behonne and landed with just enough time to refuel and rearm before joining Thénault for the scheduled morning patrol. De Laage and Chapman also took part in this patrol. Thénault was still concerned about the inexperience of the new pilots:

I gave my orders to attack only if I signaled the pilots to do so, by see-sawing my plane. . . . Having spent the first six weeks of the battle here I knew that the Boches had all their great aces, Boelcke and the rest of them, in the neighborhood, and I wanted to train my boys before trying to stack up against those dangerous foes. I did not want to go too fast, and thus have my squadron uselessly slaughtered . . .

We turned northward. Soon a strange sight met our eyes: a strip of land, several miles wide, without a tree, without grass, brown and yellow in color, the ground pitted with innumerable shell holes that touched each other; without roads, without houses, and looking as if the very bowels of the earth had been torn open. Such was the battlefield of Verdun. A few geometric lines in that chaos still indicated Fort Douaumont.

Suddenly, far away in the East, towards Etain, I noticed a dozen German two seaters, flying low over their own lines, so low that they seemed like sheep grazing on the green meadows far from the cannon-ravaged zone.

They were too low, too numerous, and too distant for us to attack on this first expedition, especially over German positions. My pilots had yet to get thoroughly acquainted with an enemy not to be despised. For when a single seater flies low over hostile territory, one must always remember the danger which may come from a plane above, against which there is almost no defense and which may oblige one to land.[15]

Despite Captain Thénault's explicit orders, one of the pilots broke formation and dove toward the German two-seaters. Thénault always insisted that he didn't know which pilot it was, but others identified the rogue as Victor Chapman. The other pilots were not willing to let Chapman take on a dozen Germans alone, so they dove after him. Thénault had no choice but to follow, probably cursing all the while. The Nieuports fell upon the startled German planes, and the two formations dissolved into a whirling cloud of airplanes. German pilots twisted and turned, trying to evade the attacking Nieuports while giving their gunners a chance to fire back. Nieuport pilots jerked their planes across the sky, trying to throw off the German gunners' aim while centering their sights on a German plane. Thénault clearly saw German soldiers in the streets of Étain firing their rifles at the low flying Nieuports. Fortunately, there were no German Fokkers overhead, as they could have swooped down and caught the Americans by surprise. Thénault thought he saw three Germans make what appeared to be forced landings, but he also saw two Nieuports streaking toward the French lines before he was able to round up what remained of his squadron and lead them back to Behonne.

One of the pilots who was making a beeline toward friendly territory was Bill Thaw. A slug from a German machine gun had slammed into his left arm and broken the bone, just above the elbow. The wound was bleeding profusely and that arm hung limply at his side. Flying with his right hand, he struggled to remain conscious in spite of the pain and the loss of blood. He managed to cross the lines and land in the first open field he came to. French soldiers dragged his nearly unconscious body from the plane and rushed him to a field dressing station, where they staunched the bleeding. Then they put him in an ambulance for evacuation to a hospital.

The other Nieuport that left the battle was flown by Kiffin. He was firing at a German plane when a bullet exploded against the frame of his windscreen. Fragments of lead, steel, and glass ripped into his face. Blood spattered his goggles, and he thought his nose had been ripped completely off. He dove out of the fight and made it safely back to Behonne. He was convinced his plane had been hit by an explosive bullet, a projectile banned by the Hague Convention.[16] When Thénault landed, he was immediately confronted by a tall, bloody pilot who was spewing a non-stop stream of profanity in multiple languages. Kiffin took full advantage of all the invectives he had learned in the Foreign Legion to denounce Germany's use of an insidious weapon. The fact that the rant was being delivered in a thick southern accent by a pilot who had temporarily lost the use of his nose probably made the individual words unintelligible, but the gist of the message got through.

Kiffin's wounds were treated by medics from a field ambulance. As they picked fragments of the bullet and the windscreen out of his face, they assured him that his nose was, in fact, still firmly attached. Thénault wanted to send Kiffin to a hospital for fifteen days, but Kiffin insisted that he was still able to fly. The captain then suggested Kiffin go to the Nieuport factory near Paris to pick up a new plane. Kiffin agreed to that, as the trip would give him a chance to visit Paul and Mrs. Weeks and reassure them that he was all right. Victor Chapman had also been wounded during the battle, as a bullet had ripped through his flight suit and grazed his arm. Fortunately, the wound was slight, and Chapman, like Kiffin, refused hospitalization. No one in the squadron yet knew what had happened to Bill Thaw. Thénault made several phone calls trying to learn some news of him, but no one he called knew where Thaw was. A little later, as the pilots were having lunch and discussing the morning's battle, Thénault got a phone call from the evacuation hospital where Thaw had been taken. He learned that Thaw would be out of action for a while, but his life was not in danger.

Kiffin apparently did not leave for Paris until the following day and he may have gone to the Nieuport factory first, as he did not arrive at Mrs. Weeks's house until eleven o'clock that night. She described his arrival to her brother Fred:

> The other evening about eleven o'clock the Slades (Thaw's sister) came over to say they had just had a telephone call from the Captain saying that Thaw had a broken arm and that Kiffin was wounded. They assured us that he said that Kiffin was not badly wounded, but nevertheless I could not sleep. Next morning no news came, nor through the day. About eleven o'clock we heard a noise in the hall, and in walked Kiffin. It was a great shock for he had been shot in the face. While fighting one machine two more attacked him and an explosive bullet struck the fuselage, exploding in his face. He was stunned for a moment and flew across the lines for fortunately he had the fastest machine. The enemies' cannon were shooting at him from the ground. He arrived at an ambulance behind the lines. He thought his nose was off, fortunately

it was not, although his face was pretty badly disfigured. At the ambulance they took out the pieces of shell, and the Captain wished him to go at once to a Hospital for fifteen days, but he told them he wanted an eight-day leave, to come home to us. He looks terribly with those dreadful eyes men always have after going through heavy firing. I can not describe them. They are sunken and yet have a sharp look.[17]

The look Mrs. Weeks described would come to be known as the "thousand-yard stare" during World War II. It was a common symptom of combat stress and could be a precursor to what is now known as *combat stress reaction*. During World War I the psychological effects of combat were not well understood, although severe cases of what was then called "shell shock" were treated as a medical condition. Many doctors thought shell shock was the result of physical damage to the brain caused by the concussion and/or the fumes of nearby explosions, so they did not look for it in fighter pilots.

Although other pilots told Kiffin the plane he was firing at when he was hit "exploded" in the air and newspapers hailed it as his second victory, ground observers said the plane made a controlled landing, so it was not confirmed as a victory. Kiffin recuperated in Paris for a few days and then returned to Bar-le-Duc. A new moustache appeared to be the only long-term consequence of his injury. He probably began growing it because his lip injuries prevented him from shaving. Whether he kept it because he liked it or because it hid the scars of his injury, it became a permanent fixture on his upper lip. About this time Kiffin also acquired a silver cigarette case from Tiffany's of Paris, which he carried with him for the rest of his life.[18] (He may have ordered this case to commemorate his first victory, at Luxeuil.)[19]

There had been several changes in the squadron during the few days Kiffin spent in Paris. As soon as Thénault learned that Bill Thaw would be out of action for a while, he called the reserve pool and asked for more pilots. The first to arrive was Raoul Lufbery—the world traveler who discovered he was an American citizen when he tried to enlist in the French Army in August 1914. He was thirty-one years old, the oldest pilot in the squadron. He did not initially impress anyone as being a gifted pilot, but he took his time, learned his craft, and eventually became one of the top American aces of the war.

Two other new pilots joined the squadron at about the same time Kiffin returned from Paris. Clyde Balsley was born in Pennsylvania but moved to Texas with his family when he was fourteen. Early in 1915, he worked his way across the Atlantic by taking care of mules on a cargo ship. He briefly served in the American Ambulance Field Service before transfering to Aviation. After a few harrowing months flying night missions with the Paris Air Guard, he was trained on Nieuports.[20] With his elegant appearance and fondness for wearing a beret, the other pilots did not immediately suspect he was from Texas.

Charles Chouteau "Chute" Johnson was born and raised in St Louis. He had been a classmate of Jim McConnell at the University of Virginia, earned a law degree, and joined the American Ambulance Field Service in early 1915. He transferred to Aviation, but Johnson's student days were plagued by crashes. Such unfortunate incidents as getting his glove caught in the throttle linkage and jamming it so that he could neither speed up to gain altitude nor slow down to land caused him to wreck several machines—fortunately without injury to himself. He attended Nieuport training with Clyde Balsley, and the two of them arrived at the Lafayette Escadrille together.[21]

Also while Kiffin was gone, Captain Thénault gave Kiffin's plane to Norman Prince. Prince simply painted over the tail of the "R" on the plane and turned it into a "P." Bill Thaw's plane went to Elliot Cowdin. Bert Hall apparently smashed his old plane and was given a Nieuport 16. He dropped the dollar sign motif and had "BERT" painted on the sides of this plane.[22] Thus, when Kiffin returned from Paris, neither he nor any of the three new pilots had an airplane. On May 30, he belatedly wrote to his mother to tell her that he'd been injured:

I suppose the papers have given you more information than I can write, but anyway, last week was rather exciting. Last Wednesday morning, I went out and had eight fights, all of them being inside the German lines, so I couldn't tell how much damage I did. Two of the other fellows brought down one machine each, I assisting at one. Finally, I attacked a German about ten kilometers within their lines, and was following him towards the ground, when suddenly there were machines all around me shooting away and I thought for a minute or two that I was going to stay in Germany, especially when an explosive bullet came through my windshield and exploded in my face. I got four or five little pieces around my mouth, but that makes no difference, and I am most well now. But when they hit me, what with the blood and the shock, I didn't know much of what was happening. But I got back to our lines o. k. and landed where there was a field ambulance. Went to Paris for a couple of days, but am now back on the job, getting a new machine fixed up, and hope soon to be back at work.[23]

The fact that he had eight fights in one morning is a testament to his aggressiveness, as well as to the intensity of the air battle over Verdun. As noted previously, none of the planes brought down over Étain were confirmed as victories, although the Fokker that Bill Thaw shot down on his early morning patrol with Kiffin was confirmed. It's not clear what new machine Kiffin was fixing up. Perhaps that was what he expected to do, but he would not fly a patrol in a plane of his own for nearly two weeks.

As the month of May ended, Kiffin had seventeen combat patrols between the escadrille's first patrol on May 13 and his injury on May 24. This was second only to Victor Chapman, who lost no time to injuries and flew twenty-two patrols during the month. The third most aggressive pilot was Bert Hall, who flew fifteen missions in May.[24]

June 1 was a frustrating day for everyone in the squadron. It was the first really nice day with good flying weather they'd had for a while. Kiffin borrowed Bert Hall's plane for an early morning patrol, but he had no luck. He spent two hours over the lines and saw several German planes, but he wasn't able to get within range. At one point he came across three German planes, each of which was as fast as his plane. Since he was all alone and well behind the enemy lines, he admitted that he had to "run for the first time."[25] Later that morning, Jim McConnell finally arrived from Luxeuil. After having been stuck for ten days waiting for the parts he needed to repair his plane, the parts that finally arrived were for a different kind of Nieuport. Jim found a local carpenter who could improvise the parts he needed and flew to Behonne. Almost as soon as he landed, Thénault asked him to accompany the squadron on an afternoon patrol.

The afternoon patrol began taking off at 12:30. Lufbery and McConnell left first. As Bert Hall was getting ready to leave, he looked up and saw a flight of German bombers high overhead. Lufbery and McConnell flew underneath the bombers without noticing them, but Hall, Thénault, Prince, Cowdin, and Chapman climbed to intercept them. Kiffin was left standing helpless on the ground, frustrated because he had no plane. Clyde Balsley and "Chute" Johnson were in the same predicament. In a few minutes they had to dive for cover as four of the bombers flew directly over the field and bombed it, scoring a direct hit on a hangar. Debris from the explosions as well as shrapnel from the anti-aircraft shells bursting around the bombers rained down on the three pilots. The bombers then flew over Bar-le-Duc and bombed it, killing forty civilians including ten children who were play-ing in a schoolyard. The Lafayette pilots managed to climb high enough to engage the bombers as they were returning to their base, but the fighters were scattered and had lost the element of surprise. A German gunner made a sieve out of Thénault's gas tank. Fortunately, his plane did not catch fire, but he was out of the fight. Elliot Cowdin's machine gun jammed. Norman Prince thought he damaged one bomber, but as he was changing ammuni-tion drums, he accidentally bumped his ignition switch with his elbow and switched off his engine. Not realizing what had happened, he thought his engine had broken, so he glided down to land. Bert Hall and Victor Chap-man chased the retreating bombers across the lines but were never able to climb high enough to mount a successful attack.

Jim McConnell had never even seen a map of the Verdun sector until he climbed into his plane for the afternoon patrol, but he thought he'd be safe if he stuck with the formation. Since most of the formation had diverted to chase the bombers he and Lufbery had missed, just the two of them headed for the lines. Somehow Jim lost sight of Lufbery, so Jim was alone flying in what he thought was the general direction of the front. He looked down and saw an airplane underneath him, and he was startled to realize that it had the black crosses of Germany. He then realized he really didn't have any idea how he was supposed to go about attacking another plane. He'd been taught how to fly, but not how to fight. This was the first time he'd ever seen a German plane in the air, and it was about to be the first time he ever fired a machine gun. He moved his hand so he could reach the trigger, cut power, and dove toward the German plane. He discovered it was a two-seater when the observer began firing at him. McConnell opened fire at a range of 150 feet but only fired a few rounds before he overshot the German plane. He turned back toward the German and found himself flying directly into the German's fire. He heard bullets slamming into his plane, so he flipped onto his side, climbed over the German, and tried to attack from the other side. He pressed the trigger, but his gun wouldn't fire. He swerved away from the enemy plane and tried re-cocking his gun, but he still couldn't get it to fire. The gun had been damaged by a German bullet. Then he heard a "tut-tut-tut" behind him. He looked, and the German was coming straight toward him, the pilot firing his forward gun. McConnell dove and managed to lose the German, but he was lost himself. He saw several canals and towns beneath him that weren't shown on his map, so he knew he'd flown out of his map's coverage, but he didn't know which way to turn to get back to his airfield. Then his motor began to miss. He saw a field that looked like a good place to land, circled until he saw men in blue uniforms (so he knew he was on the French side of the lines), and glided in for a landing. It turned out the field had ridges hidden by grass. As McConnell later wrote, "The only way to land is from the direction I didn't take." His plane bounced into the air, flipped over, and smashed into the ground.[26] He was unhurt, but the plane was a total loss.

The pilots had nothing to cheer about that night. They had failed to shoot down any of the bombers, and two of their own planes had been put out of commission. To make matters worse, they thought the publicity given to their arrival at the front might have triggered the German raid. (The raid was more likely triggered by the fact that General Pétain's staff had just moved to Bar-le-Duc.)[27] Kiffin wrote his brother that if only he had had a plane, and if Thaw could have been there with him, they might have brought down at least one bomber. He closed his description of the day by saying, "For Christ's sake, let's try and shut down on the publicity about the Escadrille!"[28]

Paul responded to Kiffin's plea to stop the publicity by explaining that he wasn't the one giving stories to the newspapers. He said that M. de Sillac, the escadrille's sponsor within the Ministry of Foreign Affairs, was publicizing the escadrille's accomplishments. He also suspected that Elliot Cowdin was "press-agenting himself." Paul did suggest that, since the newspapers were hungry for stories about the American fliers and others were already giving out stories, they might as well join the club and earn a little money that could be shared with all the pilots. Paul also wrote that there was a rumor of a big British offensive soon to be launched north of Verdun. There was in fact a major British offensive due to be launched near the Somme River on July 1. The fact that Paul Rockwell, a civilian, knew about the planned attack and openly discussed it in early June shows how lax secrecy was regarding upcoming offensives.[29]

Kiffin's frustration at not having a plane continued. June 2 brought beautiful flying weather, but Kiffin was stuck on the airfield, unable to take to the air and hunt down the Germans who had bombed Bar-le-Duc. Then the weather turned bad. For the next two weeks there would be very little flying due to rain, winds, thunderstorms, and low clouds. Kiffin wrote to his brother and fumed:

> We are very unlucky in having a captain who is a nice fellow and brave, but doesn't know how to look after his men, and doesn't try to. I have been fighting with him ever since being back, mainly about the fact that I have no machine, he having given my old one to Prince and not managing right about getting me a new one. He acts, when I get after him about it, as if he was doing me a favor to get me one. I think that in a few weeks I will be pretty sick with the outfit. I am going to try my damnedest to get another [German] machine down well within the French lines. Then I think things will change a little.[30]

A few days later, Kiffin wrote Alice Weeks and said that Bert Hall was on leave (pilots were routinely granted leave after scoring a victory) and had allowed Kiffin to use his plane, but the weather had been too rotten to make any flights. On a brighter note, Mr. Charles Prince (the uncle of Norman Prince) visited the squadron and gave them a phonograph, which they used extensively to while away the hours on days when flying was impossible.[31] Also, two new pilots joined the squadron. Laurence Rumsey, the son of a tycoon in Buffalo, New York, and a Harvard alumnus, joined the squadron on June 4. Before the war he had been a professional polo player.[32] Dudley Hill also joined the squadron. Dudley grew up in a wealthy family in Peekskill, New York. He was studying mechanical engineering at Cornell University at the beginning of the war but soon left school to volunteer with the American Ambulance Field Service. He was totally blind in his left eye as a result of a childhood hockey accident, but by memorizing the standard French eye charts, he managed to hide this fact from the medical examiners and transferred into Aviation. He joined the squadron on June 6.[33]

Apparently Kiffin wasn't the only pilot who was feeling disgruntled. Jim McConnell wrote to Paul Rockwell on June 8 and said, "There seems to be a split-up in this outfit. Thaw & Co. vs Cowdin, Prince, et al. I don't give a damn and won't join either club." Jim also said he had a new plane to replace the one he crashed on June 1 and expected to have it ready to fly on the following day. This probably irritated Kiffin, despite the fact that he and Jim were good friends, as Kiffin had been waiting much longer for a new plane and Kiffin hadn't crashed his old one. Jim also said that, despite the fact that the terrible weather was keeping the pilots from flying, "Bar-le-Duc has been closed to us for some fool reason."[34] Trips to cafés and other establishments in Bar-le-Duc were the main source of entertainment for the grounded pilots, so this restriction couldn't have made anyone happy.

In his letters, Paul suggested that Kiffin's enforced idleness while he waited for a plane might provide a good rest, but it's not clear how much rest Kiffin got during this period. Kiffin's conviction that he was fighting "for all humanity" compelled him to fly, and when he was prevented from flying, his letters showed his irritation. He finally got his new plane (a Nieuport 16) operational late in the afternoon of June 9 and made a flight over the lines, but he wasn't able to engage any Germans in combat. He saw a few German planes in the distance, but the cloud cover was too heavy to engage them.[35] Then bad weather set in again. The pilots still pulled standby duty in case any German planes were reported, but there was very little actual flying done by either side.

The bad weather and lack of flying provided many opportunities for the pilots to get on each other's nerves. Bert Hall described two such opportunities in the villa where they were staying:

> We had a phonograph in our villa and a piano too. The phonograph was supplied with the most terrible old records, but we played them just the same. . . . The piano was most troublesome. The Commanding Officer thought he was a musician. He really wasn't. His musical efforts were limited to pounding out a few bad tunes, and when I say pounding, I mean just that—pounding! He used to use the same bass notes for everything he played. But he was the C.O, and we had to put up with it. Now and again a Red Cross man or an ambulance driver would happen in and they could oftentimes play real music.[36]

Other pilots confirmed Bert's description of Captain Thénault's musical abilities, often adding that the captain's dog Fram would howl in protest whenever his master played the piano. Victor Chapman described life in the villa during this period as follows: "I sit in an upper window with waves of leaden clouds drifting by, and the indefatigable graphophone [*sic*] churns out some vulgar tune below, and the other 'heroes' play poker, and the Captain practices scales on the piano. It is disintegrating to mind and body,—this continued inertia."[37]

Jim McConnell provided Paul Rockwell with more details about the "split-up" in the squadron:

> I don't mean that I'm neutral in opinion as to the camps here but I can't see any good in putting my voice in. Here's the way I've got the outfit sized up. Kiffin, Bill, Chapman, and Co. are the most serious, Lufbery included. They are all one could ask for. Prince and Cowdin are in it for the sport, especially the latter, and while they do their work, will never ring any gongs. Hall is minus a few cogs but runs along in the average. Johnson & Rumsey frankly dislike the game and I believe Balsley needs a new pair of drawers whenever he goes out. Hill is a nice sort and I believe will try hard. The only ones with the really right feeling are the first named. We've been trying to get "Skipper" [Paul Pavelka] out here and I guess he'll arrive soon. The general run of see-the-war boys from Amerika [*sic*] are going to hurt us like hell by coming in. It makes me sore for they are taking the place of good Frenchmen. In other words hurting the cause. I feel like a French pilot would do a better job than I am able. I do not feel that I am a good pilot but I cheer up when I think that I'm just starting. I entered aviation after all the crowd here and so being the youngest pilot have a little more to learn. At present the only way I'm clever enough to get a Boche would be to catch him sleeping. If he's awake and shooting I can't dodge well enough to keep him from filling me with holes as the first chap did.[38]

So much for the stereotype that every fighter pilot thinks he's the world's greatest flier!

McConnell and the rest of the squadron would soon change their opinion of Clyde Balsley, but Paul Rockwell wrote to Kiffin that Elliot Cowdin's nerves were giving out: "Mr. Prince says that Cowdin imparted to him that he was very nervous, could not sleep, and had absolute need of a rest!!!! Seems that worthy is always resting."[39] Whether or not Paul Rockwell considered him worthy, the symptoms Paul described were typical of pilots suffering from the stress of combat. No one is immune to such stress, but it seemed to hit some pilots harder than others, and Cowdin had been flying in combat for a year before the American squadron was formed, including several months of combat in the Verdun sector.

The weather finally improved on June 16, and the pilots were able to take to the air again. McConnell wrote that most of the pilots were in the air for six hours (three patrols) and on alert the rest of the twenty-four hours.[40] Kiffin wrote that he was attacking planes all the time and almost got shot down twice himself. Both times he was caught by surprise, even though he thought he was keeping a sharp lookout. He said the only reason he didn't get shot down was because the Boche shot poorly. He was unable to bring down any planes himself, as there were too many of them shooting back whenever he attacked. None of the Lafayette pilots scored a victory that day.[41]

In the same letter, Kiffin described fights that took place on June 17:

> Chapman has been a little too courageous and got me into one of the mess-ups because I couldn't stand back and see him get it alone. He was attacking all the time, without paying much attention. He did the same thing this morning, and wouldn't come home when the rest of us did. The result was that he attacked one German, when a Fokker which we think was Boelke (the papers say he was killed but we don't believe it), got full on Chapman's back, shot his machine to pieces and wounded Chapman in the head. It is just a scratch but a miracle that he wasn't killed. Part of the commands on Chapman's machine were broken, but Chapman landed by holding them together with his hand.

The morning flight where Chapman was "a little too courageous" was reminiscent of the melee during which Kiffin and Bill Thaw were wounded. Captain Thénault, Lieutenant de Laage, Kiffin, Chapman, and Balsley were assigned to protect French observation machines photographing territory on the right side of the Meuse River. Thénault gave his pilots strict orders not to cross over to the left side of the river. Then, as Thénault described the flight,

> Chapman saw that the Boches did not leave the left bank and, like a tiger, he dashed at a group of them. They literally swarmed on this

left bank; they reminded me of bees! With Balsley and de Laage we followed and freed him from the attack of a big camouflaged plane, a heavily armed three-seater, which we forced to dive for safety to Forges wood.[42] We turned homewards satisfied, but Chapman evidently was not. After having filled up with gas at Vadelaincourt he went off alone again. He met a Boche ace, who handled his machine "infernally well," as Chapman told us afterwards, and who was accompanied by four others. Chapman put up a good fight but bullets riddled his plane and one of them wounded him slightly in the head. He landed at Froidos, on the field of Escadrille 67, with a machine absolutely out of use; several struts had been almost completely cut through. His opponent had been Boelke [*sic*], the best German pilot, a clever veteran who recorded this fight in one of his letters. Chapman exhibited such an eagerness to keep on with the bout that my friend, Captain Jules de Saint-Sauveur, commanding the 67th, had to give him positive orders not to attempt another flight with his injured "cuckoo," as we generally termed our machines. Chapman wanted to go and have another shot at the Boches; despite his wounds he utterly declined to rest.[43]

Once again, there were no consequences for violating Thénault's orders and breaking formation. Thénault was extremely reluctant to discipline his pilots, probably as a result of the special orders he was given when the escadrille was formed. He tried to persuade Chapman to go to the hospital to have his head wound checked and to get a few days' rest, but Chapman refused to go. The captain then offered him a new Nieuport 16 as a replacement for his badly damaged Nieuport 11. Chapman eagerly agreed to this arrangement, and the captain was happy because it meant Victor would be grounded for a few days while the Nieuport 16 was set up for him. The broken "command," which Kiffin said Victor held together with one hand while flying home, was probably a wooden aileron control rod. These rods ran vertically from the joystick linkage inside the cockpit to the aileron linkage in the top wing. A portion of these rods ran between the fuselage and the upper wing and could be reached from the cockpit.

Despite the conviction of the Lafayette pilots that Victor Chapman had been attacked by Oswald Boelcke, many historians are not convinced.[44] In some ways, Boelcke was the "bogeyman" for Allied pilots over Verdun— any time they encountered an exceptional German pilot, they assumed it was Boelcke. Boelcke was the reigning German "Ace of Aces" at the time, with eighteen confirmed victories. He scored nine of these victories while flying over Verdun and received much publicity as a result. Allied newspapers described him as flying an all-black Fokker with a white skull and crossbones on the wings. Bert Hall claimed he fought with Boelcke daily and could easily recognize him because he flew a black Fokker with white crosses. Neither claim was true. Boelcke flew a white Fokker with black crosses, undistinguishable from any other Fokker monoplane. Germany's other leading ace, Max Immelmann, was shot down and killed on June 18, 1916. Not wanting to risk losing both of the Germans' premier aces, the kaiser ordered Boelcke to be grounded and sent on a tour of the Eastern Front. Boelcke managed to sneak in a few more flights and score one more victory before leaving Verdun in late June.[45]

Back at Behonne, German bombers staged another attack on the airfield on June 17 (the same day that Chapman got "a little too courageous"). Kiffin and several other pilots immediately took off to try to intercept the bombers. Kiffin's efforts were frustrated when a spark plug in his engine fouled out, preventing him from reaching the altitude of the bombers. Three of the other planes also couldn't intercept the bombers due to engine problems caused by the multiple missions they flew on the previous day and that morning, which gives an indication of how unreliable their rotary engines were. The few planes that did eventually catch up with the bombers were not able to bring any down. Kiffin closed his letter to his brother by saying:

> I had thought beforehand that yesterday and to-day I would try my damnedest to kill one or two Germans for the boys who got it this time last year [legionnaires killed in the closing phase of the Battle of Artois], but as I say had no luck. Am tired out now. Have been out four different times to-day, and all the while going up and down. One time I dropped straight down from 4,050 meters (13,000 ft.) to 1,800 meters (6,000 ft.) on top of a Boche, but he got away. It tires you out a lot, the change in heights and maneuvering.[46]

The physical demands of flying World War I planes are often overlooked. A collector who frequently flies a replica Nieuport 11 says he is in awe of any pilot who can fly it for more than one two-hour mission a day because you have to "fly" the aircraft at all times. There is never a moment when you can relax.[47] Major Keith Park, who was the commander of the British 78 Squadron during World War I, wrote:

> Two high patrols a day rendered pilots inefficient after five summer months, and necessitated their being withdrawn for a period of rest. In the autumn, winter, and early spring, when flying at lower altitudes, pilots could stand up to longer periods, eight or nine months. Continuous flying at high altitudes, over 10,000 feet, without oxygen, renders fifty percent of officers unfit for flying till after a long rest on ground duty. Unless carefully checked the high strung "enthusiast" wears himself out by extra voluntary patrols just when he has become most valuable to his squadron.[48]

Kiffin and other pilots in the escadrille routinely flew three or four patrols per day, when the weather permitted. The fighting at Verdun never let up. The day after Victor Chapman had his plane shot to pieces, Captain Thénault led the squadron on a patrol over the lines. They were protecting artillery spotting aircraft. It was Clyde Balsley's third combat patrol, and it turned into his first air battle. Kiffin described the flight in a letter to his brother on June 19:

> Well, yesterday was a rather bad day for us. You know we didn't think much of Balsley. It was because he is young and inexperienced, but when he got here to the Escadrille I began to like him fairly well and better every day, as I saw he had plenty of good will to work and was not afraid. Well, yesterday, we all left for an offensive barrage over the lines. We were all supposed to follow the Captain, but only Prince, Balsley and myself did so. We four were over the lines, when we ran across about forty Boches in one little sector, flying at different heights. At the top, where we were, there were twelve or fifteen little "Aviatiks de Chasse," which go just as fast as we do, and in addition they carry a passenger. The pilot shoots like we do, but has a man to the rear of him who has a second gun that can cover the rear and sides. We were only four and over the German lines, but we stayed close together and for ten or fifteen minutes circled around the Boches, they shooting at us nearly all the time from four or five hundred meters. Finally, we saw our chance. One of their machines crossed over between us and our

lines, while all the others were in the rear of us. We immediately went down on this one Boche, which of course caused a general mix-up, as Boches came from the sides and rear. I saw either Prince or Balsley go over in a regular death drop and thought to myself that he was killed. Then I lost sight of the other one, and only the captain and I were left, so we got out of it and finally came home, thinking the other two were killed. Prince came home soon afterwards, having had to drop straight down, owing to a Boche having the upper hand on him and putting a bullet through his casque [helmet], but not wounding him.[49]

Clyde Balsley later wrote a description of the fight from his viewpoint:

My first battle in the air was my last. I had fired one shot; my machine gun had jammed. A German was at my left, two were on my right, one was underneath me, and the man I had first attacked was still behind me. From the silence of my gun they would know there was nothing to fear. My fight was over. I was too far behind the German lines to drive [sic] straight to earth. I could only maneuver back to Bar-le-Duc, where my escadrille was stationed. I swung in every direction; I went into a cloud. Bullets followed. One scratched my machine, and I slipped away from the man who fired it, and threw the belly of my plane upward. I was then about twelve thousand feet up. It was while I was standing on my head, the belly of my machine skyward, that something struck me. It felt like the kick of a mule. With the sensation of losing a leg, I put my hand down to learn if it was still there. I had the presence of mind to cut the motor. But as my right foot went back with the shock of the bullet, my left foot sprang forward. So, with my commands reversed, my leg knocked out, still standing on my head, I fell into a spinning nose-dive.[50]

The one bullet he fired before his gun jammed would be the only bullet he ever fired in combat. Balsley had been hit from underneath by a bullet that tore through his thigh, hit his pelvis, fragmented, and sent pieces into his intestines, kidney, and lungs. Initially his right leg jerked back and threw his plane into an uncontrolled spin. He finally managed to use his hands to move his leg forward, pulled out of the spin, and crashed just behind the French front line trench. He would spend weeks in a field hospital at

Verdun and a year and a half in an American hospital in Paris, undergo multiple surgeries, and be crippled for the rest of his life. But he would live. At first he was in great pain and suffered terribly from hunger and thirst, as the doctors would not let him eat or drink until his intestinal wounds had a chance to heal. The other pilots visited him whenever they could, and Victor Chapman got the doctor to concede that Clyde could perhaps suck on an orange. Victor then began bringing him oranges.

Meanwhile, life went on for the pilots at Behonne. Didier Masson was assigned to the squadron the day after Balsley was shot down. Like Raoul Lufbery, Masson was born and raised in France but spent time in the United States before the war.[51] He was one of the few Americans whom the French accepted into Aviation before Bill Thaw, and his success flying Caudron bombers helped clear the way for other Americans to be accepted into French aviation.[52] Bill Thaw visited the squadron for a few days before going back to Paris on convalescent leave, still unable to fly with his wounded arm. Elliot Cowdin, who had engine problems and left the formation shortly before Balsley was shot down, tried unsuccessfully to convince the captain to give him a month's leave.[53] And then came the events of June 23.

Kiffin was on alert that day, so he was stuck on the airfield, waiting in case a German airplane crossed the lines and he was called to intercept it. McConnell, Chapman, and Rumsey flew an uneventful patrol in the morning. Upon landing, Rumsey crashed his plane into McConnell's, putting Jim's plane out of commission. (Crashes like that occurred periodically in the uncontrolled, open fields used for airfields, with no radio communications, no brakes, no ground control, and no marked runway or taxiways.) Chapman flared his plane a little too high in his landing, dropped hard, and broke an elastic shock-absorbing cord that held the wheels onto the landing gear. His mechanic, Louis Bley, began disassembling the landing gear to repair it. Before he had finished, Victor rushed back to the plane, threw the mechanic's tools out of the way, and ordered Louis to start the engine. Victor had heard the sound of what he thought was a German bomber headed for the airfield, and he wanted to take off to intercept the German. His mechanic refused, arguing that the wheels were not fastened securely and might fall off when Victor landed, flipping the plane. Victor insisted that if he could shoot down a German bomber, it wouldn't matter if he crashed upon landing. As they were arguing, the noise faded away and Victor realized that, whatever it was he had heard, it wasn't heading for their airfield and he wouldn't be able to intercept it. He let his mechanic get back to work while he left to get lunch.[54]

After lunch, Victor returned with a bundle of newspapers, oranges, and chocolates for Clyde Balsley. Captain Thénault, Norman Prince, and Raoul Lufbery were ready to fly a patrol over the lines. Victor told Thénault he would tag along until they got to the lines; then he would fly to an airfield near the hospital where Balsley was recovering and take the oranges to him. Victor's mechanic was happy to report that he had fixed the landing gear, replaced the spark plugs, and prepared the plane for flight. Thénault and the others took off while Victor and his mechanic stowed the oranges in Victor's plane. By the time Victor took off, the others were far ahead of him, but he was still able to follow them.

Thénault spotted a couple of German two-seaters over Fort Dou-aumont. He, Prince, and Lufbery dove to attack, but then three Fokkers who had been providing high cover dove to attack them. The Fokkers had the altitude advantage, and Thénault realized his patrol was outnumbered, outgunned, and behind enemy lines. He successfully disengaged, and, with the others, he dove for the safety of the French lines. No one realized that Chapman hadn't turned off to go to the hospital but was still following them. He had apparently seen the Fokkers dive to attack and was himself diving into the battle to help his comrades. When they disengaged, he found himself fighting alone, against five German planes. He was quickly shot down. His plane went into a dive with full power, the wings tore off, and the fuselage plummeted ten thousand feet before burying itself in the ground three miles behind the German lines.[55] There is no clear agreement among historians as to which German pilot shot down Victor Chapman.[56]

Back at Behonne, no one even knew Victor was missing. They assumed that he had flown the oranges to Clyde Balsley as planned, but as the hours ticked by and he didn't return from the hospital, they began to worry. Then a French two-seater pilot called to ask whether they were missing a Nieuport, as he had seen one shot down. That night Kiffin wrote his brother to describe the day:

> Well, I feel very blue to-night. Victor was killed this afternoon. I was the guard here today and so didn't go out over the lines. The Captain, Victor, Prince and Lufbery went out this afternoon. Inside the German lines they attacked five German machines. The Captain, Prince and

Lufbery came out all right and came home. But Victor didn't show up.
We were beginning to feel uneasy when a Maurice Farman pilot tele-
phoned that he was there and saw the fight. He said that he saw one
of the Nieuports suddenly dive straight down and then the machine
break to pieces in air. . . . If possible, try not to let anything go to the
papers in America, until his parents are notified, which we are in train
to do. After that, I would like to see every paper in the world pay a
tribute to him. There is no question but that Victor had more courage
than all the rest of us put together. We were all afraid that he would
be killed, and I rooming with him had begged him every night to be
more prudent. He would fight every Boche he saw, no matter where
or what odds, and I am sure that he had wounded if not killed several.
I have seen him twice right on top of a German, shooting hell out of
him, but it was always in their lines and there being so much fighting
here it is impossible to tell always when you bring down a machine.
His head wound was not healed, yet he insisted on flying anyway, and
wouldn't take a rest. . . . As I say, he and I roomed together and flew
very much together, so I rather feel it, as I had grown to like him very
much. I am afraid it is going to rain to-morrow, but if not, Prince and
I are going to fly about ten hours, and will do our best to kill one or
two Germans for him.[57]

Jim McConnell wrote:

We talked in lowered voices after that; we could read the pain in one
another's eyes. If only it could have been some one else, was what we
all thought, I suppose. To lose Victor was not an irreparable loss to us
merely, but to France, and to the world as well. I kept thinking of him
lying over there, and of the oranges he was taking to Balsley. As I left
the field I caught sight of Victor's mechanician leaning against the end
of our hangar. He was looking northward into the sky where his patron
had vanished, and his face was very sad.[58]

Bert Hall wrote, "One of the most ghastly things about losing a partner
in war times is rolling up his kit—packing what he left behind and sending
it back to his folks."[59] Staring at the empty bunk beside your bed, where
the night before your best friend had slept, has to be equally painful. Kiffin

experienced both when Victor was killed. In time he would write a long letter to Victor's parents, praising Victor and giving them the details of his final flight, but it would be many days before he could bring himself to do that. Kiffin described that first night in a letter to Alice Weeks:

> Victor had about the strongest character of any boy I have ever known. He was very frank, honest and never had let anything kill his ideals. . . . As we all have to die sometime, it isn't so bad, yet by living he could have accomplished a great deal in his life. Last night I went to bed, but I couldn't sleep thinking about him, especially as his bed was right beside mine.[60]

Despite the loss of Victor Chapman, life went on for the other pilots. The Battle of Verdun was still raging. The weather turned bad again, and there was very little flying. Neither Kiffin nor Norman Prince was able to kill one or two Germans for Victor. The spirit was willing, but the weather wouldn't cooperate. Bert Hall repainted the insignia on his plane, possibly in an attempt to lighten the mood of the squadron. Instead of simply writing "BERT" on both sides, he wrote "BERT" on the left side and "TREB" on the right side so enemy pilots could read his name no matter which way they passed him.[61]

On June 25, Elliot Cowdin left the squadron for health reasons. Many of his fellow pilots felt this was a "diplomatic" way to remove him while avoiding negative publicity, claiming that he flew little, quarreled with everyone, and overstayed his leave once too often. However, it's possible that this was one of the few times during the war when the effects of combat stress on a pilot were appropriately dealt with. Elliot was hospitalized for a while and then attached to the Royal Flying Corps, where he tested and delivered French aircraft being purchased by the British. In January 1917, he was deemed physically unfit for flying and discharged from the French Army. He returned to the United States and eventually joined the US Air Service, working in the Bureau of Aircraft Production. To his credit, he never tried to "cash in" on his status as a founding member of the Lafayette Escadrille and lived the rest of his life in relative obscurity.[62]

On the following day, Victor Chapman's uncle sent Kiffin 1,000 francs to be spent in the mess in Victor's name.[63] The reason he sent the money to Kiffin was because Kiffin was the "Chef de la popote" (Chief of the Mess).

Kiffin wasn't responsible for actually preparing the food, but as chef de la popote he would have handled the finances, overseen the menu, and been the person the other pilots complained to if they didn't like the food. (Jobs like this, tasks that are necessary to keep a military organization functioning but don't require enough time to be anyone's full-time job, are often called "additional duties." Commanders have probably been assigning additional duties since the time of Caesar's legions, and assignees have been complaining about them for at least as long.)

On the same day, June 26, 1916, Kiffin was promoted from the rank of corporal to sergeant, as were Jim McConnell, Chouteau Johnson, Clyde Balsley, and, posthumously, Victor Chapman. Jim McConnell mentioned this promotion in a letter to Paul Rockwell. He also tried to soften his earlier criticism of Norman Prince, saying, "Old Norman Prince isn't a bad sort at all. He's serious and works hard and tho crazy as a loon means well all the time."[64] In closing, he mentioned that they might move north for the coming fight, another sign of poor security for the upcoming Battle of the Somme.

The weather continued to be bad, and the month of June fizzled out. It was the first full month of operations for the escadrille, and it was a disappointing month for Kiffin. He was ready to give his all to win this war for humanity, but the weather wouldn't cooperate. And much of the time when the weather was suitable for flying, he didn't have an airplane to fly! He was only able to fly twenty-one missions that month, for a total of thirty-six hours over the front. Norman Prince flew forty-seven hours that month, which must have rankled Kiffin since Norman was flying Kiffin's plane.[65] Much more distressing than the lack of flying, though, was that Kiffin had lost his best friend. A new friend was lying in a hospital, often in excruciating pain, with no guarantee of survival. And Kiffin's old legionnaire buddy Bill Thaw was still recovering from a bullet that had shattered his arm. Flying was serious business.

13

July Frenzy

Intrepid, superb—but how foolish!

—RENÉ FONCK

ON JULY 1, 1916, THE ALLIED ARMIES LAUNCHED A MAJOR OFFENSIVE NEAR the River Somme. Nicknamed "The Big Push," it would go down in history as the Battle of the Somme. It had been planned as a joint British/French offensive to punch through the German lines and defeat the German Army. General Falkenhayn upset that plan when he attacked at Verdun. The French Army exhausted itself defending Verdun, so the Somme became a British offensive with limited French support. It was the first major battle for Britain's "New Army," the thousands of recruits who volunteered during the first year of the war. Because these recruits were inexperienced, British planners did not try to teach complex maneuvers such as squad tactics, covering fire, or local initiative. Instead, they relied upon a massive, week-long bombardment to obliterate the German trenches, cut their barbed wire, and destroy their machine gun nests. The British troops were then expected to rush across no-man's-land in rows so they could overwhelm any surviving German soldiers with a concentrated bayonet attack.

Security was poor. The Lafayette pilots openly discussed the coming attack in early June. Arthur Guy Empey, an American who served in the British Army, wrote that three weeks before the battle the British dug a duplicate of the German trench system about thirty kilometers behind the lines. Troops who were going to attack spent days rehearsing their advance and drawing maps of the dugouts, saps, barbed wire, and other key features they would encounter. Each section of trench was given a unique code name that allowed troops to quickly orient themselves once they captured a position. To their dismay, when these troops moved into their attack trenches, they discovered the Germans had erected signposts with the correct code name for each trench.[1]

Whatever element of surprise may have remained was forfeited by the weeklong preliminary bombardment. Many shells proved to be defective, and there were not enough large-caliber guns to destroy the deep shelters the Germans had built to protect their men. While the bombardment was destructive and demoralizing, enough German troops, machine guns, and barbed wire survived to make July 1 the bloodiest day in the British Army's history. The British suffered close to sixty thousand casualties on that one day alone, a third of whom died. There were some local successes, primarily by French troops and by experienced British commanders who used innovative tactics instead of a Napoleonic march, but there was no major breakthrough. Regardless, the British high command considered the first day to have been a success, with "acceptable" casualties, and continued to attack until mid-November.

The Battle of the Somme eventually relieved the pressure on the French at Verdun, but it had little immediate impact. For the time being, the Battle of Verdun raged on. Jim McConnell described the battlefield as seen from the air:

> Peaceful fields and farms and villages adorned the landscape a few months ago—when there was no Battle of Verdun. Now there is only that sinister brown belt, a strip of murdered Nature. It seems to belong to another world. Every sign of humanity has been swept away. The woods and roads have vanished like chalk wiped from a blackboard; of the villages nothing remains but gray smears where stone walls have tumbled together. . . . Columns of muddy smoke spurt up continually as high explosives tear deeper into this ulcerated area. During heavy bombardment and attacks I have seen shells falling like rain.[2]

The death of Victor Chapman and the wounding of Clyde Balsley didn't seem to bring the remaining pilots any closer together. McConnell described a continuing rift in a letter to Paul: "Norman predicted that Hall would follow in the footsteps of Cowdin and take the 'cure' but it's hard to say. As we all know he's an awful liar and hot air artist, and every time he sees a fire on the ground he comes rushing back and reports bringing down a Boche but I believe he has the wherewithal in a pinch."[3]

It's hard to know the truth about Bert Hall's relationship with the other pilots. Certainly he was not popular with Norman Prince or Jim McConnell. He seems to have gotten along fine with his legionnaire buddies Kiffin and Bill Thaw, and he claimed to be good friends with Lufbery. Clearly, though, he was fond of tall tales and did not have the "gentleman's" manners that most of the other pilots had. Paul Rockwell's letters show that later in the war he took a strong dislike to Bert, which is unfortunate because Paul was the official historian of the Lafayette Escadrille. He performed an invaluable service by preserving letters, newspaper articles, and other historical materials, but he also told many early historians that Bert Hall cheated at cards, forged his fellow pilots' names on chits, and had his teeth extracted to avoid combat patrols. There is absolutely no evidence to support this last charge, and his combat record shows that he not only flew more missions than most of his fellow pilots but also was one of the most successful pilots in the squadron. Kiffin said of Hall, "He may be a dastardly blowhard, but the man has skill and a killer's instinct."[4]

There's also no evidence to support or refute the claims that Bert cheated at cards and forged chits. Given Bert's rough-and-tumble background and many of the other pilots' relative naivety, he probably didn't have to cheat to win at cards. And given Bert's impoverished background and most of the other pilots' ready access to money, Bert may have felt justified in relieving them of a little of their surplus cash. Certainly he would have had ample opportunity. A Canadian pilot who was once stationed at the same airfield as the Lafayette Escadrille described their poker games thus:

> There were three so-called leagues: the small-fry, with a 5-franc ($1) limit; the small-timers, with a 20-franc limit, and the big-timers with no-limit betting. . . . In the big league, each man had by his side a roll of toilet paper, and when he made his bets he tore off a sheet upon which he wrote his I.O.U.s—sometimes they ran as high as 5000 francs, worth then at least $1,000.[5]

In such an atmosphere, it would be easy for a skilled player like Hall to win without cheating, but it would also have been easy for him to cheat or to forge chits. It would be difficult to prove that a chit scribbled on toilet paper was forged. It's also possible that debts weren't taken as seriously as they would have been under other circumstances. Although admittedly not an unbiased observer, Bert wrote:

> Aviators in groups on any of the battlefronts have an odd time of it. We play poker, dice, roulette, and if any one wins all the money, as someone usually does, it doesn't matter greatly. You go around and borrow what you want and nobody keeps any account of it, since we know this thing is going to last a good while and there will be nobody left to worry about the debts when it's over.[6]

Regardless of whatever friction existed on the ground, pilots supported each other in the air. Kiffin described a mission with Lieutenant de Laage in a letter to Paul. The date is unknown, but it seems likely that this flight occurred in early July:

> Very early one morning Lieutenant de Laage and I went on patrol together. Over Étain, I saw a Boche underneath me. I immediately dove on him, and when I was just about ready to open fire, two other Germans, whom I had not seen, attacked me, filling my machine full of holes. I thought that my last hour had surely come. Lieutenant de Laage had already had a combat and his machine-gun was jammed. But although it was impossible for him to fire even one shot, he dove on the two Boches who were trying to bring me down and drove them away. I am certain that at that moment he saved my life, as he had done many times before.[7]

That year the French tried to give as many Americans as possible a day off to celebrate the Fourth of July. American volunteers in the Legion who were attacking at the Somme were not able to get the day off, but many other Americans and Captain Thénault attended ceremonies in Paris. Aristides Briand, the prime minister of France, gave a speech at one of these ceremonies in which he called Victor Chapman "the living symbol of American idealism."[8] General Henri Gouraud, of the French General Staff, expressed France's sentiments more eloquently when he said, "When men who have no obligation to fight, who could not possibly be criticized if they did not fight—yet nevertheless decide upon their own individual initiative to risk their lives in defense of a cause they hold dear—then we are in the presence of true heroes. The young Americans who entered the Légion Étrangère and the Escadrille Américain are in every sense heroes, and France owes them all the homage that word implies."[9] Kiffin may have been technically correct when he complained that the escadrille shouldn't be given any special publicity because they weren't doing anything more than what French escadrilles were doing, but from the French standpoint that issue was irrelevant. The American pilots were volunteers, fighting for a cause they believed in. The French recognized and appreciated that fact. They also recognized and appreciated the fact that these volunteers were garnering press coverage in the United States, publicity that might help convince the United States to join the war against Germany.

Lieutenant de Laage was in charge of the squadron while Captain Thénault was in Paris. Although generally well liked, the pilots weren't entirely happy with the lieutenant's command style. Jim McConnell wrote:

> The Capt. is off on permission. Lieut. is running us. He's a wild one and needs a few bullets near him to tame him down. This morning he led us 20 kilometers [twelve miles] inside the lines and we kept diving on Boches there that were in far greater numbers. . . . He'll keep this "Nach Berlin" [To Berlin!] stuff up once too many times and about a half of us will stay over there. It's fool work and does no good. Kiffin's sore on him for being so wild. The outfit seems to have tamed down, anyway, having learned that there are certain precautions to follow. When we first got here no one knew anything about this aerial warfare as conducted at present and it took some while to learn.[10]

Lieutenant de Laage must have been exceedingly aggressive for Kiffin to object!

The death of Victor Chapman and the severe injuries to Clyde Balsley made a deep impact on Kiffin's mother, as she explained in a letter to Paul and Kiffin:

> My darling Boys, I am thinking of you a great deal. . . . Last night at supper someone handed me an afternoon paper. My eyes at once fell on the headlines "American Aviator Killed etc." I came near fainting,

all at table noticed it. Poor Chapman! It was beautiful for him to go for the oranges, but so sad for him to go down. Please let me know, if you can, if he has a mother in N.Y. and get me her name and address. It came so close home to me. I sympathize with his loved ones. I notice too that Bach is in prison [POW], Balsley wounded and lamed for life, and Thaw wounded. I thank the Lord every day my boy is spared. You have done so much already Kiffin. I do wish you could have less dangerous work now. . . . A Capt. Riley—conductor—who has a home on Peachtree Street says all Atlanta is praising you boys and claim you. Our N.C. people do not like it when Kiffin is commented on as from Atlanta. Asheville wants that honor.[11]

In early July, Paul Rockwell finally obtained permission to visit the squadron. Paul was working for what he described as the French Propaganda Ministry, and he was also a special correspondent for several American newspapers, so it would seem that this would be a great opportunity to generate favorable publicity. In general, though, the French Army did not allow reporters anywhere near the front for fear they would write pieces that were critical of the army. Paul didn't receive permission to visit Behonne until he promised not to write about anything he saw while he was there.[12] He arrived on July 6, and while he may not have written anything, he took a great number of photographs.[13] Low clouds, winds, and bad weather kept the pilots from doing much flying during Paul's visit, but Kiffin borrowed Bert Hall's plane for staged pictures and a short flight. Unfortunately, this turned out to be Kiffin's day to fall victim to the wretched crosswinds at Behonne. He rammed Bert's plane into a visiting Bregeut bomber when he landed. The damage was not serious, but the incident embarrassed Kiffin and Captain Thénault.

Loula wrote to Kiffin and Paul on July 6. It had been two years since they'd seen her last, shortly before they set out for Europe to join the Foreign Legion. A lot had happened during those two years, and they would have been dismayed if they had known the war would continue for two more years. Loula wrote:

I remember the last time I saw you, two years ago yesterday, while we were waiting for a street car you asked me to come to Atlanta and make a home for you boys and quit working. That was very sweet of you. I told you I wanted you boys to get married and have your own home. Do you remember? It seems so long ago. Surely you will be spared to come to me again. . . . Has Kiffin found some girl in France he loves, or have you been too busy, my baby? How old I feel! I want so to cling to some one of you, and yet I know it would not be right. My heart goes out to all the soldiers, especially to our Americans. If any of them have mothers or people you would have me write to, just send me the address. Give Mrs. Weeks my warmest love and don't forget to write me a long letter. Devotedly, Mamma.[14]

Paul Rockwell left Bar-le-Duc on July 10, just after Charles Nungesser arrived. Nungesser was one of France's leading aces. He was an old friend of Captain Thénault's, and he was the one who had told Mata Hari that Bert Hall was a famous American millionaire. Nungesser was nothing if not intrepid. After completing Nieuport training, he celebrated his arrival at his first fighter squadron, N65, by putting on an impromptu aerobatics show before landing. His new commanding officer chewed him out for this, finishing his tirade by telling Nungesser that if he wanted to impress someone with his flying skills, "frighten the enemy!" Nungesser immediately got back into his plane, flew to a German airfield, and put on a low-altitude aerial display that included flying upside down past the German hangars. He then flew back to his new airfield and reported that he had successfully completed his assigned mission. His commander placed him under arrest for eight days—the first of several such punishments Nungesser would earn.[15]

In between punishments, Nungesser proved adept at shooting down enemy planes. When he visited the Lafayette Escadrille, he already had ten confirmed victories, but in achieving those victories he had suffered enough injuries to keep a small hospital fully occupied. Among his more serious injuries, on January 29, 1916, he broke both legs, suffered multiple internal injuries, and shattered his jaw.[16] He was rushed to the hospital but wasn't expected to survive. Eight weeks later, he was flying combat missions again. He crashed and broke his jaw once more after being shot in the face, but he soon returned to active duty with a mouth full of gold teeth.[17] On June 22, he shot down two German Aviatiks but crash landed near his victims, this time suffering a broken nose and jaw, a dislocated knee, and bullet fragments in his lip.[18] It was while recovering from this crash that he decided to visit the Americans at Behonne. Ostensibly he was there on convalescent leave, but in less than a week he asked to be put on the squadron roster and began flying combat missions.[19] He hobbled to his plane using two canes and had to be helped into the cockpit, but he could still fly.

Some sources credit Nungesser with "revitalizing" the escadrille following the weeks in early July when the escadrille didn't score any confirmed victories, but that seems unlikely. There is no indication that Nungesser flew any missions with the Lafayette pilots during the time he was attached to the escadrille.[20] He undoubtedly discussed flying with the pilots over dinner and drinks, but he flew solo missions. It's probably just as well that he didn't try to teach them how to shoot down German planes. His style was to attack immediately, regardless of the odds. The squadron already had considerable experience with that tactic, thanks to Chapman, de Laage, and, at least on his early missions, Kiffin. Nungesser's style was similar to that of the celebrated French ace Georges Guynemer, who managed to achieve fifty-four victories before he was shot down and killed in September 1917. Their "attack at any cost" tactics were in stark contrast to those of France's leading ace René Fonck. Fonck patiently stalked enemy aircraft, waited for an opportunity when the odds were in his favor, and then attacked. Fonck survived the war with seventy-five confirmed victories and sixty-seven unconfirmed claims. He sometimes boasted that his plane had never once been hit by a German bullet. He described Guynemer's tactics as "intrepid, superb—but how foolish!"[21] Incredibly, Nungesser survived the war, with forty-three confirmed victories and a medical record that spanned multiple volumes. In 1927, he disappeared without a trace during an attempt to fly the Atlantic, two weeks before Lindbergh's historic flight.

When Nungesser visited the Lafayette Escadrille, he was flying a Nieuport 17, an evolutionary development of the Nieuport 11s and 16s that the squadron was then flying. It had the same 110-horsepower Le Rhône rotary engine as the Nieuport 16, but with an airframe that was designed to handle the more powerful engine. With a top speed of 110 miles per hour and a service ceiling of more than seventeen thousand feet, it offered improved performance in all categories. Most important, it had a belt-fed Vickers machine gun mounted in front of the pilot and synchronized to fire through the propeller. This provided a more stable gun platform than the Lewis gun on the top wing, was easier to aim, and used a five-hundred-round belt instead of forty-seven-round drums that needed to be changed in the middle of a dogfight. Captain Thénault received a Nieuport 17 the same day that Nungesser arrived, but the other pilots would have to wait many weeks before they could get their hands on one.

The bad weather didn't mean the Americans were doing no flying. They flew whenever they could and fought with the Germans whenever they found them. There were just fewer opportunities to score victories than there had been when the weather was better.

Pilots still reported encounters with Captain Boelcke on the days when they could fly, despite the fact that Boelcke was in Budapest at the time, as part of his forced removal from combat. Jim McConnell wrote, "I saw the black plane of the famous Capt. Boelcke. The white crosses stand out very clearly."[22] Loula quoted a newspaper report that he had shot down Victor Chapman in a letter to Kiffin and Paul:

> Miss Champion sent me a clipping from one of the Asheville papers, headed "Kiffin Rockwell Saves Comrade." It tells—copied from New Orleans Picayune—of his attacking Capt Boelcke and saving Victor Chapman when his head was wounded. I guess that happened before Chapman was killed. The papers said it was Capt Boelcke who got Chapman at last. I hope Kiffin can get the Capt, though I guess I ought to be happy if the Capt fails to get Kiffin.[23]

(Victor Chapman was flying alone when he was wounded in the head, and historians are still debating whether Boelcke was involved in that battle. Boelcke had been pulled from Verdun and ordered not to fly before Chapman was killed, so he definitely wasn't involved in that battle. Kiffin wasn't involved in either dogfight, but other than that the newspaper story was correct.)

Another news story that must have worried Loula ran in several US newspapers that week, datelined Paris, July 13:

> Another thrilling battle has been fought between American and German aviators and the Americans have won. For the first time in several days the American aviation escadrille in the service of France made a volunteer sortie over German lines and ran into a bunch of Teutons. Corporal Dudley Hill of Peekskill N.Y. and Sergeant Kiffin Rockwell of Atlanta attacked an observation machine at once. Sergeant Norman Prince of Boston joined them, while a powerful aeroplane rushed up

to aid the German side. All of the American machines were hit several times. Sergeant Rockwell got a bullet through his machine which also took a piece out of his coat over his heart, but he was untouched.[24]

In addition to describing what must have been a frightening experience for Kiffin, this story illustrates how the Lafayette Escadrille was providing good publicity for the French. The Americans, with their home towns prominently listed to help garner local support, were portrayed as heroically attacking the "Teutons" and winning. In this case, their victory seems to have been that they weren't shot down, but the overall tone of the piece is that the Americans successfully defended France against an attack by a barbaric horde.

The weather turned bad again after this battle against the Teutons. Kiffin and Jim McConnell wrote several letters to Paul complaining that there was very little flying going on, and when they did manage to fly they didn't encounter any enemy planes. Jim McConnell got a letter from "Skipper" Paul Pavelka, who was still at the flight school in Pau, cooling his heels while waiting for orders to join the other pilots at Behonne. Flight training was obviously improving, as Skipper had received training on aerobatics and air-to-air combat, and he scored at the top of his class in aerial gunnery. Things weren't all moonlight and roses at Pau, however. Skipper wrote to McConnell:

> Oh! I tell you this is some hell hole. One fellow hung himself in the jail yesterday. Four of them smashed up and one went into a *vrille* [tailspin] and fell into the road, and is expected to die. Still another took a notion to go to Spain and was brought back to the school by gendarmes. To make things still worse, one of the pencil-pushing *embusqués* [embedded—that is, a permanent staff member] cleared out with 1200 francs of the payroll. Therefore, no pay this 10th for some of us.[25]

Skipper also relayed the astonishing (to him) news that Fred Zinn, the legionnaire who snored so badly, had washed out of pilot training and been made an observer/gunner. "Hell, he couldn't hit the side of a barn if he was on top of it!" Skipper wrote. (As it turned out, Zinn could shoot well enough to defend his airplane, and by the end of the war he was one of the top US experts in aerial photography.)

The weather cleared on July 21 and the pilots got busy again. Kiffin described the renewed activity in a letter to Paul:

Have been rather busy lately flying. Friday had a very interesting day. Flew six hours, and attacked four different machines. The first one certainly had a lot of luck. Right over the lines I attacked him first. Went within ten or twenty meters of him, shot forty-four rounds straight into him, then turned off. Lieut. de Laage then arrived just as close to him and shot over eighty shots into him; then came Bert Hall with about twenty more shots, but the damned Boche went on as if nothing had happened.

In the middle of the day Bert and I went out alone. I found an Aviatik and dived on him. Two Fokkers dived on me; Bert dived on the two Fokkers, and two more Fokkers went on him. In that line of battle we went down through the air about two thousand meters. I got within about ten meters of my Aviatik, shot all my shots into him, and he began to fall in the clouds, and then I disappeared in the clouds. I thought that I had gotten the Aviatik, but a post of observation that saw the fight said he readdressed [recovered]. As for Bert, he shot his shots into one Fokker, then the other two got right on his back. They came damned close to getting him, plugged a lot of bullets around him in the machine, but he wasn't touched.

Yesterday, I flew for over eight hours. One machine attacked by the Lieut. de Laage, Hill and me was forced to land immediately in the German lines. We gave Hill the credit for it, as he was the closest to the German, and more likely to have hit him. But it doesn't count anything officially, but will help him toward a citation. None of this for publication. I only write it that it might interest you.[26]

The Aviatik that the post of observation said recovered before hitting the ground did not count as a confirmed victory for Kiffin, but newspapers in the United States hailed it as his third victory. Despite the fact that Kiffin said none of this was for publication, the newspapers quoted a postcard from Paul Rockwell as the source of the story.[27] Newspapers also described the fact that Kiffin and Bert Hall dove into a cloudbank as a "Yankee Trick" that outwitted the Germans.[28] This battle prompted Kiffin to write, "Hall saved my skin, no doubt about it. When we returned both our ships were more hole than whole."[29]

Norman Prince tried a new tactic in his effort to score his first aerial victory. Both sides made extensive use of observation balloons during the war. These giant, sausage-shaped balloons were filled with hydrogen and tethered to a winch on the ground. They kept a close watch on the enemy's trench system and called for an artillery barrage if anything looked suspicious. They were obvious targets, but it was difficult to shoot them down. Hydrogen is very flammable, but only when mixed with oxygen. The pure hydrogen inside the balloon would not ignite. There was an ignitable mixture of hydrogen and oxygen at the surface of the balloon, where hydrogen that seeped out mixed with the air. However, conventional tracer ammunition flew through this layer so quickly that it seldom ignited the hydrogen. Sometimes a pilot could ignite a balloon by concentrating a long burst of fire on one small spot, but balloons were surrounded by anti-aircraft guns and often protected by fighters, which made it extremely difficult (and unhealthy) for a pilot to sustain an attack long enough to set the balloon on fire. Also, the high-speed winches could pull the balloon down very quickly. If a pilot didn't set the balloon ablaze on his first pass, it would be pulled so low and the anti-aircraft fire would be so intense that a second attempt would be suicidal.

On May 22, the French unveiled a new weapon for attacking balloons. Lieutenant Yves Le Prieur developed an electrically ignited "skyrocket" that could be mounted on the struts of a Nieuport and fired at an enemy balloon. A knife-edged spear point on the rocket sliced through the balloon fabric and the rocket itself ignited the hydrogen. The rockets tended to twist and turn in flight like a Fourth of July bottle rocket, so their maximum effective range was about one hundred yards. They were most accurate if fired straight down, so, to have success, a pilot had to dive vertically on a balloon and hold his fire until he was within, say, two seconds of colliding with it before firing his rockets. Nevertheless, on May 22 eight French pilots attacked eight German balloons and successfully shot down six of them.[30] When Norman Prince heard of this encounter, he talked Captain Thénault into getting Le Prieur rockets for the squadron.

When the rockets arrived, Norman put them on the "Hoodooed" machine, the ex–Bill Thaw / Elliot Cowdin / "Chute" Johnson Nieuport 16. The machine soon lived up to its reputation, as Jim McConnell wrote, "Prince damn near ran into me on landing and made a swerve with result he tipped over."[31] This did not discourage Prince, as in the same letter Jim wrote, "De Laage and Kiffin have just gone out to act as guards for Prince who, loaded down with sky rockets, is off after a Boche observation sausage." Bert Hall wrote that Prince succeeded in igniting a balloon on August 1, but the victory was unconfirmed.[32] Hall's fondness for tall tales makes his books of questionable historical value, except when the events he describes can be verified by other sources. In Jim McConnell's *Flying for France*, he wrote that Prince once fired his rockets at a balloon and "when he looked again, the balloon had vanished."[33] McConnell didn't mention this event in any of his letters, though, and balloons that caught fire didn't just vanish; they burned brightly and fell slowly, leaving a huge plume of black smoke.[34]

The wretched field conditions at Behonne continued to take a toll. Raoul Lufbery narrowly escaped serious injury when he had to take evasive action to avoid hitting a Maurice Farman that was landing from the opposite direction. Lufbery tried to pull up and bank away from the Farman, but his wingtip hit the ground and the plane cartwheeled across the ground at one hundred miles per hour, smashing itself into "bits of wood, iron, and cloth."[35] Lufbery emerged from the wreckage without a scratch, but he was sick from gasoline he had swallowed during the impact. In his letter describing these crashes, McConnell commented that out of eleven planes in the squadron, only four were in flyable condition.[36]

The lack of flyable aircraft was not just a result of accidents: the frantic pace of activity during good weather was wearing out the planes faster than the mechanics could repair them. The sun rose early and set late during the summer months, and there were missions to be flown from dawn to dusk. Kiffin wrote of getting up at 3:00 a.m. to be ready for dawn patrols. Captain Thénault wrote that pilots scarcely had time to sleep or to eat, and they sometimes slept underneath their planes, dressed in their leather flight suits, to be ready to take off at the first glimpse of dawn.[37] They would take off as soon as there was enough light to see the airfield and climb to the maximum altitude of their aircraft in hopes of catching a German pilot who had slept in a little longer and was at a lower altitude.

The fighting on the ground continued unabated, which meant reconnaissance and artillery-spotting planes were in the air from sunup to sundown. These planes needed protection, so fighters were scheduled to provide escort throughout the day. Fighter pilots were typically scheduled to fly one or two escort patrols per day. They were free to fly additional missions to find and attack enemy aircraft if they wished, but, as Ted Parsons put it, "a buzzard had to be mighty ambitious to want to make patrols for which he wasn't scheduled."[38] Kiffin frequently flew additional patrols. A Nieuport carried enough fuel to fly for roughly two hours, so when Kiffin wrote that he spent eight hours in the air, that meant he flew four patrols, two or three of which were voluntary. Add in the time required to service his plane between flights, and it made for a very long day indeed. As Captain Thénault said, he would barely have had time to sleep or eat. Keeping up with this exhausting schedule was bound to take its toll.

While Kiffin and Norman Prince may not have received credit for victories during this period of intense activity, others in the escadrille had better luck. Charles Nungesser, still temporarily assigned to N124, scored his eleventh confirmed victory when he shot down an Aviatik on July 21.[39] Two days later, Bert Hall shot down what he described as a "new type Fokker fighter, all decorated up like a new saloon." Hall said the victory wasn't much to crow about. The German opened fire when they were still a long way apart, giving himself away as a beginner. Hall dove on the Fokker, the Fokker dove away and turned, and Hall shot him as he was coming out of the turn. Bert checked his new watch, which he had won playing poker against an ambulance driver, and noted the time was 3:00 p.m.[40] The victory was confirmed by ground observers. His fellow pilots might dismiss him as a blowhard, but he now had more confirmed victories than any other American pilot.

Lieutenant de Laage was the next Lafayette pilot to score a victory. On the morning of July 27, 1916, he was flying with Kiffin when he shot down an Aviatik. This was his first confirmed victory with the Lafayette Escadrille. When Kiffin described this latest victory in a letter to his brother, his tone was unusually harsh. Certainly Kiffin had never been shy about expressing his opinion to Paul, especially when dealing with people or situations that he felt were holding him back. But Lieutenant de Laage was a friend, and Kiffin's main complaint was that he didn't feel his efforts were being recognized. This was an odd reaction from someone who frequently complained that the squadron was receiving too much publicity.

Some of Kiffin's frustration is understandable, given the incredible risks he and the other pilots were taking. His fellow pilots claimed that Kiffin had shot down several planes so far behind the lines that they could not be confirmed, but confirmed victories eluded him.[41] Jim McConnell wrote, "Kiffin Rockwell is a wonder at this game and it is only hard luck that has kept him from bringing down four or five Boches instead of one. He's in the air all the time."[42]

However, the anger in Kiffin's letter to Paul seems to go beyond his frustration with a lack of confirmed victories:

> Am pretty disgusted; have been working my fool head off lately, and don't even get thank-you for it. I may ask any day to change Escadrilles. This outfit is on the bum. Everyone is scrapping and discontented, and me about the worst of any. This damn Capt. does everything in the world to discourage me from trying to do anything. It is hard to understand him except that he is a selfish stupid fool.
>
> I have had about twenty fights lately, sometimes going as close as ten meters to the Germans, and I almost ran into one two days ago. But I haven't had the luck to have one of them smash to pieces in our trenches, so as far as thanks go could not have done anything. This morning the Lt. de Laage and I brought one down in their lines. I attacked him first and he went over on his nose. As he came up, the Lieut. opened up on him and he fell. The Lieut. deserves all the credit one gives him, but I certainly ran the most risk this morning, and if I didn't hit him myself, which I may have, I made it possible for the Lt. to hit him. Yet do you think I got any credit for it? Not at all! Fifteen minutes later I made another German land just within his own lines, having attacked two, and was seen by Prince, but nothing is said about it.[43] The trouble is that I fight all the time with the Captain instead of taking him down to a whore house and buying him a drink.
>
> I had a hell of a scrap with the captain about the popote [squadron mess] right after you left, and refused to have anything more to do with it.
>
> I think the best thing I can do is to go to another Escadrille, but I hate to lose what work I have done here, and to tell you the truth, I want the *Légion d'Honneur* and a Sous-Lieut.'s grade. I don't give a damn how conceited it may appear, but I think I have well earned the two.[44]

Kiffin's bitterness, complaints about Captain Thénault, complaints about his fellow pilots, complaints that he was not getting enough credit for the work he was doing, and fixation on how much work he was doing (hours flown, number of fights, etc.) would grow worse in the weeks to come. Photographs also show he was losing weight, with his face becoming drawn and furrowed. While it is risky to diagnose a medical condition based upon letters, particularly when the author is not a medical doctor, it seems possible that Kiffin was beginning to exhibit stress-related symptoms.

At the beginning of the war, very little was known about the effects of combat stress. During the war doctors began to recognize "shell shock" as an actual medical condition in ground troops. This condition was seldom diagnosed until it had reached the point where the patient was trembling uncontrollably or otherwise incapable of continuing to serve. It was thought to be caused by nearby explosions and therefore not something that would affect pilots. Aviation medicine, like all other aspects of aviation, evolved during the war. By the end of 1917, all the belligerents had established some form of medical service specifically for aviators, but during Kiffin's time at Verdun very little was known about the medical effects of combat flying.

Historian Steve Ruffin wrote an excellent series of articles on the medical effects of flying during the First World War.[45] His series was subtitled "Rx for Misery" in recognition of the fact that pilots were subject to extreme physical and mental stresses. The concept of flying an open cockpit airplane in a clear blue sky, high above the battlefield below, sounds thrilling. The reality is that it was exhausting, nerve-wracking work that wore down the pilots day after day, mission after mission. The physical stresses Ruffin described included:

- Noise and vibration: The noise and vibration from the unmuffled engine, machine guns, and wind could easily exceed 130 decibels, louder than a jackhammer or artillery fire.
- Toxic fumes in the cockpit, including castor oil and carbon monoxide: These fumes could cause inattentiveness, poor coordination, drowsiness, headache, depression, and gastric distress.
- G-forces: During violent maneuvers such as pulling out of a dive, pilots experienced G-forces that could exceed 6G and possibly reach as high as 9G. Pilots could and did black out momentarily, which could prove fatal in a dogfight or cause the pilot to crash. Less violent maneuvers didn't cause blackouts but added to fatigue and headaches.

- Altitude sickness: At eleven thousand feet, the oxygen available to the brain is decreased by one-third; at eighteen thousand feet, it's decreased by half. Some pilot candidates proved unable to function above altitudes of eight thousand feet, and a quarter of the candidates in one study were unable to function at an altitude of fifteen thousand feet. For those who could tolerate the higher altitudes, the lack of oxygen led to shortness of breath, sleepiness, fatigue, muscular weakness, confusion, lack of coordination, inattentiveness, and giddiness. In all probability, toxic fumes made the altitude sickness worse. The symptoms became more pronounced if the pilot flew repeated missions at twelve thousand feet or higher, and it could take up to seventy-two hours of rest on the ground to completely recover.
- Cold: Air temperature decreases steadily with altitude at a rate of roughly 3.5°F per one thousand feet. Thus, if it was 60°F on the ground at Behonne (a typical July morning), the temperature at twelve thousand feet would only be 18° above zero. On a winter morning, if the ground temperature was 20°F, the temperature at twelve thousand feet would be -22°F. The effects of these temperatures were made much worse by the 100+ miles per hour winds swirling around the open cockpit, as well as by the fact that the pilot was strapped into his seat and could not move around to improve circulation. The cold temperatures also increased his body's demand for oxygen, but oxygen was scarce at high altitudes. This made it even harder to stay warm, and it made altitude sickness worse.

These were the physical effects. Some of them were understood at the time, others were undetected, but the net effect was to wear down a pilot's constitution over time and leave him exhausted, irritable, and increasingly vulnerable to the mental stress of combat. We tend to romanticize World War I pilots as being "fearless knights of the sky," but to call them "fearless" is to trivialize what they experienced. No sane person could dive into a dogfight, a firefight with no cover, a situation in which they were vulnerable to fire from all directions including above and below, without feeling fear. World War I aviators experienced fear, and they had to overcome it every time they flew a mission. That fear, and their struggle to fly missions in spite of it, gnawed at their guts.

Symptoms of this stress could include personality changes, depression, irritability, tremors, tic-like movements, stomach upset, loss of appetite, headaches, insomnia, and nightmares. Pilots suffering from combat stress tended to be either excessively cautious (as was the case with Elliot Cowdin) or excessively rash, exhibiting what amounted to a death wish (Victor Chapman?). Pilots who continued to fly in combat without a break would eventually break down and become ineffective, suffering from what was variously called "flying sickness," "flyers neurasthenia," or "flying fatigue." The Germans called it *Überflogen*, which meant "flown out." During World War II, it was commonly known as "combat fatigue" or, among aviators, "flak happy." Today it is referred to as combat stress reaction (CSR). Combat stress reaction is similar to the more widely known posttraumatic stress disorder (PTSD) except that CSR is usually a temporary ailment that occurs during or immediately after the stress of combat, whereas PTSD can occur months or years after the traumatic event.

A classic description of being "flown out" is given in a 1918 aviator's diary in the book *War Birds*:

It's only a question of time until we all get it. I'm all shot to pieces. I only hope I can stick it [out]. I don't want to quit. My nerves are all gone and I can't stop. I've lived beyond my time already. It's not the fear of death that's done it. I'm still not afraid to die. It's this eternal flinching from it that's doing it and has made a coward out of me. Few men live to know what real fear is. It's something that grows on you, day by day, that eats into your constitution and undermines my sanity. ... Here I am, twenty-four years old, I look forty and I feel ninety. I've lost all interest in life beyond the next patrol.[46]

Kiffin was certainly not "flown out" in July, but he was beginning to exhibit some symptoms of combat stress. These symptoms grew worse as the month progressed, particularly in late July, when the weather allowed him to fly multiple patrols every day. He frequently complained about being tired or needing sleep. His personality was changing. He became harshly critical of the squadron and his fellow pilots, and especially of Captain Thénault. Kiffin's descriptions of Thénault went from being "a pearl of a fellow" in late April to "a nice fellow and brave [but] who doesn't know how to take care of his men" in June to "a selfish stupid fool" in late July. Kiffin's letters don't mention losing his appetite, but photos show he was losing weight and looking careworn. Like the description from *War Birds* quoted above, he was twenty-three years old but he looked forty.

One symptom of combat stress that Kiffin did not exhibit was excessive caution. If anything, he became excessively rash in that he flew a great number of voluntary patrols. His idealistic conviction that he was fighting "for all humanity" probably played a role here, as he felt as if the fate of the world rested on his shoulders. Adding to that was his frustration at not scoring confirmed victories. Lacking victories, the proof that he was doing everything he could to win the war became the amount of flying he was doing. In his letters, he repeatedly described how many patrols he flew, or how many hours he spent in the air. This was not a common theme in other pilots' letters, but Kiffin almost seemed obsessed with flying more hours than any other pilot and frustrated that others were not recognizing his achievements in this area by giving him medals and promotions.

Kiffin's insistence upon flying as much as possible undoubtedly made his stress worse. The primary treatment for combat stress was rest. Pilots were routinely given short leaves to visit Paris or otherwise unwind for a few days, and later in the war it became common to give them longer leave periods every few months and to rotate them into non-combat jobs after six to nine months at the front. Captain Thénault normally rewarded pilots with an eight-day leave after they scored a confirmed victory. Kiffin never took this leave after his victory in May, and he refused Thénault's urging to go to the hospital and take convalescent leave after he was wounded in the face. That was a traumatic event that probably affected Kiffin more than he realized. It was obviously just sheer luck that the bullet hit his windscreen frame rather than killing him. Any illusions Kiffin may have had that he was invulnerable, that he led a charmed life, or that he was too good a pilot to be shot down would have been shattered with that bullet. But after a quick trip to Paris to reassure Paul and Mrs. Weeks that he was all right, Kiffin was back at Behonne ready to fly more missions. Thénault's tardiness in getting Kiffin a new plane may have been an attempt to force Kiffin to take a break, but it only seems to have added to his frustration and stress. Indeed, Kiffin's criticism of Thénault and his fellow pilots began during this period. Similarly, it appears from Kiffin's letters that the bad weather they experienced in June and July left him frustrated at the forced idleness, rather than grateful for a chance to relax.

Regardless of what drove Kiffin, or what his inner feelings were, by mid-July he was doing a lot of flying. In late July, he wrote to his mother:

Have been so busy for the last week that I haven't kept up with anything going on around me. The weather has been fine and I have flown between forty and fifty hours over the lines, and have attacked over twenty German machines, shooting a lot of them up very badly, but never having the luck for one of them to fall over the trenches.[47] What time I have not been in the air I have not had energy enough even to look at a paper.[48]

The weather would stay fine, and he would fly many more hours before the month ended.

Kiffin's complaints about Captain Thénault and the friction between some of the pilots were probably made worse by the fact that Bill Thaw was still recuperating from his arm injury. As the senior American pilot in the escadrille, Bill was in many ways the glue that held the squadron together. It was not just Bill's rank that made him the senior officer but also his personality. (Bill was actually a year younger than Kiffin and was almost the youngest pilot in the squadron. Kiffin was twenty-three, and Bill twenty-two. It's easy to forget how young these pilots were.) Bill Thaw had earned the respect of all of the pilots. He was the type of leader who was friends with everyone but still unquestionably in charge. Bill often acted as the "go between" for Captain Thénault, who seems to have been an effective but not particularly charismatic leader. Bill also helped maintain camaraderie among the extremely diverse group of pilots in the squadron. In the months and years to come, the Lafayette Escadrille would endure many stressful times, but these times would not cause the friction and complaints that characterized the months at Verdun when Bill Thaw was on convalescent leave. Lieutenant de Laage also served as an intermediary for Thénault and, like Thaw, was very well liked and respected by the American pilots. Ironically, de Laage was a good friend and frequent flying partner of Kiffin, but in this case he doesn't seem to have soothed the friction between Kiffin and Thénault. De Laage was flying the same hectic schedule that Kiffin was, and it's possible that he was too exhausted to see what was happening to squadron morale.

The rash of landing accidents continued. This time it was Jim McConnell's turn. He was returning from the last patrol of the day, and the stars were becoming visible in the darkening sky when his engine began to fail. He described his forced landing:

> I made for a field, but in the darkness I couldn't judge my distance well and went too far. At the edge of the field there were trees, and beyond, a deep cut where a road ran. I was skimming the ground at a hundred miles an hour and heading for the trees. I saw soldiers running to be in at the finish and thought to myself that Jim's hash was cooked, but I went between two trees and ended head-on against the opposite bank of the road. My motor took the shock and my belt held; as my tail went up it was cut in two by some very low telephone wires. I wasn't even bruised.[49]

Jim may not have been bruised, but his back was severely wrenched. It did not bother him at first, but as the days and weeks went by, it grew progressively worse. Eventually Jim would be hospitalized as a result of this accident.

Back in Paris, Paul Rockwell was trying to make things better for Kiffin. When Kiffin was in the Legion and it became obvious that the Second Regiment was not up to par—especially after René Phélizot was killed by a fellow legionnaire—Paul had worked to get Kiffin transferred to another unit. Now Paul had a much more influential job, and he had powerful friends in high places. Kiffin may have just been "venting" to relieve stress when he complained about Captain Thénault in his letters to Paul, but Paul took him seriously. In late July, Paul wrote, "I hear that you and Bert had a hot scrap with the Huns the other morning, and that you shot one down back of their lines. Everyone speaks of your good work, but I don't seem to hear much about the others. . . . I cannot connect with Mr. Leygues, the Chambre meets soon and he'll have to return. I want to speak to him personally."[50]

Mr. Leygues was a French deputy and president of the Foreign Affairs Committee. He was active in getting the Lafayette Escadrille formed, and he was the father of Paul's fiancée. A few days later, another letter from Paul made it clear why he wanted to speak to Mr. Leygues:

> Take the permission [leave] due you and come on in to Paris, and we will get that damn Capt. thrown out and a decent one put in, so by the time you get back the boys will get credit for their work. I haven't as

yet been able to do anything, but M. L—is in town. I'll see him first of the week. But you can tell him better than I how things stand and there is no use you're not taking the leave due you and coming on in. You might work out there forever but with an ass in charge it'd be no use. We will get a good Capt. put in, but frankly the best way is for you to come here and talk.[51]

Since Paul was a civilian, he was probably not breaking any laws by trying to get Captain Thénault fired, but the fact that he tried certainly does not reflect well on him or on Kiffin. The impetus for this action seems to have been Paul's, as in the coming weeks he would repeatedly ask Kiffin to come to Paris to talk to Leygues. Kiffin didn't do anything to encourage Paul, but he was obviously aware of Paul's efforts and made no effort to stop him. In most of Kiffin's letters, he simply ignored Paul's efforts to replace Thénault.

In their correspondence, Paul and Kiffin talked as though many of the other squadron's pilots also wanted to replace Thénault. It's possible that was true, as Paul talked to the other pilots when he visited the squadron in early July and he met with them individually when they took leave in Paris, but there is no surviving correspondence from other pilots to support this idea. Even Jim McConnell, who in some ways was the squadron gossip, did not write about replacing Thénault.

Kiffin's response to Paul's initial suggestion that he talk to Leygues was the only letter in which Kiffin specifically addressed this issue.[52] That letter also illustrates Kiffin's increasing irritability, and his focus on the amount of flying he was doing:

Received your letter this morning. The weather was good yesterday and to-day, but my machine is worn out, and I won't do much until I get a new one. They are repairing it now, but the Captain made a demand for a new one for me, as he couldn't help it, owing to the amount of flying I have done. I took out another machine yesterday, but couldn't do any good with it, as it was not arranged right for me.

Right now I don't care to take a permission, as I want to keep up with everything that goes on around here. You can just tell M. Leygues that I want to be changed to a French escadrille unless the Captain is changed and that several others will follow my example and that there is not a man here who likes the Captain. That Colonel Barès [director of French Aviation] did not want to give him to us at first but only did it because Thaw asked it. I think I have the most hours and the most fights for the month of July on the Verdun front of any Nieuport pilot, but am not sure. I don't think, however, that a full report of my work has gone out of this office, and a number of times my report on a fight has been changed.[53] The machine that Hall brought down the Captain did his damnedest to prove that it wasn't brought down, and so far hasn't proposed Bert for even a citation.

But this morning he showed a change. Lufbery is a quiet boy who does good work and when he says he has done something we all believe him. He doesn't like Thénault but doesn't show it so openly as some of us so Thénault kisses his ass. This morning Lufbery brought down a German machine ten kilometers in the German lines. We all know he did because he wouldn't lie about it, yet not a soul saw it. If any of the rest of us had done it and even if it was seen by a second one of us T. would only sneer about it yet he immediately went in an automobile to the Commandant of this Armée, and proposed Lufbery for the Médaille. All of us will be damned glad to see him get it, as he deserves it yet the principle is all wrong.[54]

Lufbery's victory was the first in what was to be a long string of victories to avenge Marc Pourpe's death. This first victory occurred on July 30, when he shot down a German two-seater over the Bois de Macé, inside the German lines. Lufbery described it as "I precipitated a one-on-one combat without giving him time to prepare,"[55] meaning that he took the German by surprise. The plane broke apart when Lufbery attacked.

On the following day, Lufbery proved his first victory was no fluke. On this occasion, he attacked four enemy machines at close range, bringing down one of them.[56] He was now tied with Bert Hall in terms of the number of planes shot down, and of course no other Lafayette pilot had shot down two planes in two days. In the weeks to come, Lufbery would threaten to drain the "Bottle of Death."

And so the month of July came to an end with a flurry of action. Kiffin flew forty-one missions during that month, spending more than eighty-one hours in the air.[57] It's not clear whether this really was more than any other Nieuport pilot on the Verdun front, as Kiffin had claimed, but it was more than any other pilot in the squadron. Lieutenant de Laage was close, with 79.6 hours in the air, which was not surprising since he and Kiffin often flew together. Norman Prince was third, with 66 hours. The other eight pilots in the squadron averaged 31.8 hours in the air. Kiffin flew more than 2.5 times that average, and roughly 25 percent more hours than Prince. His drive to fly more than anyone else was succeeding, but it was taking its toll.

14

Summer Heat

To fight has grown to be a kind of habit, and I don't suppose we'd know what else to do.

—KIFFIN ROCKWELL

THE GOOD FLYING WEATHER CONTINUED INTO AUGUST, SO THE PILOTS followed the same grueling schedule that had ruled their lives in July: Up well before dawn,[1] grab some coffee, and rush to the car that took them to the airfield. There the mechanics would already be wheeling the Nieuports out of the hangars, getting them ready for the first patrol of the day. Four or five pilots were usually scheduled for this dawn patrol, which sometimes meant every pilot who had a flyable airplane and wasn't assigned to alert duty was scheduled for the patrol.[2] Typically one pilot would be on alert duty. That pilot would stand by his plane, ready to take off and intercept any German planes that crossed the lines. The rest would take off as soon as there was enough light to see the airfield, which in early August was around 5:00 a.m. The squadron might be scheduled to fly a second patrol that day, a patrol that could return as late as 10:00 p.m., when the evening twilight faded. Pilots were free to fly additional patrols if they wanted to. Kiffin generally wanted to.

While Kiffin was flying combat missions from dawn to dusk, his brother was pulling strings behind the lines, trying to get Captain Thénault replaced. On August 1, he wrote to Kiffin:

I have just been talking with Mon L. [Leygues] and he is seeing the Min. de la Guerre [Minister of War] this afternoon on that subject of making a change. His advice is that you not tell anyone the complaint came from you, so don't speak to any of the boys about it. An investigation will surely be made, and I believe a new man will take T's place. If Norman Prince wants his friend from N69 put in charge of the escadrille, why doesn't he write his uncle Charles Prince about it? Mr. Prince knows many political people, and if Norman only wrote him the Escadrille wants a new Capt. he'd get busy. But don't let on that you have had me say anything too. The more people there are working this thing the quicker it'll go then. I know you have been given a damn rotten deal, but I didn't mention it. Your reward will come later, I am sure.[3]

Paul also complained that someone else had been sending reports to the papers about the escadrille's activities, including the victories of Hall and Lufbery. The reporters Paul worked with were complaining to him because they were getting scooped. Paul asked Kiffin to send him a card or a note whenever anyone in the escadrille did anything of interest.

Kiffin did not respond to Paul's efforts to get Thénault removed—at least, not in any letters that have survived. Kiffin did respond at length to Paul's request for news updates, though he was not interested in being the conduit for publicity:

In regard to the news from this escadrille and all, I think you had better fix up an arrangement with Jim or someone to keep you posted, or quit trying to handle it. When I have a machine that flies all right, I fly two or three times more than most of them, and for that reason don't have time to write letters or think much about it, and I don't go to Bar-le-Duc once a week whenever I am flying, whereas the others do. Then another thing, you never know when a machine brought down is official or not, and I don't care to write about them when they are not. . . .

Last month, I had from thirty to forty fights, twenty-one of them being officially reported, yet they did not give me credit for any machines brought down, so I don't see why they should be written up, as after one or two are told of it is the same with all. Now this morning, Lufbery and Jim attacked a machine which they think fell; later Lufbery and some pilot from a French escadrille had the same experience. Then Bert Hall thinks he brought one down also. Yet so far none of them is officially confirmed, so they may report three machines brought down or they may not report any. Sometimes they report a machine brought down without anyone seeing it, and then again they don't.

One day, Lieut. de Laage and I attacked two machines. At the end of the fight he [one plane] went straight down and I thought the pilot had been killed, but he readdressed close to the ground with nothing wrong. He was seen going down by a post of observation which did not see him readdress. This post sent in a report that a German machine had been brought down in the German lines. They wanted to give us credit for the machine but we both knew we had not brought down a machine, and told them so, and explained the circumstances. Yet two well-known French pilots claimed it the following day, and were given credit as having brought down a German machine. So all in all, you can't tell much about what is going on in the aviation. Sometimes a man will work his head off and get no credit or recompense, and then later, when he least expects it, he will get everything. I worked damned hard last month and got no credit for it. Well, now I am going to take it easier this month and I bet I gain more by it. I stayed in bed this morning until ten-thirty, and am taking life easy at present until they give me a new machine.[4]

Kiffin's rising level of stress is evident in this letter. He was particularly frustrated by the seemingly random way in which victories were confirmed.[5] His closing comments about taking life easy and staying in bed until ten-thirty appear to be a dramatic change in behavior that would have given him a much-needed rest, but it was not exactly a voluntary change. He wrote his mother on the same day to say that he was waiting for a new machine,[6] and Jim McConnell wrote to his girlfriend Marcelle Guérin the following day to say that there were only four flyable airplanes in the entire squadron, so they were all getting enforced idleness as they took turns flying those four planes.[7]

Kiffin described several aerial combats in that letter to his brother, but only the one by Lufbery and "some pilot from a French escadrille" was eventually confirmed. Lufbery found himself attacking a German two-seater at the same time it was being attacked by Adjutant Victor Sayaret of Nieuport squadron N57. Together the two men succeeded in downing the German plane. It was the third confirmed victory for each of them.[8]

Lufbery had now scored three confirmed victories in six days to become the squadron's highest-scoring pilot. He was scoreless for his first two months with the squadron, but he had used that time to carefully learn how to be a successful fighter pilot. Just four days later, on August 8, he scored his fourth victory. Lufbery was flying with Jim McConnell, but despite exceedingly clear visibility, they became separated. Lufbery then climbed until he was three miles above the earth (sixteen thousand feet) and throttled back while he searched for an enemy plane. He zigzagged as he flew, scanning the horizon and the skies above to make certain no enemy plane was stalking him. Then he spotted a German two-seater about three thousand feet below. He described his attack in the French magazine *Guerre Aerienne*:

As a matter of prudence, I looked around me to make sure the machine had no protectors. It would be stupid to fall into a trap, especially now that I knew the enemy's favorite ruse, having several times been a victim of it.

Evidently the occupants of the suspicious-looking machine had not seen me. I must make the most of the occasion. I stopped my motor and *piqued* [dove] towards it. As I drew nearer I saw the Boche's black crosses showing through the camouflage. I placed myself about thirty yards in the rear of the fuselage, just a little below, so that its fixed plane and helm would serve me as a shield. Finally my adversary saw me, but it was then too late. Vainly the pilot sought to turn his machine in order to enable his gunner to fire. It was no use. Their lack of vigilance was to cost them their lives. I pressed the trigger of my gun. Pan! Pan! Pan! In a few seconds forty-seven bullets were fired. We were now so close together I was forced to dive to my left to avoid a collision. I righted my machine and looked down for my adversary. He was still there, but now to my surprise, his machine was white. I removed my glasses [goggles] the better to examine it. To my great satisfaction I found it was upside down; I could see its chassis and wheels. It remained thus as it continued to fall. Black smoke and fire spurted from it. Its descent grew more rapid as the fire became more intense. Finally, in a mass of flames, it fell in a ravine only a few yards from our trenches.[9]

It's clear that Lufbery used tactics similar to René Fonck's—that is, carefully stalking his opponent and waiting to strike until all the elements were in his favor. Contrast this method with an attack that Jim McConnell, no longer a novice, made during the same general time frame:

De Laage (our Lieutenant) and I made a sortie at noon. When over the German lines, near Côte 304 [Hill 304], I saw two Boches under me. I picked out the rear chap and dived. Fired a few shots and then tried to get under his tail and hit him from there. I missed and bobbed up alongside of him. Fine for the Boche but rotten for me! I could see his gunner working the mitrailleuse [machine gun] for fair, and felt his bullets darn close. I dived, for I could not shoot from that position, and beat it. He kept plunking away and altogether put seven holes in my machine. One was only ten inches from me.[10]

McConnell makes no mention of checking to see whether there were fighters protecting this two-seater. He was not able to take his intended victim by surprise, probably because he alerted the crew by firing while he was diving. He tried to maneuver into a favorable position, but either he misjudged his speed and overshot or the alerted enemy pilot took evasive action. Whatever the cause, the result was that McConnell became the prey rather than the hunter. Where Lufbery carefully planned and executed his attack, McConnell seems to have followed a strategy of "See German, Shoot!"

Paul Rockwell wrote to Kiffin and backed off a bit in his pressure for news of the squadron, saying, "I agree with you about the news, and shall not bother with the aviation except when I get a story that I know is good." American newspapers were hungry for news about the American flyers, however, and other reporters were not as careful about verifying stories as Paul was. They would rush to telegraph the latest rumor to the United States, which sometimes caused problems. In the same letter, Paul complained, "Just the other day the report came in that Prince was missing, it was sent to America and caused his family much anxiety. Mr. Charles Prince [Norman Prince's uncle] wired me from the country about it." He concluded the letter by asking, "Have you heard anything about the matter I interested M. L— [Leygues] in? He is still in the South, but spoke to the Minister of War before he left. If things are not bettered soon, let me know. I have about a half dozen people I can interest, and if several kicks go in, a change is bound to be made."[11]

One minor change had been made. After Kiffin argued with Captain Thénault about the squadron mess and declared that he would have nothing more to do with it, Didier Masson replaced Kiffin as "Chef de Popote [mess officer]."[12] Of more importance, Kiffin's good friend from the Legion, "Skipper" Paul Pavelka, finally arrived at the escadrille. Pavelka was initially assigned the "Hoodooed" plane, the Nieuport 16 that Bill Thaw had been injured in. After Bill's injury, the plane was assigned to Elliot Cowdin. Elliot was discharged from the escadrille shortly thereafter. Chouteau Johnson flew the plane after Elliot left, and he decorated it with his personal "Snake Eyes" dice motif. Johnson seems to be the only pilot who didn't have any problems with this plane. He was eventually given a newer plane. Norman Prince mounted Le Prieur rockets on Johnson's old plane for his experiments in balloon strafing, but he soon flipped the plane when he swerved to avoid crashing into Jim McConnell while landing. The wings were replaced after that accident, and the plane was assigned to Paul Pavelka.

Pavelka loved his new assignment. He wrote to Mrs. Weeks:

Life here is splendid, beats anything I have run across. I have been out twice, on the first occasion with Kiffin and the Lieutenant. I reached a height of 4400 meters [14,500 feet] in order to survey the surroundings, and to acquaint myself with some of the landmarks. Yesterday I went out in the clouds on my own, flew from Verdun to St.-Michel which is in the hands of the Boches. I came down to 300 meters and tried my mitrailleuse [machine gun] on a German battery. It choked [jammed] on me so I made away and landed at Commercy at an Escadrille of Farmans, where I took in some essence [gasoline] and had lunch with a Lieutenant. I was gone three hours. Everyone thought I was lost and worried about my landing in Germany.[13]

The "Hoodooed" plane lived up to its reputation a few days after Pavelka joined the squadron. On August 15,[14] he was flying over Verdun at about nine thousand feet when a valve broke on his rotary engine. Due to the unusual design of the engine, this created an open hole in the top of the cylinder. There was no exhaust manifold or other barrier between the piston, which was rapidly pumping a raw fuel/air mixture onto the hot engine, the spark plug (which was still actively sparking with every revolution), and the engine cowling (which was liberally smeared with castor oil). The engine caught fire almost immediately, and the wind fanned the flames back into Pavelka's face. This was one of the most terrifying things that could happen to a pilot, and Pavelka later said it was far more terrifying than anything that happened to him in the infantry.[15] If the fire had been caused by a bullet hole in the fuel tank (a very real possibility during a dogfight), there was virtually nothing any pilot could do to extinguish the flames. The pilot could stay in the plane and be burned alive, or jump to a certain death. Pavelka was lucky. Initially, only the engine and the cowling were on fire. He immediately shut off the fuel and ignition and put his plane into a sideslip so the wind would stop blowing the flames directly into his face. Instead, the wind now blew the flames onto his lower wing, where they began burning away the fabric. He had to put the plane down in a hurry. He glided back to friendly territory and crash landed in a swamp. At this point, the flames enveloped the fuel tank, but Pavelka managed to get out of the plane and slog his way through the swamp to a safe distance before the fuel tank exploded. The smoke attracted the attention of German artillery spotters, and they added to the festivities by immediately shelling the area.[16]

Fortunately, Pavelka escaped the shelling. His helmet and goggles protected most of his face, although he did have second-degree burns on the lower portion of his face and on his hands.[17] The next day he was flying again, having been given "Bert Hall's old bus." He painted this airplane in a distinctive brown and white "cowhide" pattern, probably to commemorate the time he spent working as a cowhand out west. He wrote Paul Rockwell to say that his new plane could climb to fifteen thousand feet in twenty-five minutes. (This was considered an excellent rate of climb in 1916.) He complained that the Boche seemed to remain at home since he came to the escadrille, and he said the only excitement he'd had was "a little cannonading." That may have been the shelling that followed his crash landing in the swamp. Other than that, his letter made no mention of the fact that his engine caught fire. Apparently he didn't consider that exciting.[18]

On August 15, Jim McConnell began a seven-day leave in Paris. He had been looking forward to this leave and had been writing about it in letters to his girlfriend Marcelle since early August, but his plans were spoiled when his back injury from the crash landing in July flared up. (Jim blamed his back problems on a recurrence of a rheumatism attack he'd had twelve years previously.) Paul Rockwell described Jim's condition in a magazine article:

About the end of the month, he and Kiffin came to Paris on seven days' leave. Jim's back grew worse and worse, and often he sat up all night, unable to sleep because of the pain. Of a morning Kiffin and I had to help him put on his clothes, and he could walk only with the support of a cane. Yet, when his seven days were up, he insisted on returning to the escadrille. When he got there he was unable to walk at all, and the captain at once sent him off to a hospital.[19]

Paul was apparently writing from memory, as he got a few of the details wrong. Jim and Kiffin didn't come to Paris together, but their leaves probably overlapped a day or two. And the captain didn't send Jim to a hospital immediately, but after Jim had been back for a few days, it was obvious that he was in no condition to fly. The captain then sent him to the hospital, but before he left Jim gave testimony to the rancor that still existed within the squadron. On August 25, he wrote to Paul Rockwell:

I gave Norman [Prince] the hell of a call down at supper last night. He denied the "'Cowdin to be shot" rumor. Says all he had against you was that you wanted to send cable about Cowdin being in jail. That it hurt [the] escadrille. I gave him the hell of a call down and put in all the details you wanted. I haven't seen him today. He was out in the morning and claims to have brought down a Boche. He acted like a wild man on landing, turned summersault and yelled. Boche was so far in lines no one saw him. Don't know if it will be official or not but any way Norman beat it immediately on permission.[20]

It's not clear what the "Cowdin to be shot" rumor was about, but it's clear that tempers were flaring and there were hard feelings between Norman Prince and Jim McConnell, and possibly also between Norman and Paul Rockwell. Jim's comments about Norman Prince's victory are also interesting. Prince had worked very hard to bring the Lafayette Escadrille into existence and understandably considered himself the "founder" of the unit. He was an aggressive pilot, and it must have been frustrating to him to have not yet scored a victory. On August 25, he attacked a German two-seater approximately ten miles behind the German lines. Most sources agree that he killed the observer and forced the pilot to land.[21] Some sources say Prince forced the German pilot to fly to French territory and land there, but there doesn't seem to be any evidence to support that theory. Noted World War I aviation historian Alan Toelle provides a more believable version of events: Norman Prince killed the observer and forced the German plane to land in the Bois d'Hingrey, about six miles behind the German lines.[22] That explanation is consistent with Jim McConnell's statement that the fight occurred so far behind the lines that nobody saw it. A plane that was forced to land within its own lines was usually not considered a victory, since neither the pilot nor the aircraft were destroyed. Nevertheless, even though the event was not confirmed by ground observers, Captain Thénault obtained a citation for Norman dated September 26, 1916,[23] which essentially confirmed it as a victory. Perhaps he did this as a favor to Norman, who had worked long and hard to secure a victory. And, of course, the publicity value of having the "founder" of the escadrille score a victory may have made it easier for Thénault to secure the citation.

Kiffin returned from his leave a few days after Norman Prince's victory and, not surprisingly, he was not happy about the way the captain had handled the incident. It's not known whether he joined Paul in lobbying for Thénault to be replaced while he was in Paris, but Kiffin had repeatedly complained about the fact that his unconfirmed victories weren't even being reported. It must have been particularly galling to him that Prince had witnessed Kiffin forcing an enemy plane to land but hadn't bothered to report it.[24] The idea that the captain would give Prince a medal for doing the same thing did not sit well with Kiffin. On September 1, 1916, Kiffin wrote to Paul:

> No one thinks Prince got a German, in fact, everyone is sure he didn't; yet the Captain proposed him for a citation, wanted to propose him for the Médaille, but everyone said if he did they would quit. I am going to have to murder him [Prince] when he gets back, as he talked awfully big about you and me behind my back when I was away. We have all agreed to try to run him out of the Escadrille.[25]

On a happier note, Bill Thaw was finally back with the escadrille. He initially returned without having bothered to go through the formal process of being released from the hospital. Thénault objected to his intention to fly missions with one arm still in a cast and sent him back to Paris. He returned within a week, minus the cast, and began flying patrols.[26] Also, Bert Hall scored his third confirmed victory on August 28, shooting down a German photographic reconnaissance aircraft northeast of Fort Douaumont.[27]

Kiffin's September 1 letter to his brother also contained news of an upcoming move:

> It has been bad weather ever since I have been back, except late yesterday afternoon. I went out then and found a number of Germans and fought with them for a long time, but couldn't do much as I was all alone.
>
> We are getting ready to leave here, and are going by Le Bourget, everyone to get new machines. Will be there two or three days, which time will be spent in Paris. Probably leave here in two or three days. I don't like it much for I lose all the work I have done here, as far as citations or anything go. If anyone asks you where we are going, say Dunkirk, although that is not right.

The escadrille pilots expected that they would be moved to the Somme, as the battle there had forced the Germans to concentrate their flying units on the Somme and it was becoming harder and harder to find German airplanes over Verdun. Kiffin had the presence of mind not to disclose their new destination in an unclassified letter, although, as it turned out, neither the destination nor the timing was what the pilots expected. In the meantime, the squadron continued to fly patrols over Verdun. Kiffin flew multiple patrols per day, searching for the increasingly elusive enemy aircraft.

Paul Pavelka didn't show as much concern over security as Kiffin, as he wrote to both Mrs. Weeks and Jim McConnell (who was in a hospital, getting frustrated because the doctors couldn't figure out what was wrong with his back) to say the squadron would be in Paris on Monday, September 4, on their way to the Somme. He also said the captain had recalled de Laage, Prince, and Lufbery from leave so they could move with the squadron.[28] The rumor that the squadron was going to depart on September 4 turned out to be false, which was probably just as well because de Laage, Prince, and Lufbery did not make it back to the squadron until September 8.

Since the squadron had not yet received any definite orders to move, the pilots continued to fly combat patrols over Verdun. Kiffin flew four patrols on September 3. The first patrol, with Bill Thaw, was uneventful. His second patrol, with Thaw and Pavelka, saw both Kiffin and Thaw engage enemy aircraft, but with no luck. When they returned, Kiffin refueled and almost immediately went out on a solo patrol. He attacked an enemy aircraft but had to break off combat when his machine gun jammed. Late that afternoon, Kiffin went on a patrol with Bill Thaw and Dudley Hill, but he had to return because of engine problems. (Thaw also returned for the same reason.) There was no flying on September 4 or 5 due to rain. On September 6, Kiffin spotted an enemy plane while flying a voluntary patrol, maneuvered into a favorable position, and had his machine gun jam after firing one bullet. He cleared the jam and attacked again, with the same result. Once more he cleared the jam and attacked, and once more his gun jammed. At this point he disengaged and returned to Behonne.

A few days later, the squadron's luck improved. In the morning, Norman Prince was flying a solo patrol when he spotted four enemy aircraft over Fort Rozelier. Another French pilot, Lieutenant V. Régnier of Escadrille N112, spotted the same aircraft, and together they attacked the rearmost airplane. The squadron had recently been equipped with new ammunition drums for the Lewis that held ninety-seven rounds, and Norman got behind the German and fired all ninety-seven rounds into the plane. The enemy plane rolled over and fell, trailing gray smoke. Norman and Lieutenant Régnier shared credit for this victory, which was confirmed by the same citation as Norman's first victory. A few minutes later, Norman attacked three planes over Ancemont, but he was forced to break contact and make an emergency landing at a nearby French airfield when a German bullet disabled his engine.

Later that same morning, Kiffin attacked an enemy two-seater at ten thousand feet over Vauquois. He killed the observer with his first burst, and the enemy pilot dove for home. Kiffin followed him down, firing intermittently, as his gun jammed three times during this pursuit. He had to pull out of the fight when he saw two other German planes diving to the rescue, but ground observers confirmed that his victim went down in the Boyeau des Houris.[29] This was Kiffin's second confirmed victory, although newspapers of the day proclaimed it his fourth. That evening, Kiffin wrote Paul to describe the fight:

Just a few lines. We have not left yet, but hope to be in Paris in a couple of days. This morning I attacked a Boche at 3000 meters high, killed the *observateur* [with] the first shot. After that followed the machine down to 1800 meters, riddling it with bullets. At that height I was attacked at very close range by two other German machines. I succeeded in getting back home. My first machine fell just in the German trenches, and the artillery fired on it.[30]

German records indicate this plane was probably a Roland C-II "Walfisch" (whale), which British ace Albert Ball once described as the best plane Germany had. The other two planes forced Kiffin to break off combat, but ground observers said the plane crashed and confirmed the victory. The plane did not crash, however, as the pilot apparently recovered at low altitude and made a forced landing. Neither the pilot (Unteroffizer Ruckdeschel) nor the observer (Lieutenant Brixle) were killed. Lieutenant Brixle had to be hospitalized for the injuries he sustained during the battle, but he recovered. The plane had a full load of bombs that Kiffin prevented them from delivering.[31]

The escadrille continued to fly patrols over the next couple of days. They had several combats, but without result. Then, on September 11, 1916, they turned their airplanes over to Escadrille N12 and caught a train to Paris.[32] For them, the Battle of Verdun was over. Captain Thénault summed up their experiences:

> Our Escadrille had become famous all over the world, but no one ever knew its real achievements, for many of the planes we brought down could not be added to our record, owing to the lack of necessary confirmation. We had fought 146 combats,[33] destroyed 13 enemies— officially sanctioned victories only. This record was not so bad. One pilot had been killed, three wounded, and four mechanics had been killed. . . . The Escadrille's baptism of fire at Verdun was an undying memory for all the pilots who took part in it, and the survivors always recalled this terrible period during which they scarcely had time to sleep or to eat; when they used to rest it was fully dressed in their flying suits beneath their planes, so as to be ready to start at the first glimpse of dawn. . . . These were the heroic days of the Escadrille, its glorious prime. Thaw, Prince, Lufbery, Rockwell, Chapman and the others, were you not worthy rivals of the greatest heroes of any age and country?[34]

15

Déjà-vu

Cut off from the land that bore us,
Betrayed by the land that we find,
The good men have gone before us,
And only the dull left behind.
So stand by your glasses steady,
The world is a web of lies.
Then here's to the dead already,
And hurrah for the next man who dies.

—MESS SONG OF THE LAFAYETTE ESCADRILLE

IN WARTIME FRANCE, ALL ROADS LED TO PARIS. OR AT LEAST, ALL ROADS traveled by pilots on leave. Infantry troops might sing about their "Mademoiselle from Armentières," but Paris was the gathering spot for aviators. They could afford the hotels, bars, theaters, and other sources of entertainment in the City of Lights, and they also enjoyed meeting other aviators to discuss shared experiences, evolving tactics, and the newest aircraft developments. Most of all, they enjoyed leaving the stress of combat behind them. For a few precious hours, they weren't faced with imminent death. They could forget about their fragile mortality and enjoy the pleasures of life. This was a rare treat for an individual pilot, but the move from Verdun gave the Lafayette pilots an extraordinary opportunity to spend seven days in Paris as a unit—to party with their friends. Captain Thénault described the situation:

The front was almost "no woman's land" but here in the Champs Elysées, everywhere women and girls were present. You were shot by admiring glances, cast from beautiful, unknown eyes at medals and uniforms, as you leisurely strolled on the graveled alleys or the asphalt curbs. Those looks made you almost believe you were a hero! An extra visit to Paris, all in a body, was appreciated as a special treat: on the regular leave, which came every four months, you had a sense of loneliness far from your friends of the battle front, and I have heard of soldiers who returned before their leave was up because they were homesick. My men had friends and acquaintances, of course, ready to take them about and help them, but they felt lost without their usual comrades.[1]

Most of the pilots stayed in hotels while they were in Paris. Kiffin and Paul Pavelka stayed with Paul Rockwell in Mrs. Weeks's apartment. (Mrs. Weeks was in England when they first arrived.) Regardless of where they slept, they gathered for lunch at the bar of the Chatham Hotel. There they met with other pilots who were on leave in Paris, pilots from the entire length of the Western Front. Sometimes they also met with reporters, although usually not by choice. Aviation was new and exciting in 1916, and combat aviation was one of the few colorful aspects of an otherwise brutal war. Reporters frequently visited the Chatham bar, hoping to pick up a story.

Sometimes pilots obliged the reporters, but not always with the truth. Aviation was a new science, and reporters knew nothing about airplanes or aerial warfare. If a reporter was pestering a pilot for a story, and the pilot had enjoyed a few martinis with his lunch, the pilot might be tempted to see how wild of a story the reporter would swallow. Usually the story involved a pilot who wasn't present, as that made it an opportunity to pull a prank on the absent pilot as well as on the reporter. Bill Thaw, for example, was amazed to read that he had once become so enraged by a German anti-aircraft battery that he landed his plane next to the battery, ripped the machine gun off his top wing, and wiped out the battery. Satisfied that the battery would pester him no more, he took off and resumed his patrol.[2]

Kiffin apparently missed one of the sessions at the Chatham Bar, as the following newspaper story appeared shortly after his Paris leave:

Kiffin Rockwell, another of the Esqaudrille [*sic*] Americaine, like Thaw, bagged three flyers in a single day, but they tell a story of him that is even more thrilling. As I heard it, he was once forced to descend behind the German lines and one of the Kaiser's aviators who had been following him at once swooped down and made him a prisoner. "You are a brave man," said the German, with that chivalry of the aerial fighters. "I shall not have you taken off by soldiers, but shall ride you back to our flying camp." And quite pleased at the prospect of bringing in a prisoner in his machine, the German made Rockwell climb into the observer's car in front of him. "I shall send soldiers to bring in your machine," the German remarked with an exasperating smile. "We shall be able to make good use of it." Rockwell ground his teeth. The German began his flight. He was about a thousand meters high when Rockwell began to shift in his seat, rocking the machine. In alarm, the German reached forward to tap him on the shoulder. "Stop," he shouted, "you'll upset us." But Rockwell had other ideas. Having lured the German into reach, he lunged backward with his arms, turned, clutched the German around the throat, choked him into unconsciousness (all the while the machine was hurtling through space eighty miles an hour), and then when he saw him collapse, Rockwell calmly worked the duplicate control and brought one German and one German machine into the French lines as prisoners. No wonder the French chose the Esquadrille Americaine for Verdun![3]

The squadron gained a new member in Paris, one who was destined to become at least as famous as any of its pilots. Bill Thaw was reading the Paris edition of the *New York Herald* and saw an ad posted by a Brazilian dentist who was selling a baby lion cub. The dentist had bought the cub, who was born in captivity, because he thought it would be a novelty that would attract patients to his office. Instead, it terrified them. Thaw got with Kiffin, Norman Prince, and Bert Hall, and together they raised the 500 francs needed to buy the cub.[4] Jim McConnell, who was still in the hospital because of his back problems, later wrote, "He was a cute, bright-eyed baby lion who tried to roar in a most threatening manner but who was blissfully content the moment one gave him one's finger to suck."[5] Shortly after they arrived at their next duty station, one of the pilots put a saucer of whiskey on the floor. The cub sniffed it warily at first but soon began to lap it up. Afterward, he "roared the way a lion should."[6] The lion was immediately named "Whiskey," and the squadron had a mascot. Jim McConnell wrote, "Whiskey got a good view of Paris during the few days he was there, for someone in the crowd was always borrowing him to take him some place.

He, like most lions in captivity, became acquainted with bars, but the sort 'Whiskey' saw were not for purposes of confinement."[7]

Kiffin seems to have been relaxed and happy during his leave in Paris. His quarrels with Thénault and his fellow pilots were apparently forgotten. Thénault wrote that "the joys of Paris were shared in the finest spirit of comradeship."[8] (To be fair, Thénault also wrote that at Verdun "a splendid spirit of solidarity prevailed" and "arguments were extremely rare."[9] He wrote that after the war, however, and time has a way of softening unpleasant memories.) Kiffin wrote to his mother on September 14, and his letter shows no hint of dissatisfaction. Perhaps the fact that Thénault had finally recommended him for promotion to *sous lieutenant* (under lieutenant—that is, second lieutenant) had something to do with it:

> Well, I am in Paris again. We stayed at Bar-le-Duc a week longer than we expected, but I didn't mind it, as last Saturday morning I brought down a German machine which fell in their first-line of trenches. I am proposed for Sous-Lieutenant for having done it, and am well pleased.
>
> We don't know where we are going and are waiting here for orders. But we are afraid that we are going to Luxeuil, where we were last spring. I like the town, but right now don't think there will be much work to do there so had rather go to the Somme.[10]

Kiffin's spirits may have been excellent, but photographs taken in Paris clearly show how stress had aged his body. He had always been thin (Bert Hall jokingly called him "the living hall tree" and said if he could just turn sideways, it would be impossible for the Germans to hit him),[11] but in Paris he almost looked emaciated.

In Kiffin's letter to his mother, he said the pilots were "afraid" they were going to Luxeuil-les-Bains, the location where they flew their first combat mission the previous May. That rumor was soon confirmed. Luxeuil was a wonderful location from the standpoint of comfort, but none of the pilots had any idea why the French needed a combat-hardened fighter squadron in Luxeuil. The battle of the Somme was still raging, and that's where the pilots felt they were needed.

Mrs. Weeks soon returned from England and was surprised to see her new house guests—one in particular. She wrote to her son Allen, "I found a number of the boys home when I returned. They have bought a small lion cub which was advertised in the New York Herald. My cook told me she was frightened to death, as they brought it immediately to the apartment and it paced up and down the salon with a very good imitation of a roar."[12]

The week in Paris wasn't totally a pleasure trip, as several of the pilots visited the Nieuport factory and testing grounds, roughly a twenty-minute drive from Paris. There they discussed their needs with aircraft designers, gave them feedback on what they thought of the current aircraft, and saw what was on the drawing boards for the future. They also got a good look at the latest version of the Nieuport 17, the plane they would be flying at Luxeuil. This plane could climb nearly twice as fast as the Nieuport 11 and was twelve miles per hour faster in level flight. Most important, it had a belt-fed Vickers .303 caliber machine gun mounted directly in front of the pilot. No more changing Lewis drums in flight! Or at least that was the promise. Unfortunately, the early Vickers guns were even more likely to jam than the Lewis, and some jams were impossible to clear in flight. When the squadron received their new planes at Luxeuil, they elected to mount a Lewis gun on the top wing for use as a backup in case the Vickers failed.[13] When the Vickers worked, it was a much better weapon. The belt held five hundred rounds, enough for nearly a minute's continuous firing. Since it was mounted in front of the pilot, it was easier to aim and easier to clear simple jams while in flight.[14]

One of the escadrille pilots didn't share in the Paris adventure. Raoul Lufbery had a *marraine* (godmother) in Chartres, and he asked Captain Thénault whether he could visit her. The unit's orders specified they were to go to Paris en route to their next duty station and Thénault couldn't approve a change in destination, but he unofficially told Lufbery that he could travel to Paris by way of Chartres. Chartres is roughly fifty miles southwest of Paris, so only a very circuitous route from Verdun to Paris would go through Chartres, but they didn't think anyone would question it. A French railway official proved them wrong. As Lufbery was boarding a train to go from Chartres to Paris to join the other pilots, this official questioned Lufbery about his leave status. Lufbery, who was wearing an impressive array of medals on his uniform, was insulted that this civilian would imply that he, a veteran of more combat than the railway official ever dreamed of, was absent without leave. When the official put his hand on Lufbery, Lufbery put his hand on the official. The difference was that Lufbery's hand left the official unconscious and missing a few teeth.

Thénault's holiday in Paris was interrupted by a telegram informing him that his highest-scoring pilot was in jail. Fortunately, he was able to convince the Chartres officials that the cause of justice and the cause of France would be served best if this very effective *American* pilot spent the next thirty days fighting Germans in the skies over the Western Front instead of languishing in a Chartres jail.[15]

On September 17, Mrs. Weeks woke up at 4:00 a.m., worrying because Kiffin and Pavelka had to return to the front that morning. She tossed and turned until 6:00 a.m., and then she got up to make their breakfast. Afterward, she saw them off to the train station. Later that day, she wrote her son Allen, "Kiffin has brought down another German machine, and has another palm, and has been made Sous-Lieutenant, and now I have to be very polite to him."[16] (Kiffin hadn't actually been promoted yet; he'd just been recommended for promotion.)

When the pilots boarded the train, Whiskey sat quietly on Bill Thaw's lap. Bill assured the conductor that Whiskey was a dog. When the conductor asked what kind of a dog, Bill replied, "An African dog." At that point Whiskey roared and bared his claws. Passengers screamed, and Bill was forced to take Whiskey off the train. Bill built a cage for Whiskey and accompanied him in the baggage car the following day.[17]

At Luxeuil, the pilots were quartered in the Grand Hôtel de la Pomme d'Or (Golden Apple Hotel), an elegant family business run by a man named Auguste Groscolas.[18] Captain Thénault was very impressed by this hotel, describing it as

> a perfect example of the "hostelleries" of old France, the owners of which succeed one another from father to son in unbroken line for centuries; every visitor there was treated as a member of the family! The cooking was unexcelled—delicious trout from neighboring streams, fat luscious chickens, game, hares, wild fowl, dishes carefully concocted by a chef too old to go to war, who considered his work an art; lunches and dinners washed down with a generous Burgundy wine, whose aroma alone was a delight! And withal extraordinarily cheap: "Board and lodging, four francs a day."[19]

Whiskey seemed to appreciate the accommodations too: "At the Pomme d'Or Hotel 'Whisky' won the hearts of the two attractive daughters of the proprietor. They put a pink ribbon around his neck, and took great trouble to find out what he liked best to eat. His preferences? After several experiments it was discovered that he had a strong inclination for a mixture of bread and milk."[20]

It was fortunate that the pilots were quartered in a good hotel, as there was little for them to do except enjoy their surroundings. Once again, they had no airplanes. Bill Thaw went trout fishing in the local streams, Lufbery hunted mushrooms, and Kiffin chafed at the forced idleness.

It didn't take long for the pilots to figure out why they had been sent to Luxeuil. In addition to Captain Happe's bomb squadron, there were now dozens of British bombers, more than fifty pilots, and roughly a thousand enlisted men at the Luxeuil airfield. Mostly Canadians, the men made up the Number 3 Wing of the Royal Naval Air Service (RNAS).[21] The RNAS was at Luxeuil to launch a massive long-range strategic bombing raid against the German Mauser factory at Oberndorf. Both sides had engaged in tactical bombing—that is, attacking military targets and transportation hubs that directly supported a battle, since the war began. Strategic bombing, however, was intended to destroy the enemy's ability to wage war by knocking out key industrial targets that supported their war effort. Captain Happe and other pioneers had been doing this on a small scale for a long time. Strongly encouraged by First Lord of the Admiralty Winston Churchill, the RNAS intended to do this on a large scale.[22]

Just as the escadrille had been sent to Luxeuil in April to provide protection for Captain Happe's French bombardment squadron, they were now expected to provide protection for this much larger bomber force. But their ability to do that would have to wait until they had airplanes. In the meantime, they hunted, fished, fretted, and organized dances in Luxeuil. Captain Thénault described the latter as follows: "At Luxeuil we organized dances in a big hotel, and often danced one steps and waltzes, or initiated our unsophisticated partners, young ladies of Luxeuil, to the new steps of the fox trot. If you told them that you knew the tango, then you were wonderful."[23]

The pilots, however, didn't seem to recall these elegant dances as vividly as they recalled their parties with the RNAS pilots. British flying units have long had a reputation for destroying crockery and otherwise cutting loose during squadron parties, and the Canadian pilots at Luxeuil upheld this tradition. Bert Hall tells some probably exaggerated tales of flying glassware and drunken target practice in his memoirs, but even Thénault admitted that things got a bit raucous when the RNAS invited the Lafayette pilots to dinner at their mess. Fortunately, the RNAS mess was an improvised wooden structure and not the elegant dining room of the Pomme d'Or. Thénault wrote, "I remember one Homeric football match between British and Americans, played about midnight with all lights out in the English-men's shed. Following a scrimmage the walls yielded to our shoulders and the players stumbled head over heels outside. The reader can imagine the condition of the furniture and the shed. Personally I felt deeply gratified that our quarters had not been selected for the game."[24]

On a personal level, the RNAS pilots and the Lafayette pilots got along great. On a professional level, the RNAS pilots were not impressed with the training, teamwork, and especially leadership of the Lafayette Escadrille. One Canadian pilot commented:

From the point of view of discipline, the situation was practically impossible for the French. Imagine a body of financially well-off Americans—basking in the knowledge they were volunteers from a neutral country—who habitually played no-limit poker, who imported unlimited booze and food and who comprised a body of men far superior educationally and possessing a far greater experience of the world than their French companions in arms—a French commander would have experienced great difficulty controlling such a body of men if they had been French citizens and fully subject to French army regulations. The pilots gave the impression of being very war-like, even amongst themselves. . . . There was a tendency to resolve themselves into cliques, wherein individuals of similar tendencies grouped and lambasted the others. Consequently, teamwork suffered. Although the early members of the Escadrille comprised pilots of high potential in every way . . . their French commander seemed helpless to cope with such independent, high-spirited men. Moreover, the French Army Administration, not unnaturally, were very anxious to sustain sympathetic responses in the United States. The general result was that the American pilots enjoyed a wide measure of freedom of action.[25]

Aviation historian Arch Whitehouse, who was himself a World War I pilot and who flew with the British throughout the war, agreed with this assessment. He was not a member of the No. 3 Wing at Luxeuil, but later in the war he was stationed on the same airfield as the Lafayette Escadrille. He blamed the French training schools in particular for emphasizing individual combat instead of formation flying and team tactics. He said the Americans were not unaware of these shortcomings, and that Bill Thaw, Raoul Lufbery, and Didier Masson in particular spent hours visiting British squadrons to discuss flying strategy and tactics.[26]

Fortunately, the Lafayette pilots didn't have to wait weeks for their airplanes to arrive, as they had during their first visit to Luxeuil. Six brand-new Nieuport 17s arrived on September 19.[27] As before, they arrived disassembled and couldn't be flown until the mechanics assembled them. The mechanics said they could have the first two planes ready to fly in three days. It made sense to concentrate on getting two planes ready, as, although they had received six planes, they had only received ammunition belts for two. Thénault assigned the first two planes to Kiffin and to Raoul Lufbery.

The next day Kiffin wrote to Paul. While it was obvious Luxeuil wasn't his first choice, he seemed to have accepted the fact that they would be there for a while and he was ready to take it easy over the coming winter:

Received your letter this morning. The weather has been cold and bad ever since we arrived here. I have gotten my machine, which is the best they have, and have fixed it up with two machine-guns [i.e., installed a Lewis on the top wing in addition to the factory Vickers]. But I don't expect much work here, as I think the weather is going to be bad most of the time. I found a number of people glad to see me back, and think that I can get along all right if we are forced to stay for the winter.

At present am staying at this hotel [letter written on Pomme d'Or stationery] but am looking around for a nice quiet little place to live, unless Captain Happe tries to make us live at the field, which will be foolish.

Nothing new of my promotion. Should hear now in a few days. If I don't you must see that Mon. L. pushes it through. The Captain said that the only thing that could stop it was that a foreigner was supposed to have the grade of sous-off. [under-officer—that is, NCO] for one year before passing officer, unless he came to France as an officer, but that is bull.[28]

Kiffin's letter referenced a note from Paul that he had received that morning, but that note has not survived. Chances are it included a birthday greeting, as September 20 was Kiffin's birthday. He was twenty-four years old.

On the following day, Kiffin wrote to Jim McConnell, who was still in the hospital:

> On arriving here found everyone surprised but glad to see me and they have all asked about you and send their best regards. I have not as yet seen Rosa but if I do I will tell her you are on your way here. All the same old girls are here but some a little worked out after the summer.... So far we have six machines for the escadrille, all of them Vickers, but we haven't the cartridge bands for them. . . . From now on here it will be bad weather and no flying, so take your time and get fixed up right.[29]

On September 22, the mechanics had two Nieuports ready to fly, as promised. Captain Happe had asked Thénault not to let his pilots fly any patrols before the raid on the Mauser factory, as he didn't want the Germans to see new planes in the air and get suspicious. Thénault refused to ground his pilots, especially since there was still no date scheduled for the Mauser raid. He explained this decision in his book: "But how could two such ardent souls like Lufbery and Rockwell be held in restraint when they had at their disposal superb machines, fitted with the latest devices?"[30]

Kiffin and Lufbery made two patrols that day, a short morning patrol over Mulhouse and a longer evening patrol over Mulhouse, Altkirch, and Guebwiller. All of these locations were behind the German lines, but apparently they didn't even see a German plane during their patrols. The operations log doesn't even include the customary "RAS" entry for *rien à signaler* (nothing to report). Nevertheless, it was obvious that Kiffin was happy to get back in the air again. His mechanic, Michel Plaa-Porte, took a photograph of him standing next to his new plane, and the smile on his careworn face clearly shows he was a happy man. At some point during this period he visited a woman in town and gave her his *Fix Bijou* pin, a gilt metal eagle worn over the left breast pocket. This was not an official Air Service insignia, but it was often worn by French pilots, and photos of Kiffin clearly show him wearing this pin.[31]

Even though they had encountered no opposition during their patrols, the flights over enemy lines reminded Kiffin of just how dangerous their occupation was. After dinner that night he turned to Paul Pavelka and said, "Paul, if I'm ever shot down make sure I'm buried where I fall. And just in case I am killed, I want you all to take whatever money you happen to find on me and drink to the destruction of the damned Boche."[32]

The next morning, Kiffin and Lufbery again flew a patrol over the enemy lines. Near Hartmannswillerkopf they encountered three Fokkers. Thénault described the battle:

> Kiffin and Lufbery ran into a patrol of three Fokkers, evidently being flown by very skillful and experienced pilots. Almost as soon as the fight began, Lufbery's gun jammed. This was all too common with the early Vickers guns, as the canvas belts, freezing oil, and vibrations frequently caused jams. Lufbery and Rockwell managed to disengage, but a bullet broke a wing spar in Lufbery's plane. Kiffin escorted him back to Fontaine.[33]

Lufbery landed at Fontaine to have his wing spar repaired and to clear the jam in his Vickers machine gun. Kiffin remained in the air, and once he saw that Lufbery had landed safely, he headed back to the German lines, looking for trouble. He soon found it. Kiffin was flying at about twelve thousand feet when he spotted a German Albatros two-seat observation plane well below him. The German was flying over Roderen, just a few miles from where Kiffin had shot down his first plane the previous May. The situation was very similar to that previous victory, except this time the German plane was still over French territory. None of the planes Kiffin had shot down, confirmed or unconfirmed, had come down on the French side of the lines. He had often written about how he wanted to down a plane on the French side of the lines, where there could be no doubt about confirmation.

We'll never know what made Kiffin decide to plunge into a headlong attack instead of stalking the plane to get into a more favorable position. Perhaps that was just his style, although it's doubtful that he could have lived through the scores of dogfights he had already survived if he attacked every plane he saw with reckless abandon. Maybe this situation reminded him so much of his first victory that he tried to repeat that feat. Maybe he was feeling invulnerable because he had a new plane with a synchronized machine gun. Maybe he hadn't fully recovered from the months of stress at Verdun, threw caution to the winds, and rushed in to shoot down the

German plane before it could cross the lines. In any event, Kiffin put his plane into a dive and headed straight for the enemy plane, ignoring the machine gun fire from the observer. A French infantry officer watched the battle through field glasses. Once again, Kiffin held his fire until a collision seemed imminent. Only then did he begin firing. The German plane jerked violently and the infantry officer thought it had been hit, but it was just maneuvering to avoid a collision. Kiffin's plane nosed down and began an even steeper dive. The hands that should have controlled it were now lifeless. A wing broke off at ten thousand feet and fluttered slowly to the ground. The plane began to spin violently until it slammed into the earth just behind the French lines, near the village of Roderen. French artillerymen braved the threat of German fire to retrieve Kiffin's body and carry it to a civilian doctor in Roderen. A gaping hole in Kiffin's chest showed that he must have died long before he hit the ground.[34]

The civilian doctor called Captain Thénault and told him Kiffin Rockwell had been killed. The captain gathered his pilots together and tearfully announced, "The best and bravest of us all is no longer here."[35] Thénault sent a car to Roderen to retrieve Kiffin's body. Bill Thaw traveled to Paris to notify Paul Rockwell and Mrs. Weeks in person. While he was in Paris, he sent a telegram to Mr. Jacob Susong, Loula Rockwell's brother-in-law, and asked him to tell Loula that Kiffin had been killed.[36] Unfortunately, Loula had temporarily left her home in Asheville, North Carolina, and was staying in Winston-Salem at the time, so Mr. Susong was not able to break the news to her in person. Instead, she received a telegram from an influential friend of the family in Paris that said simply "Kiffin Rockwell killed this morning in aerial battle in Alsace."[37] Only a few hours earlier, she had received the letter that Kiffin had written her while he was on leave in Paris, in which he said he was afraid there would not be much work to do in Luxeuil.[38]

The following day, Paul Rockwell accompanied Bill Thaw when he returned to Luxeuil. Thénault took Paul to the crash site, where the wreckage of Kiffin's plane still lay where it had fallen. They approached it cautiously, as it was within sight of German artillery spotters, but the gunners left them alone as they stared at the wreckage in silent grief.[39]

Kiffin had asked to be buried where he fell, but that was impossible. The crash site was within sight of the German lines, and any large gathering would be certain to draw fire. Despite Kiffin's aversion to publicity, his death made headlines all over the world, and the French could not pass up the opportunity to gain support from the American public through a lavish funeral. More important than that, his fellow pilots needed closure. Jim McConnell wrote, "No greater blow could have befallen the escadrille. Kiffin was its soul. He was loved and looked up to by not only every man in our flying corps but by every one who knew him."[40] Lieutenant de Laage said, "Kiffin was for me a veritable friend, and he was more, the bravest man I ever met."[41] Bert Hall wrote that, as Kiffin's frequent flying partner, de Laage was a wreck. Bert said he himself felt like a sonovabitch because he wasn't there to help when Kiffin dove to attack, and he kept thinking about how Kiffin was alive and having a great time at the RNAS party just a few nights before.[42]

Raoul Lufbery, uncharacteristically, let his emotions override his careful approach to aerial combat when he learned Kiffin had been killed. He took off and flew to the German aerodrome at Habsheim, daring any German to come up and fight.[43] Fortunately, none of them took the bait, as Lufbery was alone. None of the other pilots could have accompanied him, as he was the only pilot with a flyable airplane and with ammunition for its machine gun. The fact that they had no way to avenge Kiffin's death aggravated the pilots' grief and frustration.

Paul Pavelka wrote to Jim McConnell, "God almighty! Jim I feel terribly broken up about Kiffin's death. Today Paul, the Captain, and I went down to where he fell and looked at that sacred piece of earth."[44]

Charles "Chute" Johnson wrote to his mother to describe how he felt:

Yesterday we were bereaved of one of our comrades and best pilots, Kiffin Rockwell. While flying over the lines he attacked a German plane and was brought down. . . . I am awfully upset about it as he was one of my best friends in the Escadrille and we went around a lot together. There isn't space to tell you what a man he was. A man all the way through, hard to know at first but once your friend he would stick all the way through. Brave to the core, never flinching. . . . You may wonder why I write at such length about a fellow you don't know from Adam. Simply to let you and everyone know the type of Americans giving their all for a cause which is for the freedom of the world over a greedy, foul enemy who carries on warfare in a way the savage would be ashamed of.[45]

Norman Prince wrote to Mrs. Weeks in the name of the entire squadron:

> For the loss of poor Kiffin we wish to express to you the deepest sympathy of all of us. We have lost a friend, one of us, and the best one of us. You have, however, lost more than us, lost one who was probably as dear to you as would be your own son. Our heartfelt sympathy goes forth to you and his brother Paul in your bereavement over his loss.[46]

On September 25, 1916, Kiffin Rockwell's body was laid to rest in a lavish funeral at the Luxeuil-les-Bains cemetery. Jim McConnell described it thus:

> He was given a funeral worthy of a general. His brother, Paul, who had fought in the Legion with him, and who had been rendered unfit for service by a wound, was granted permission to attend the obsequies. Pilots from all near-by camps flew over to render homage to Rockwell's remains. Every Frenchman in the aviation at Luxeuil marched behind the bier. The British pilots, followed by a detachment of five hundred of their men, were in line, and a battalion of French troops brought up the rear. As the slow moving procession of blue and khaki-clad men passed from the church to the graveyard, airplanes circled at a feeble height above and showered down myriads of flowers.[47]

Kiffin's orders for promotion to sous lieutenant had finally come through, and he was posthumously awarded this rank. (After the war he was also made a Chevalier [Knight] in the Legion of Honor.)[48]

Captain Thénault gave an emotional eulogy to Kiffin at the grave site, including phrases such as

> Never did Rockwell consider that he had done enough. His courage was sublime and when the flights prescribed by the Commandant were accomplished he would set out again on his "Baby," barely allowing his mechanic time to refill his tanks. . . . He was a great soldier with a high sense of duty. This he accomplished simply and valiantly, without boasting and without ambition. "I am paying my part of our debt to Lafayette and Rochambeau," he would say. He gave himself to France

and for France he sacrificed himself. . . . And to thee, our best friend, in the name of France I bid thee a last farewell. In the name of thy comrades, who have so often proved that they know how to keep their promises, I salute thee reverently.[49]

During his eulogy Thénault also paid tribute to Kiffin's herculean efforts at Verdun. Recalling General Nivelle's stirring orders ("They shall not pass!") to the defenders of Verdun, Thénault said, "Where Rockwell was, the German could not pass." He might well have added, as Jim McConnell did later, "and he was over their lines most of the time."[50]

After the funeral, Paul Rockwell and Norman Prince patched up their differences. Paul Pavelka described it as "Norman Prince apologized, and Paul's kind heart, forgave him for all the injustice that he had done."[51] A few days later, Paul took a train back to Paris. Under his arm he carried a box with Kiffin's personal effects, including the Médaille Militaire, a Croix de Guerre, some personal letters, a fountain pen, a silver cigarette case that had been crushed and twisted, and a wristwatch with the hands stopped at 9:50.[52]

Loula Rockwell received many letters of condolence. Some were from Kiffin's fellow pilots and his friends in the Legion. A letter from Lieutenant Pechkoff is particularly eloquent. Pechkoff was one of Kiffin's friends in the Legion and was later commissioned in recognition of his heroic actions. After explaining how he came to know Paul and Kiffin, he wrote, "I do not intend to speak to you words of consolation—a mother of such a noble hero must be heroic herself."[53] Although the handwriting in the letter is beautiful, he added, somewhat apologetically, that he was writing the note with his left hand because his right arm had recently been amputated at the shoulder.

Letters of condolence also came from friends in the United States. Some were from people who had never met Kiffin but felt as if they knew him because they had followed his exploits in the newspapers. One letter from Huntersville, North Carolina, shows how the publicity given to the Lafayette Escadrille was influencing America's views of the war. That letter read in part:

I have followed his career through the papers so closely that he seemed to be a friend instead of one whom I'd never met. While you cannot but feel keenly so great a loss still there should be a great consolation in the fact that your boy met so gallant a death fighting for right and at the same time helping pay American debt to good old France. Reading the exploits of Kiffin should stir up the blood of patriotism in all the young men of our land. I thank God that North Carolina can call Kiffin Rockwell one of her sons.[54]

These letters reside today in the North Carolina Historical Archives in Raleigh.[55] Looking at the addresses, one can see how famous Kiffin and his mother were, as many letters were delivered to her with an incomplete or incorrect address. One envelope said, "street number not known but this is for the mother of Kiffin Rockwell the aviator." A note from a nurse in France, who had attended Kiffin after he was wounded in May 1915, was addressed to "Mrs. Rockwell—the aviator's mother—Atlanta, Georgia, USA." It was delivered in spite of being addressed to the wrong city and the wrong state. The nurse told Mrs. Rockwell, "I like my country very dearly and admire our brave French soldiers. Still, how much more to be admired are those who could have remained absolutely out of the war and instead, came forward for the triumph of a great ideal: freedom and civilization!"

Mrs. Weeks in Paris also received many letters of condolence. She felt as though she had lost a second son to the war, and she lost this son very suddenly. A few days after Kiffin was killed, she wrote to her brother and commented, "Only Sunday he was singing around the house."[56]

Among all the letters of condolence that were written, a letter from Billy Thorin was surprisingly eloquent. Billy was the legionnaire who was always getting into bar fights, who stole the heart of Mrs. Weeks's maid, and the man who decided he'd rather spend eight days in jail than spend the ten francs Paul Rockwell had given him to "fix things up" with his corporal. Billy had been wounded again, and he wrote to Mrs. Weeks from the hospital:

I can pretty well imagine how you feel about it. Even a fellow like me that has seen all kinds of sights and lost plenty of comrades both on land and at sea, cannot help feeling sorry, because it ain't every day you meet fellows like Kiffin. At the same time we must remember it is war. Kiffin knew very well what he was doing when he joined this outfit; but like a man he done his duty. Yes, even more than his duty as he wasn't obliged to serve this country, but being a man and knowing right from wrong, he couldn't stand out of it, so I think you would rather sooner like to see any of us die like men than be cowards and hide behind neutrality.[57]

~

After Kiffin's funeral, the escadrille pilots decided they'd like to decorate Kiffin's gravesite with a fence and some landscaping. It took several days to make the arrangements, but eventually everything was ready. When they got to the gravesite, however, they met with a surprise. Paul Pavelka described the incident in a letter to Paul Rockwell:

Lufbery and I met with a great surprise to-day. We had fixed it up with the Parc de Aviation [engineers responsible for the airfield] for three carpenters, and lumber, to arrange Kiffin's grave. This morning we went down to commence working on it, and on arriving there found that some one had beaten us to it. I was there yesterday with Dudley, and everything was still untouched, but this a.m. it is all changed. All of the flowers are removed and the grave itself trimmed up most wonderfully. We asked the man in charge of the cemetery and he told us a gardener from town had been there, very early this a.m. and had arranged it. So we were obliged to lay aside our plans. Then we went to town and found the florist who had done the work and he told us that a lady, who had come from Paris the day after the funeral, had left orders for him to take care of the grave, and to place cut flowers on it every week. He refused to tell us who she was, only saying, that she was a cousin of Kiffin. Do you by any possible chance know who it could be? If so, would you please let us know, that the boys and I could thank her for her kind interest in Kiffin? To us it is all a mystery. We shall leave it as is with the exception of adding cut flowers from time to time.[58]

Just who this "cousin" of Kiffin's was remains a mystery to this day.

Epilogue

In May 2014, my wife and I celebrated our thirtieth anniversary by seeing whatever sights in Europe caught our fancy. Among the sights that caught my fancy were battlefields at Verdun and the Somme, and the town of Luxeuil-les-Bains. (I have a very understanding wife.) I hadn't yet started to research this book, or even decided for certain that I would write a book, but I have had a lifelong interest in Kiffin Rockwell and the Lafayette Escadrille. The Lafayette Escadrille still exists as a French Air Force unit, and until recently they flew Mirage jets out of Luxeuil. My purpose in visiting Luxeuil was not to visit the airfield, however, but to pay my respects to Kiffin. I had downloaded a very rough sketch from the internet that showed the location of the cemetery. My wife had saved a handful of roses from the anniversary bouquet I'd given her a few days previously, and she planned to place those flowers on Kiffin's grave. We wandered through the town following the map, and on a cloudy afternoon we found the cemetery. Once inside, among the weathered markers of generations of Luxeuil families, we saw rows of white crosses marking the graves of World War I soldiers. I began looking at the dates on the crosses, hoping to discover a pattern that would help me find Kiffin's grave. It was a classic case of not being able to see the forest for the trees. Only after examining multiple crosses did I notice that, near the center of the military section, there were two tall flagpoles flying the French tricolor—the flag Kiffin was serving when he gave his life. They flanked a single grave, one with memorial plaques in addition to the traditional military cross. It was Kiffin's grave. The French were paying special homage to the American volunteer who gave his life for France.

My wife and I approached the grave and were astonished to discover that a fresh bouquet of flowers had recently been placed at his grave by a veteran's group from the current Lafayette Escadrille. It wasn't a French holiday; they had placed the flowers there in observance of our American Memorial Day. It had been nearly one hundred years since Kiffin's death, but the French people had not forgotten him.

As my wife knelt down to place her flowers on his grave we heard the rumble of aircraft above us. We looked up and saw two jets, flying in formation, as if keeping watch over their fallen comrade. They were too high up for us to see any markings, but the military formation was unmistakable.

Billy Thorin was right. It ain't every day you meet fellows like Kiffin.

Notes

Chapter 1: The Education of an Idealist

1. Rockwell, *War Letters of Kiffin Yates Rockwell*, xvii. Paul described this lunch as occurring on the last Sunday in July, but he goes on to say that the next day was August 3. His sequence of events and a subsequent entry in the *Atlanta Journal* make it clear that the lunch probably took place on August 2. He also said the lunch was in their apartment, but that's at odds with a later conversation where he told historian Arch Whitehouse that the conversation was "overheard" by a nearby reporter.
2. "Three Young Atlantians Would Shoulder Arms in Defense of France," *Atlanta Journal*.
3. Whitehouse, *Legion of the Lafayette*, 41
4. Rockwell, *War Letters of Kiffin Yates Rockwell*, xviii.
5. "Paul Ayres Rockwell," *Sigma Phi Epsilon Journal*, 136.
6. "Lincoln Opposed by Three Generations," unknown newspaper clipping; Dickert, *History of Kershaw's Brigade*.
7. Rockwell, *Three Centuries of the Rockwell Family in America*, 81. In this book Paul Rockwell states that all of Enoch Shaw's younger brothers and sisters died during this epidemic, but ancestry records show that one younger sister survived the war, along with two older sisters and an older brother.
8. Ibid., 82.
9. Ibid., 83.
10. "Lincoln Opposed by Three Generations," unknown newspaper clipping.
11. "The Rockwell Family in America," North Carolina State Archives; House, "Kiffin Yates Rockwell," *Documenting the South* (online), 152.
12. Biographical information from Tucker, "Rockwell, James Chester," *NCpedia* (online), and an unpublished biography of Kiffin Rockwell written by Loula Rockwell in the North Carolina State Archives.
13. "History of First Baptist Church," *Cocke County Banner*.
14. Tucker, "Rockwell, Kiffin Yates," *NCpedia* (online).
15. There are various stories as to the origin of Kiffin's name. The *North Carolina Booklet* claims he was named Kiffin in honor of William Kiffin, an English home missionary

in the fifteenth century who was a key figure in the founding of the Baptist Church, and Yates for Mathew Yates, a foreign missionary from North Carolina in the nineteenth century. Other sources say he was named in honor of two of his father's favorite poets. While the poet explanation seems more logical given his father's interests, it's hard to identify famous poets with the name "Kiffin" or "Yates." Kiffin's great-grandmother's maiden name was Yates, and it's possible that Kiffin was also the name of a family friend or relative, but none are known. Kiffin is extremely unusual as a first name. An electronic search of all digitized newspapers in the Library of Congress from 1900 to 1916 does not reveal anyone except Kiffin Rockwell with "Kiffin" as a first name.

16. "Dr. Loula Rockwell Dies Here at Age 92," *Asheville Citizen*.
17. "Addenda to Rockwell Material," North Carolina State Archives.
18. "Mountain Topics," *Asheville Citizen-Times*.
19. Wynne, "History of the Escadrille Lafayette."
20. "Skill in Riding Bucking Pony Revealed Kiffin Rockwell's Will to Fly," *Newport Plain Talk*.
21. Ibid.
22. "Local Happenings," *Newport Plain Talk*, December 4, 1902.
23. "Local Happenings," *Newport Plain Talk*, July 13, 1901.
24. "Local Happenings," *Newport Plain Talk*, September 21, 1905.
25. "Local Happenings," *Newport Plain Talk*, July 10, 1902.
26. "Local Happenings," *Newport Plain Talk*, May 4, 1901.
27. "Newport's Kiffin Rockwell Carried on Family's Military Tradition," *Newport Plain Talk*, January 28, 2010.
28. "Paul Ayres Rockwell," 136.
29. Marc McClure interview with Vance Brown, Asheville, NC, May 9, 2017.
30. Loula Rockwell, unpublished biography of Kiffin Rockwell, 2, North Carolina State Archives.
31. March 10, 2016, email to the author from the Registrar's Office, A. T. Still University, Kirksville, Missouri.
32. Letterhead on multiple letters from Loula and Agnes Rockwell, Washington and Lee University.
33. Interview with Paul Rockwell by Louis D. Silveri, 22.
34. Herring, "If I Had a Dozen Sons I Should Want Them to Fight for France," *Philadelphia Public Ledger*.
35. "Paul Ayres Rockwell," 136.
36. Washington and Lee University, *Catalog* for 1909, 208; and 1910, 198.
37. Wellesley College, *Legenda, 1912*.
38. House, "Kiffin Yates Rockwell," 152.
39. Loula Rockwell to Robert B. House, August 4, 1920, North Carolina State Archives.
40. "Addenda to Rockwell Material." This document may have been notes taken by Mr. House after reviewing an early draft with Loula.
41. Loula Rockwell to Supt. Hunter Pendleton, undated, VMI Archives.
42. Virginia Military Institute, *Official Register*, 1905–1906, 49.
43. VMI Class Standings, 1908–1909 school year, provided by Virginia Military Institute.

44. Robert N. Bond to his father, September 12, 1915, Robert N. Bond Collection, Manuscript # 0435, VMI Archives.

45. Rockwell, *War Letters of Kiffin Yates Rockwell*, xiii.

46. Ibid., xiii.

47. Ibid., xiv.

48. "Paul Ayres Rockwell," 137.

49. Loula Rockwell, unpublished biography, 2, North Carolina State Archives.

50. Rockwell, *War Letters of Kiffin Yates Rockwell*, xv.

51. Family lore says that Kiffin decided to move to Atlanta because Loula caught him in a pool hall and was so incensed that he would frequent such a place that she drove him out with a horsewhip. Supposedly, this caused a family rift and Kiffin never saw her again (author's interview with Vance Brown, Kiffin's grand-nephew). While the story is probably based upon a true event, it may have grown in the retelling over the years. Loula was certainly strict, but there are no other stories of her being violent. Paul and Kiffin returned to Asheville a few months after this incident and there did not appear to be any rift, as they asked Loula to move to Atlanta and live with them (Loula Rockwell to Kiffin and Paul Rockwell, July 6, 1916, Washington and Lee University). This incident is not mentioned in any of the surviving letters from Kiffin, Loula, or Paul, and the letters between Kiffin and Loula certainly do not indicate there were any hard feelings between them.

52. Craig, "Paul Rockwell Tells Story of Kiffin's Death," *Atlanta Constitution*.

53. Mason, *Lafayette Escadrille*, 11.

54. US Passport #39116, Washington and Lee University.

55. Before World War I, US passports did not include a photograph. Photographs would not be required until after the war began and Allied governments complained that German reservists in the United States were using other people's passports to return to Germany (see Blum, *Dark Invasion*, 86). The passport Kiffin obtained in 1914 wasn't even labeled as a passport; it was a "to whom it may concern" letter stating that Kiffin was a citizen of the United States and should be allowed to freely pass to other countries.

56. Enoch Shaw Ayres estate records, Dillon County, South Carolina.

57. Summary of Kiffin Rockwell by St. Elmo Massengale, September 1, 1917, North Carolina State Archives.

58. Rockwell, *War Letters of Kiffin Yates Rockwell*, 116. Paul included this phrase in his published version of Kiffin's February 17, 1916, letter to his mother, and it has been widely quoted. However, the original copy of that letter in the North Carolina State Archives does not include this phrase. Paul often deleted extraneous or unflattering passages from Kiffin's letters when he published them in *War Letters*, and he sometimes toned down Kiffin's colorful language, but he did not, as a rule, insert new material. The key may lie in a note Loula inserted with Kiffin's letters when she donated them to the North Carolina State Archives: "Most of Kiffin's letters to me are of such an intimate personal nature that I can not let them be open to public eyes. These contain enough of his life and experiences to show any one interested something of Kiffin's life and ideals from Aug 6-1914 to Sept-1916." It is possible that Kiffin included the sentence about fighting for the cause of all humanity in one of the letters that Loula did not want to share with the public, but she allowed Paul to instead insert it in a different letter.

Chapter 2: War!

1. Lamszus, *The Human Slaughter-House*.
2. Ferguson, *The Pity of War*, 8.
3. Rockwell, *American Fighters in the Foreign Legion*, 5.
4. Tuchman, *The Guns of August*, 123.
5. Liddell Hart, *The Real War 1914–1918*, 100.
6. Tuchman, *The Guns of August*, 32.
7. Horne, *The Price of Glory*, 12.
8. Kiffin Rockwell to Loula Rockwell, August 6, 1914, North Carolina State Archives.
9. "German Machine Brought Down," *Twin City Daily Sentinel*, North Carolina State Archives. No source is quoted for this article, but based upon the level of detail about their trip, it is probable that Paul Rockwell was the source.
10. Mosier, *The Myth of the Great War*, 60.
11. Trouillard, "August 22, 1914."
12. Flammer, *The Vivid Air*, 1.
13. Pardoe, *The Bad Boy*, chap. 3, Kindle location 695.
14. Mason, *Lafayette Escadrille*, 5.
15. Ibid., 6.
16. "Addenda to the Rockwell Material," North Carolina State Archives.
17. Rockwell, *American Fighters in the Foreign Legion*, 6.
18. Pardoe, *Lost Eagles*, 33.
19. Rockwell, *American Fighters in the Foreign Legion*, 88.
20. Ibid., 21.
21. Gordon, *The Lafayette Flying Corps*, 436.
22. Pardoe, *The Bad Boy*, chap. 2, Kindle location 558.
23. Rockwell, *American Fighters in the Foreign Legion*, 8.
24. Gordon, *The Lafayette Flying Corps*, 290.
25. Whitehouse, *Legion of the Lafayette*, 95.
26. "American Flyer Thought He Was Native of France," *Harrisburg Telegraph*, October 20, 1916. This newspaper article does not cite any sources for the claim that Lufbery did not know he was American, and it is at odds with a statement from Raoul's older brother Julien, who said that Raoul renounced his French citizenship and declared himself an American at the French consulate in Cairo, Egypt, on June 26, 1906. Raoul was twenty-one at the time, and had he been French, he would have had to return to France to fulfill his national service requirement. (Per September 10, 2018, email from Raoul Lufbery III to the author.)
27. August 11, 2016, email from US CIS historian to the author. Some sources claim Lufbery became a naturalized citizen when he joined the US Army, but according to the laws in effect at the time, he was a US citizen from the day of his birth.
28. Hall, *One Man's War*, 33.
29. Kiffin Rockwell to Loula Rockwell, August 31, 1914, North Carolina State Archives.
30. King, *L.M. 8046*, 6.

31. Rockwell, *American Fighters in the Foreign Legion*, 6. By the time the war ended, all Allied troops on the Western Front would become intimately familiar with the French "Forty and Eight" boxcars, and a veterans group in the United States would be named after these aromatic transports.

32. After the recruits left Rouen, the German right wing turned south. Rouen was not overrun.

33. Liddell Hart, *The Real War 1914–1918*, 61.

34. Flood, *First to Fly*, 12.

35. Liddell Hart, *The Real War 1914–1918*, 47.

Chapter 3: Life in the Foreign Legion

1. Mason, *Lafayette Escadrille*, 13.

2. King, *L. M. 8046*, 9.

3. "Monkey meat" was boiled or corned beef. The troops called it monkey meat because a popular brand was Madagascar, and they assumed that if it came from Madagascar, it was probably made from monkeys.

4. Mason, *Lafayette Escadrille*, 15.

5. Hall, *One Man's War*, 35.

6. Mason, *Lafayette Escadrille*, 15. Mason claimed the gear weighed one hundred pounds, but Bert Hall and others complained about their seventy-pound packs. Seventy pounds seems more reasonable.

7. Ibid., 16.

8. King, *L. M. 8046*, 14.

9. Rockwell, *American Fighters in the Foreign Legion*, 13.

10. Ibid., 19.

11. Kiffin Rockwell to Loula Rockwell, September 17, 1914, North Carolina State Archives.

12. Weeks, *Greater Love Hath No Man*, 5.

13. A full regiment consisted of about four thousand men. In the Legion, there were two hundred fifty men to a company, four companies in a battalion, and four battalions to a regiment. The Legion had sixteen regiments, or roughly sixty-four thousand men. ("With the French Foreign Legion," *Norwich Bulletin* newspaper interview with Lieutenant Pechkoff.)

14. Hall, *One Man's War*, 35.

15. Hall, *En l'air*, 10.

16. King, *L. M. 8046*, 16.

17. Rockwell, *American Fighters in the Foreign Legion*, 19.

18. King, *L. M. 8046*, 22.

19. Ibid., 19.

20. Mason, *Lafayette Escadrille*, 18.

21. Kiffin Rockwell to Loula Rockwell, September 25, 1914, North Carolina State Archives.

22. "Atlanta Boy, Wounded on French Battlefield," *Atlanta Constitution*.

23. Rockwell, *American Fighters in the Foreign Legion*, 22.

24. King, *L. M. 8046*, 23.
25. Ibid., 25.
26. Rockwell, *American Fighters in the Foreign Legion*, 23.
27. Ibid., 31.
28. Hall, *En l'air*, 31.
29. Kiffin Rockwell to Loula Rockwell, October 16, 1914, North Carolina State Archives.
30. Rockwell, *American Fighters in the Foreign Legion*, 25.
31. King, *L. M. 8046*, 26.
32. Rockwell, *American Fighters in the Foreign Legion*, 26.
33. Hall, *En l'air*, 17.
34. King, *L. M. 8046*, 27; Rockwell, *American Fighters in the Foreign Legion*, 27.
35. Rockwell, *American Fighters in the Foreign Legion*, 28.
36. Rockwell, *American Fighters in the Foreign Legion*, 34.
37. King, *L. M. 8046*, 33.
38. Hall, *One Man's War*, 52.
39. "Atlanta Boy, Wounded on French Battlefield," *Atlanta Constitution*.
40. Rockwell, *American Fighters in the Foreign Legion*, 38.
41. Ibid., 39.
42. Paul Rockwell interview by the Cross & Cockade Society.
43. Miller, *Like a Thunderbolt*, chap. 2.
44. King, *L. M. 8046*, 38.
45. Hall, "Three Months in the Trenches."
46. Thénault, "The Story of the Lafayette Escadrille" (unpublished draft), 11, Washington and Lee University.
47. Hall, *En l'air*, 25.
48. King, *L. M. 8046*, 40.
49. Rockwell, *American Fighters in the Foreign Legion*, 40.
50. King, *L. M. 8046*, 34.
51. Rockwell, *American Fighters in the Foreign Legion*, 43.
52. Kiffin Rockwell to Loula Rockwell, November 14, 1914, North Carolina State Archives.
53. "Atlanta Boy, Wounded on French Battlefield," *Atlanta Constitution*.
54. Mason, *Lafayette Escadrille*, 35
55. Kiffin Rockwell to Loula Rockwell, December 1, 1914, North Carolina State Archives.
56. Loula Rockwell to Paul and Kiffin Rockwell, November 20 and 26 and December 1, 1914, North Carolina State Archives.
57. Loula Rockwell to Paul and Kiffin Rockwell, December 3, 1914, North Carolina State Archives.
58. Kiffin Rockwell to Loula Rockwell, December 10, 1914, North Carolina State Archives.
59. Weeks, *Greater Love Hath No Man*, 11.
60. Rockwell, *American Fighters in the Foreign Legion*, 43.
61. Chapman, *Victor Chapman Letters from France*, 72.
62. Kiffin Rockwell to Loula Rockwell, December 26, 1914, North Carolina State Archives.
63. Kiffin Rockwell to Paul Rockwell, December 26, 1914, Washington and Lee University. The actual letter differs from the one Paul published in *War Letters of Kiffin Yates*

Rockwell in that the published letter says Kiffin considered giving the English his name but decided to stay with the French.

CHAPTER 4: THE FORTUNES OF WAR

1. Kiffin Rockwell to Paul Rockwell, February 1, 1915, Washington and Lee Archives.
2. Loula Rockwell to Paul and Kiffin Rockwell, December 29, 1914, Washington and Lee University.
3. Kiffin Rockwell to Agnes Rockwell, January 7–11, 1915 (the first part of the letter was written on January 7, but the last part was written on January 11), Washington and Lee University.
4. King, *L.M. 8046*, 42.
5. The Germans maintained that the soft lead slugs fired by a shotgun flattened out inside the body, making them the equivalent of soft-nosed or "Dum-Dum" bullets. Those had been banned by the Hague Convention of 1899. (The Hague Convention was an early international agreement on the laws of war and a precursor to the Geneva Convention.) This became a bigger dispute later in the war, as the US Army issued shotguns to US troops for use in trench raids.
6. "Coolness of Americans Saves Outpost in France," *New York Post.*
7. Kiffin Rockwell to Agnes Rockwell, January 7, 1915, North Carolina State Archives.
8. In addition to the sources already cited, Kiffin wrote about this attack in a January 11 letter to his brother and in a February 5 letter to Massengale. Both letters are in the Washington and Lee University Archives. This attack is also well documented in Herbert Mason's book *The Lafayette Escadrille*, 31–32. Paul published the January 11 letter from Kiffin in *War Letters of Kiffin Yates Rockwell*, in which he inserted a sentence that said Kiffin's rifle jammed during the attack. That sentence is not in the original copy of the letter, and Kiffin did not say anything about his rifle jamming in his letters to Agnes or Massengale.
9. Kiffin Rockwell to his sister Agnes Rockwell, January 7, 1915, North Carolina State Archives.
10. Rockwell, *War Letters of Kiffin Yates Rockwell*, 20.
11. Kiffin Rockwell to Paul Rockwell, January 19, 1915, Washington and Lee University.
12. Kiffin Rockwell to Paul Rockwell, January 21, 1915, Washington and Lee University.
13. Undated biography of Paul Rockwell, Virginia Military Institute Archives.
14. Loula Rockwell to Kiffin and Paul Rockwell, January 6, 1915, Washington and Lee University.
15. Loula Rockwell to Kiffin and Paul Rockwell, January 11, 1915, Washington and Lee University.
16. It's not clear that Loula discovered this connection. She may very well have been responding to a connection discovered by Paul. While Paul was recovering from his wounds, he fell in love with his nurse, Mademoiselle Marie Francois Jeanne Leygues, whom he would later marry. Her father was Monsieur Georges Leygues, an influential French politician who would become the French prime minister after the war. As a result, Paul Rockwell had more connections than most privates in the Foreign Legion.
17. Kiffin Rockwell to St. Elmo Massengale, February 5, 1915, Washington and Lee University.

18. Kiffin Rockwell to Loula Rockwell, February 27, 1915, North Carolina State Archives.
19. Rockwell, *American Fighters of the Foreign Legion*, 10.
20. Kiffin Rockwell to Paul Rockwell, February 16, 1915, Washington and Lee University.
21. Kiffin Rockwell to Paul Rockwell, February 28, 1915, Washington and Lee University.
22. Pardoe, *Lost Eagles*, 50.
23. Lockjaw is a common name for tetanus, which is a bacterial infection commonly caused when contaminated dirt enters a wound, especially a deep puncture wound. The widespread use of manure as fertilizer in pre-WWI France led to a large incidence of tetanus following the early battles of 1914. An effective, though impure, form of anti-tetanus serum had been developed in the 1890s, and it quickly became standard practice to inject wounded soldiers with this serum. This treatment greatly reduced deaths due to lockjaw. Obviously, the doctor at Phélizot's infirmary had not given him this serum.
24. Similar versions of René Phélizot's death are given in Rockwell, *American Fighters of the Foreign Legion*, 55–56; King, *L.M. 8046*, 60–62; and Mason, *Lafayette Escadrille*, 33–34. This account is taken from all three sources.
25. Rockwell, *American Fighters in the Foreign Legion*, 57.
26. King, *L.M. 8046*, 62.
27. Mason, *Lafayette Escadrille*, 34.
28. Kiffin Rockwell to Paul Rockwell, March 11, 1915, Washington and Lee University. The author also has a photograph of Kiffin Rockwell with a note on the back written by Kiffin's mother. The note mentioned a barely noticeable chip on one of Kiffin's teeth, which Loula said "was done in the trenches in 1915." While there are many ways Kiffin could have chipped a tooth in the trenches, he wasn't engaged in the type of hand-to-hand fighting that typically causes such an injury. He almost certainly was involved in the brawls that broke out over René Phélizot's death, however, and it would have been very possible to have chipped a tooth during one of those fights. Sometimes a boy doesn't tell his mother everything.
29. Kiffin Rockwell to Loula Rockwell, March 21, 1915, North Carolina State Archives.
30. Gordon, *Lafayette Flying Corps*, 408.
31. Rockwell, *American Fighters in the Foreign Legion*, 65.
32. "Guttman," *SPA124 Lafayette Escadrille*, 10.
33. http://patch.com/connecticut/madison-ct/madison-historical-society-pumpkin-blaze-and-ghost-walk.
34. Gordon, *Lafayette Flying Corps*, 347.
35. "Paul Pavelka, Soldier of Fortune," *New York Sun*, December 30, 1917.
36. Sometimes spelled Zinovy Peshkov.
37. Rockwell, *American Fighters in the Foreign Legion*, 62.
38. Kiffin Rockwell to Paul Rockwell, April 17, 1915, Washington and Lee University.
39. Technically it would be called the Second Battle of Artois. The First Battle of Artois was a much smaller, indecisive campaign that occurred in December 1914–January 1915.
40. Rockwell, *American Fighters in the Foreign Legion*, 70.
41. Kiffin Rockwell to Loula Rockwell, May 2, 1915, North Carolina State Archives.
42. Ibid.
43. Kiffin Rockwell to Paul Rockwell, May 5, 1915, Washington and Lee University.
44. Paul Rockwell interview by the Cross & Cockade Society.

45. Weeks, *Greater Love Hath No Man*, 50.
46. Rockwell, *American Fighters in the Foreign Legion*, 71.
47. Kiffin Rockwell to Paul Rockwell, May 13, 1915, Washington and Lee University.
48. Ibid.

CHAPTER 5: RECOVERY

1. The name comes from the fact that the infection created gas bubbles in the wound. It had nothing to do with the poison gasses used as weapons during the war. Gas gangrene was caused by an anaerobic bacterium that lived in the manure-fertilized fields of France and Belgium. When the ground was disturbed (say, by digging trenches or exploding shells), this bacteria came to the surface. Bullets and shell fragments carried dirt, bits of uniform, and other debris into wounds, which could cause an infection.
2. Kiffin Rockwell to Paul Rockwell, May 15, 1915, Washington and Lee University.
3. Opening a wound to clean it was standard practice by that time in the war. Early in the war they sutured wounds closed as soon as possible, but that often led to gangrene.
4. Rockwell, *American Fighters in the Foreign Legion*, 78.
5. Kiffin Rockwell to Loula Rockwell, June 8, 1915, North Carolina State Archives.
6. Rockwell, *War Letters of Kiffin Yates Rockwell*, 50.
7. Kiffin Rockwell to Loula Rockwell, January 11, 1915, North Carolina State Archives.
8. Her advice had been to tell the Germans they were Americans and beg to be sent home. The Germans executed mercenaries.
9. Kiffin Rockwell to Loula Rockwell, May 21, 1915, North Carolina State Archives.
10. Loula Rockwell to Paul Rockwell, February 2, 1916, Washington and Lee University.
11. Herring, "If I Had a Dozen Sons I Should Want Them to Fight for France," *Philadelphia Public Ledger*.
12. Loula Rockwell to Mr. Olds, August 18, 1917, note, North Carolina State Archives.
13. Mr. House later became the chancellor of UNC Chapel Hill.
14. Loula Rockwell to Robert B. House, August 4, 1920, note, North Carolina State Archives.
15. J. A. Susong to Paul Rockwell, January 15, 1916, Washington and Lee University.
16. Herring, "If I Had a Dozen Sons I Should Want Them to Fight for France," *Philadelphia Public Ledger*.
17. Loula Rockwell to Robert B. House, August 4, 1920, note, North Carolina State Archives.
18. Kiffin Rockwell to Loula Rockwell, May 30, 1915, North Carolina State Archives.
19. Rockwell, *War Letters of Kiffin Yates Rockwell*, 54.
20. Kiffin Rockwell to Loula Rockwell June 15, 1915, North Carolina State Archives.
21. Ibid.
22. Kiffin Rockwell to Paul Rockwell, June 15, 1915, Washington and Lee University.
23. Paul Pavelka to Kiffin Rockwell, June 20, 1915, Washington and Lee University.
24. Kiffin Rockwell to Paul Rockwell, June 22, 1915, Washington and Lee University.
25. Paul Pavelka to Kiffin Rockwell, June 24, 1915, Washington and Lee University.
26. Paul Pavelka to Paul Rockwell, June 26, 1915, Washington and Lee University.

CHAPTER 6: MAMAN LÉGIONNAIRE

1. Gordon, *Lafayette Escadrille Pilot Biographies*, 259.
2. Weeks, *Greater Love Hath No Man*, 14.
3. Ibid., 38.
4. Ibid., 33.
5. Ibid., 33.
6. Ibid., 35.
7. Ibid., 37.
8. Ibid., 38.
9. A few Zeppelins were damaged by anti-aircraft fire and had to make forced landings following raids on Paris, but none caught fire and produced the spectacular "fireworks" displays that were seen later in the war when airplanes set fire to Zeppelins raiding England.
10. Weeks, *Greater Love Hath No Man*, 43.
11. Ibid., 41.
12. Ibid., 44.
13. Flammer, *The Vivid Air*, 6.
14. Weeks, *Greater Love Hath No Man*, 102.
15. Ibid., 124.

CHAPTER 7: BACK TO THE LEGION

1. Kiffin Rockwell to Loula Rockwell, July 8, 1915, North Carolina State Archives.
2. Mason, *Lafayette Escadrille*, 40.
3. Kiffin Rockwell to Loula Rockwell, July 31, 1915, North Carolina State Archives.
4. Weeks, *Greater Love Hath No Man*, 53.
5. Rockwell, *War Letters of Kiffin Yates Rockwell*, 67.
6. Kiffin Rockwell to Paul Rockwell, August 1, 1915, Washington and Lee University.
7. Kiffin Rockwell to Paul Rockwell, August 6, 1915, Washington and Lee University.
8. Weeks, *Greater Love Hath No Man*, 57.
9. Ibid., 63.
10. Kiffin Rockwell to Paul Rockwell, August 15, 1915, Washington and Lee University.
11. Weeks, *Greater Love Hath No Man*, 60.
12. Kiffin Rockwell to Paul Rockwell, August 26, 1915, Washington and Lee University.
13. Ibid.
14. Kiffin Rockwell to Paul Rockwell, September 1, 1915, Washington and Lee University.

CHAPTER 8: FROM FLYING BIRDCAGES TO WAR MACHINES

1. Clark, *Aces High*, 136.
2. Hale, "A Few of the First."
3. *Encyclopedia Britannica Online*, s.v. "The Royal Air Force," https://www.britannica.com/topic/The-Royal-Air-Force.

4. Thénault, "The Story of the Lafayette Escadrille," unpublished draft.

5. Sumner, *German Air Forces, 1914–18*, 5. This was the authorized strength "on paper." The number of actual flyable aircraft was probably much smaller.

6. Nolan, "The Bitter Bird Man," M4.

7. King, *The Skies over Rhinebeck*, 10.

8. Cameron, *Iron Men with Wooden Wings*, 12.

9. King, *The Skies over Rhinebeck*, 74.

10. Graham Mottram provides details on these developments in an excellent paper "Early Aero Engines." See also W. O. Bentley's book *My Life and My Cars*.

11. Flood, *First to Fly*, 10.

12. Reynolds, *They Fought for the Sky*, 16.

13. Flammer, *The Vivid Air*, 35. The Battle of the Marne was in reality a series of battles in which General Galliéni's Army of Paris played a small but important role. The use of taxicabs was a colorful but mostly ineffective way to move this army, but they helped create a wonderful myth.

14. Flammer, *The Vivid Air*, 35.

15. Thénault, "The Story of the Lafayette Escadrille," iii. French casualty records show an unnamed Maurice Farman airman as a casualty on August 4, 1914, and a Bleriot pilot named Captain Tiersonnier as wounded by flak on August 6, but there is no indication as to whether these pilots were actually shot down. Bailey and Cony, *The French Air Service War Chronology 1914–1918*, 1.

16. Strange, *Recollections of an Airman*, 46.

17. Thénault, "The Story of the Lafayette Escadrille," iv.

18. Roberts, *A Flying Fighter*, Kindle location 1380.

19. An exception was the great German ace Oswald Boelcke, who early in his career liked to use a single-seat Fokker for short-range artillery spotting. Boelcke, *An Aviator's Field Book*, 47 (entry dated December 9, 1914).

20. Flammer, *The Vivid Air*, 42.

21. Ibid., 43.

22. Strange, *Recollections of an Airman*, 42.

23. Roberts, *A Flying Fighter*, Kindle location 1162.

24. Boelcke, *An Aviator's Field Book*, 129 (entry dated June 2, 1916).

25. "Synchronization gear," Wikipedia, https://en.wikipedia.org/wiki/Synchronization_gear #The_Franz_Schneider_patent_.281913-14.29.

26. Guttman, *The Origin of the Fighter Aircraft*, 20.

27. Flammer, *The Vivid Air*, 47.

28. Fokker, *The Flying Dutchman*, 124–38.

29. Among other problems, Fokker claimed that he turned his first plane with a synchronized machine gun over to Oswald Boelcke in April 1915 and that Boelcke shot down an Allied plane on his third flight with it, but that story doesn't match Boelcke's field notes. Boelcke doesn't mention meeting with Fokker, and he recorded no victories in April, May, or June. During those months he mostly flew unarmed reconnaissance planes. Boelcke does, however, describe getting his first armed "battle plane" on June 14, 1915. It was a two-seater, and his observer had the only gun.

30. Strange, *Recollections of an Airman*, 112–15.
31. MacLanachan, *Fighter Pilot*, Kindle location 466.
32. Ibid., Kindle location 454.
33. Flammer, *The Vivid Air*, 49.
34. Rogers, *L'Escadrille Lafayette*, chap. 3.
35. Flammer, *The Vivid Air*, 52.
36. Lee, *No Parachute*, appendix C.
37. Parsons, *I Flew with the Lafayette Escadrille*, 32.
38. Fryer, "Bravery of British WWI 'Suicide Club.'"
39. Gordon, *Lafayette Escadrille Pilot Biographies*, frontispiece quote.
40. Parsons, *I Flew with the Lafayette Escadrille*, 240.
41. Gordon, *Lafayette Escadrille Pilot Biographies*, 39.
42. Jim McConnell to Paul Rockwell, October 11, 1915, Washington and Lee University.

CHAPTER 9: LEARNING TO FLY: THE PENGUINS

1. Parsons, *I Flew with the Lafayette Escadrille*, 48.
2. Ibid., 47.
3. Undated note inserted into letter, Kiffin Rockwell to Paul Rockwell, September 1, 1915, Washington and Lee University.
4. Kiffin Rockwell to Loula Rockwell, September 8, 1915, North Carolina State Archives.
5. Rockwell, *War Letters of Kiffin Yates Rockwell*, 81.
6. Ibid., 82.
7. Pilots were treated like officers in that they had to buy their own uniforms.
8. Later in the war, a group of influential Americans and French officials called the Franco-American Committee would provide funds to American volunteers to help pay for uniforms. This committee was influential in forming the Lafayette Escadrille, and later, with the help of a generous donation from William K. Vanderbilt, it would provide a monthly stipend to American pilots and student pilots. The financial assistance hadn't yet started when Kiffin was in flight training, so he had to borrow money from his brother to buy a new uniform. When Paul Pavelka finally made it to flight training, Kiffin collected money from friends to buy a uniform for Pavelka.
9. Kiffin Rockwell to Paul Rockwell, September 19, 1915, Washington and Lee University.
10. The "stick" is the propeller. With the engine off, the propeller is not moving and hence is a "dead stick."
11. Kiffin Rockwell to the Vicomte and Vicomtesse Peloux, September 19, 1915, Washington and Lee University.
12. Kiffin Rockwell to Paul Rockwell, September 15, 1915, Washington and Lee University.
13. Rockwell, *War Letters of Kiffin Yates Rockwell*, 86.
14. Kiffin Rockwell to Paul Rockwell, September 27, 1915, Washington and Lee University.
15. Jim McConnell to Marcelle Guérin, January 24, 1916, University of Virginia Archives.
16. Rockwell, *American Fighters in the Foreign Legion*, 113.
17. Ibid., 127.

18. Ibid., 149–52.
19. Ibid., 119.
20. Gordon, *Lafayette Escadrille Biographies*, 33.
21. Chapman, *Letters from France*, 14.
22. Ibid., 15.
23. Ibid., 117.
24. Ibid., 120.
25. Ibid., 16.
26. Ibid., 18.
27. Kiffin Rockwell to Paul Rockwell, September 27, 1915, Washington and Lee University.
28. Chapman, *Letters from France*, 156.
29. Rockwell, *War Letters of Kiffin Yates Rockwell*, 79.
30. Kiffin Rockwell to Paul Rockwell, October 5, 1915, Washington and Lee University.
31. *Asheville Gazette*, October 6, 1915, 1.
32. Weeks, *Greater Love Hath No Man*, 80.
33. Kiffin Rockwell to Paul Rockwell, October 16, 1915, Washington and Lee University.
34. Ibid.
35. Kiffin Rockwell to Loula Rockwell, October 18, 1915, North Carolina State Archives.
36. Kiffin Rockwell to Agnes Rockwell, October 21, 1915, North Carolina State Archives.
37. Rockwell, *War Letters of Kiffin Yates Rockwell*, 103.
38. Jim McConnell to Paul Rockwell, October 25, 1915, Washington and Lee University.
39. Rockwell, *War Letters of Kiffin Yates Rockwell*, 105.
40. Kiffin Rockwell to Paul Rockwell, November 6, 1915, Washington and Lee University.
41. Winslow, *With the French Flying Corps*, 216.
42. Hudson, *Hostile Skies*, 32.
43. Rockwell, *War Letters of Kiffin Yates Rockwell*, 107.
44. Kiffin Rockwell to Paul Rockwell, November 18, 1915, Washington and Lee University.
45. Kiffin Rockwell to Paul Rockwell, November 22, 1915, Washington and Lee University.
46. Weeks, *Greater Love Hath No Man*, 85.
47. Ibid., 91.
48. Ibid., 94.
49. Rockwell, *American Fighters in the Foreign Legion*, 152.
50. Billy Thorin to Kiffin Rockwell, November 22, 1915, Washington and Lee University.
51. Helen Gurphue (?) to Kiffin Rockwell, December 2, 1915, Washington and Lee University.
52. Helen Gurphue (?) to Kiffin Rockwell, December 14, 1915, Washington and Lee University.
53. At this point in time, the term "ace" was popularly used to describe being the best in anything. Only later would it become a standard term for a fighter pilot who had shot down five or more enemy aircraft.
54. Rockwell, *War Letters of Kiffin Yates Rockwell*, 111.
55. Parsons, *I Flew with the Lafayette Escadrille*, 219.
56. Gordon, *The Lafayette Flying Corps*, 384.

57. Kiffin Rockwell to Loula Rockwell, December 14, 1915, North Carolina State Archives. Some pilots stationed at Camp Le Bourget after Kiffin left were tasked with protecting Paris against German night-bombing raids, but there is no indication that Kiffin was assigned such duties.

58. Weeks, *Greater Love Hath No Man*, 99.

59. Rockwell, *American Fighters in the Foreign Legion*, 149.

CHAPTER 10: AN AMERICAN ESCADRILLE

1. Weeks, *Greater Love Hath No Man*, 102.

2. Pardoe, *The Bad Boy*, chap. 4, Kindle location 1272.

3. Jim McConnell to Paul Rockwell, undated letter (est. January 9, 1916), Washington and Lee University.

4. Weeks, *Greater Love Hath No Man*, 103.

5. Jim McConnell to Paul Rockwell, January 15, 1916, Washington and Lee University.

6. Rockwell, *War Letters of Kiffin Yates Rockwell*, 114.

7. Rockwell, *American Fighters in the Foreign Legion*, 152.

8. Billy Thorin to Kiffin Rockwell, January 12, 1916, Washington and Lee University.

9. Jim McConnell to Paul Rockwell, March 30, 1916, Washington and Lee University.

10. Whitehouse, *Legion of the Lafayette*, 2.

11. Mason, *Lafayette Escadrille*, 43.

12. Gordon, *Lafayette Escadrille Pilot Biographies*, 106.

13. Flammer, *The Vivid Air*, 15; Pardoe, *The Bad Boy*, chap. 4, Kindle location 1046.

14. Whitehouse, *Legion of the Lafayette*, 1. A description of this victory is given on pages 5 and 6, but the description makes it appear that Jimmy's observer really deserves credit for the victory.

15. Ibid., 11.

16. "Drop Polite Notes between Air Fights," *Leavenworth (WA) Echo*.

17. Bill Thaw presumably to his parents, December 28, 1914, Heinz History Center archives.

18. Gordon, *Lafayette Escadrille Pilot Biographies*, 57.

19. Flammer, *The Vivid Air*, 25.

20. Babbitt, *Norman Prince*, 56.

21. Ibid., 26.

22. Ibid., 27.

23. Ibid., 30.

24. Flood, *First to Fly*, 43.

25. Ruffin, *The Lafayette Escadrille*, 32.

26. "Intern American Flyers, His Cry," *New York Tribune*, 4.

27. "New Demand Made for the Internment of William Thaw," newspaper clipping, appears to be *New York World*, December 29, 1915, Heinz History Center archives.

28. "Fliers Can't Drink Says Lieut. Thaw," newspaper clipping, appears to be *New York World*, December 31, 1915, Heinz History Center archives.

29. Rockwell, *War Letters of Kiffin Yates Rockwell*, 115.

30. Horne, *The Price of Glory*, 36.

31. Reynolds, *They Fought for the Sky*, 73.
32. Horne *The Price of Glory*, 328.
33. Olley, "The Forbidden Forest."
34. Horne, *The Price of Glory*, 171.
35. Flood, *First to Fly*, 156.
36. Wilberg, *Jean Navarre: France's Sentinel of Verdun*, 49.
37. Guttman, *SPA124 Lafayette Escadrille*, 13.
38. Babbitt, *Norman Prince*, 32.
39. Flood, *First to Fly*, 96.
40. Guttman, *SPA124 Lafayette Escadrille*, 16.
41. Rockwell, *War Letters of Kiffin Yates Rockwell*, 117.
42. Henri Saint-Sauveur to Kiffin Rockwell, April 12, 1916, Washington and Lee University.
43. Chapman, *Victor Chapman's Letters from France*, 169, 165.
44. Thénault, "The Story of the Lafayette Escadrille," unpublished draft, 31.
45. Flammer, *The Vivid Air*, 103.
46. Over the years, *Lafayette Escadrille* became the name that was remembered, and it has commonly been used as a general term in book titles, journal articles, and other media to refer to the unit and its pilots throughout the squadron's existence, even though the squadron was officially known as the *Escadrille Américain* and the *Escadrille des Volontaires* during its early months. This book will follow that convention, although *Escadrille Américain* may be used in direct quotes.
47. Mason, *Lafayette Escadrille*, 71.
48. Hall, *One Man's War*, 123.

Chapter 11: Luxeuil Luxury

1. McConnell, *Flying for France*, 21.
2. Thénault, "The Story of the Lafayette Escadrille," unpublished draft, 36.
3. Jim McConnell to Paul Rockwell, undated postcard, Washington and Lee University.
4. Jim McConnell to Marcelle Guérin, April 20, 1916, University of Virginia Archives.
5. Weeks, *Greater Love Hath No Man*, 128.
6. Guttman, *SPA124 Lafayette Escadrille*, 16.
7. Ruffin, *The Lafayette Escadrille*, 15.
8. Kiffin Rockwell to Jim McConnell, September 21, 1916, Washington and Lee University. In Captain Thénault's book, he says the pilots stayed and ate at the Hotel Pomme d'Or (Golden Apple), but Kiffin's letter and the writings of other pilots make it clear that they didn't stay there until their second tour at Luxeuil.
9. Thénault, "The Story of the Lafayette Escadrille," unpublished draft, 51.
10. McConnell, *Flying for France*, 26.
11. Winslow, *With the French Flying Corps*, 167.
12. Mason, *Lafayette Escadrille*, 57.
13. Parsons, *I Flew with the Lafayette Escadrille*, 69.
14. Thénault, "The Story of the Lafayette Escadrille," unpublished draft, 30.
15. Weeks, *Greater Love Hath No Man*, 128.

16. Thénault, "The Story of the Lafayette Escadrille," unpublished draft, 41.
17. Jim McConnell to Paul Rockwell, April 25, 1916, Washington and Lee University.
18. Kiffin to Paul Rockwell, April 29, 1916, Washington and Lee University.
19. Kiffin to Loula Rockwell April 28, 1916, North Carolina State Archives.
20. Paul Rockwell to Kiffin Rockwell, May 1, 1916, Washington and Lee University.
21. Ibid.
22. Jim McConnell to Paul Rockwell, April 30, 1916, Washington and Lee University.
23. Thénault, "The Story of the Lafayette Escadrille," unpublished draft, 38.
24. Jim McConnell to Paul Rockwell, April 30, 1916, Washington and Lee University.
25. Kiffin Rockwell to Paul Rockwell, May 6, 1916, Washington and Lee University.
26. Kiffin Rockwell to Paul Rockwell, May 10, 1916, Washington and Lee University.
27. Jim McConnell to Paul Rockwell, April 30, 1916, Washington and Lee University.
28. Flammer, *The Vivid Air*, 57.
29. Thénault described this flight as occurring on May 10, but letters from Kiffin and McConnell set the date as May 5.
30. Thénault, *The Story of the Lafayette Escadrille* (published version), 33–34.
31. Ibid., 33.
32. Several books about the Lafayette Escadrille credit Kiffin with making unarmed patrols over the lines, sometimes flying with Victor Chapman. The dates given for some of these patrols are before the squadron received its first planes. These reports are probably based upon letters published in Alice Weeks's book *Greater Love Hath No Man*. For some reason several letters in that book have incorrect dates. Events that clearly happened in June and July are given April and May dates, causing confusion. Neither Kiffin nor Victor Chapman mentions unarmed flights over the lines in their letters, and Chapman specifically mentions adjusting his machine gun before his first trip over the lines on May 12.
33. Hall, *One Man's War*, 129.
34. Thénault, "The Story of the Lafayette Escadrille," unpublished draft, 45.
35. "Regulating" the gun involved adjusting it for an individual pilot so it would hit a target the pilot was aiming at and so it swung down for reloading into a position that was easy for the pilot to reach.
36. Kiffin to Loula Rockwell, May 8, 1916, North Carolina State Archives.
37. Guttman, *SPA124 Lafayette Escadrille*, 17.
38. Thénault, "The Story of the Lafayette Escadrille," unpublished draft, 48.
39. *Albuquerque Morning Journal*, May 1, 1916, 1.
40. Thénault, "The Story of the Lafayette Escadrille," unpublished draft, 36 and 50.
41. The photo of Kiffin with a note from Kiffin's mother on the back, noting that Kiffin's tooth had been broken "in the trenches," is a still from this newsreel.
42. Chapman, *Letters from France*, 178.
43. Pardoe, *The Bad Boy*, chap. 6, Kindle location 2122.
44. Hall, *One Man's War*, 126.
45. Parsons, *I Flew with the Lafayette Escadrille*, 92.
46. Ibid., 87.
47. Weeks, *Greater Love Hath No Man*, 135.

48. Thénault, "The Story of the Lafayette Escadrille," unpublished draft, 52.
49. Jim McConnell to Marcelle Guérin, May 19, 1916, University of Virginia Archives.
50. Hall, *One Man's War*, 131.
51. Kiffin Rockwell to Paul Rockwell, May 18, 1916, Washington and Lee University.
52. To date, no corresponding loss has been found in German casualty records. It's possible that the records have been lost, or it's possible that Kiffin and the ground observers were mistaken and the crew survived the crash.
53. Kiffin was not the first American to shoot down an enemy plane, although there is considerable debate about who was the first. Questions such as "Does the pilot of a two-seater get credit for shooting down an enemy plane if the shots were fired by his observer?" and "Is a pilot still considered American if he had to renounce his citizenship to join the British Army?" cloud the issue. Some historians don't consider victories scored by the Lafayette Escadrille in this debate because even though they did not renounce their citizenship, they were flying in a French unit. Kiffin was also not the first American fighter pilot to shoot down an enemy plane, as Elliot Cowdin was given credit for shooting down a German plane on April 20, 1916, before he joined the Lafayette Escadrille. (Some pilots in the Lafayette were skeptical of that claim, but it was cited in the award of a second palm to his Croix de Guerre.) Kiffin did, however, score the Lafayette Escadrille's first victory.
54. McConnell, *Flying for France*, 34.
55. Jim McConnell to Paul Rockwell, May 18, 1916, Washington and Lee University.
56. Paul Rockwell to Kiffin Rockwell, May 20, 1916, Washington and Lee University.
57. Ruffin, *The Lafayette Escadrille*, 38.
58. Captain Thénault claimed the bottle contained eighty-year-old bourbon, but that probably indicates that he was more familiar with brandies and cognacs than with bourbon. Ted Parsons simply referred to it as a "very old Bourbon," which, in 1916, probably meant eight or ten years old. Perhaps Captain Thénault, thinking of very old wine spirits, misheard "eight" as "eighty." Also, while it's satisfying to think that this celebration occurred on the night of Kiffin's first victory, it probably would have taken a couple of days for Paul Rockwell to ship a bottle of bourbon from Paris to Luxeuil. The celebration may even have been delayed until they reached their next duty station.
59. Nurse to Kiffin Rockwell, June 2, 1916, Washington and Lee University.
60. Jim McConnell to Paul Rockwell, May 20, 1916, University of Virginia Archives.
61. Jim McConnell to Marcelle Guérin, May 19, 1916, University of Virginia Archives.
62. Rickenbacker, "Fighting the Flying Circus," 26.
63. Boelcke, *An Aviator's Field Notes*, entry for June 2, 1916.

Chapter 12: Into the Furnace

1. Thénault, "The Story of the Lafayette Escadrille," unpublished draft, 58.
2. Guttman, *The Origin of the Fighter Aircraft*, 43.
3. Ibid., 48.
4. Flammer, *The Vivid Air*, 63.
5. Thénault, "The Story of the Lafayette Escadrille," unpublished draft, 56.

6. Hall, *One Man's War*, 139.
7. Thénault, "The Story of the Lafayette Escadrille," unpublished draft, 59.
8. Hall, *One Man's War*, 135.
9. Horne, *The Price of Glory*, 236.
10. Mason, *Lafayette Escadrille*, 67.
11. Kiffin Rockwell to Paul Rockwell, May 22, 1916, Washington and Lee University.
12. Horne, *The Price of Glory*, 240.
13. Toelle, "A White-Faced Cow," 295.
14. Thénault, "The Story of the Lafayette Escadrille," unpublished draft, 60.
15. Ibid., 61.
16. True "explosive" bullets, carrying an explosive charge, did not come into use until the British introduced the Pomeroy bullet later in the war. That bullet was only intended for use against Zeppelins or observation balloons, as the rules of warfare permitted the use of explosive bullets against machines but not against people. Often the term "explosive" was used to describe a soft-nosed or hollow-point bullet, often called a "dum-dum" bullet because they were once manufactured at the British Dumdum arsenal in India. These were outlawed by the Hague Convention. Airmen on both sides of the conflict frequently accused the other side of using explosive bullets, but many historians are skeptical of those claims because of a lack of evidence to support them. Conventional steel-jacketed bullets and tracer rounds could cause massive wounds that looked like the result of an explosive bullet. The pioneering World War I aviation historian Arch Whitehouse, himself a British World War I pilot, stated flatly, "There is no reliable record of explosive bullets in the air armament of the Germans during 1914–1918" (Whitehouse, *Legion of the Lafayette*, 115). During the war, however, the Lafayette pilots did not have time to calmly study these reliable records, and they firmly believed the Germans were using illegal projectiles.
17. Weeks, *Greater Love Hath No Man*, 138.
18. Tiffany's of Paris to Kiffin, May 30, 1916, Washington and Lee University.
19. In addition to a monthly stipend of 100 francs, the Franco-American Committee paid a bonus of 1,000 francs (about $200) for each confirmed victory. It's possible that Kiffin used this bonus to buy the cigarette case.
20. Gordon, *Lafayette Pilot Biographies*, 87.
21. Ibid., 93.
22. Toelle, "A White-Faced Cow," 296.
23. Kiffin Rockwell to Loula Rockwell, May 30, 1916, Washington and Lee University.
24. Toelle, "A White-Faced Cow," 335.
25. Weeks, *Greater Love Hath No Man*, 131. The letter is incorrectly dated April 29, 1916, but the events in the letter occurred on June 1, 1916.
26. This summary of the events of June 1 is pieced together from several sources, most notably Clyde Balsley's Diary for June 1, 1916; a letter from *Victor Chapman's Letters from France* to his father written on June 1, 1916; and letters from Jim McConnell to Paul Rockwell on June 3, 1916, and to Michelle Guérin on June 4, 1916, both letters in the University of Virginia Archives.
27. Chapman, *Victor Chapman's Letters from France*, 184.
28. Kiffin Rockwell to Paul Rockwell, June 2, 1916, Washington and Lee University.

29. Paul Rockwell to Kiffin Rockwell, June 5 and 7, 1916, Washington and Lee University.
30. Kiffin Rockwell to Paul Rockwell, June 5, 1916, Washington and Lee University.
31. Weeks, *Greater Love Hath No Man*, 140.
32. Gordon, *Lafayette Pilot Biographies*, 97.
33. Ibid., 101.
34. Jim McConnell to Paul Rockwell, June 8, 1916, University of Virginia Archives.
35. Kiffin Rockwell to Paul Rockwell, June 11, 1916, Washington and Lee University.
36. Hall, *One Man's War*, 139.
37. Chapman, *Victor Chapman's Letters from France*, 187.
38. Jim McConnell to Paul Rockwell, June 15, 1916, University of Virginia Archives.
39. Paul Rockwell to Kiffin Rockwell, dated "Monday," probably June 12 or 19, 1916.
40. Jim McConnell to Marcelle Guérin, June 18, 1916, University of Virginia Archives.
41. Kiffin Rockwell to Paul Rockwell, June 17, 1916, Washington and Lee University.
42. Chapman was credited with forcing the enemy plane to land. This did not count as a confirmed victory, as the enemy plane was not destroyed. Bailey and Cony, *The French Air Service War Chronology*, 53.
43. Thénault, "The Story of the Lafayette Escadrille," unpublished draft, 69.
44. Guttman, *SPA124 Lafayette Escadrille*, 21, gives credit to Lieutenant Walter Höhndorf. Bailey and Cony, *The French Air Service Chronology*, 54, also credit Höhndorf. Toelle, "A White-Faced Cow," 304, disputes this contention, providing documentation that Höhndorf was at the time stationed far from Verdun. Toelle believes that Boelcke was indeed the one who damaged Victor Chapman's plane that day. The author of a forthcoming biography of Oswald Boelcke, in correspondence with this author, contends that the references in Boelcke's *Field Notes*, which link him to this incident, are a mistranslation of Boelcke's original notes.
45. Werner, *Knight of Germany*, 149–80.
46. Kiffin Rockwell to Paul Rockwell, June 17, 1916, Washington and Lee University.
47. Wilberg, *Jean Navarre: France's Sentinel of Verdun*, 50.
48. Hart, *Aces Falling*, 161.
49. Kiffin Rockwell to Paul Rockwell, June 19, 1916, Washington and Lee University.
50. Hall and Nordhoff, *The Lafayette Flying Corps*, 2:60.
51. Although Didier Masson is commonly described as being a naturalized American, neither this author nor other historians I have corresponded with, nor the US Customs and Immigration Service, can find records to support this contention. It's possible that Didier was the one exception to the "All American" squadron makeup. Given Captain Thénault's desperate need for experienced pilots at the time, he may have arranged for the assignment of an experienced French pilot who had lived in America and was very familiar with American language and customs.
52. Gordon, *Lafayette Pilot Biographies*, 105.
53. Jim McConnell to Paul Rockwell, June 21, 1916, University of Virginia Archives.
54. Chapman, *Victor Chapman's Letters from France*, 193.
55. Mason, *Lafayette Escadrille*, 80.
56. Guttman, *SPA124 Lafayette Escadrille*, 24, and Bailey and Cony, *The French Air Service Chronology*, 55, give credit to Lieutenant Kurt Wintgens, one of the top German aces

flying over Verdun. Toelle, "A White-Faced Cow," 307, disputes this claim, providing evidence that Lieutenant Wintgens was stationed far from Verdun.

57. Kiffin Rockwell to Paul Rockwell, June 23, 1916, Washington and Lee University.
58. McConnell, *Flying for France*, 44.
59. Hall, *One Man's War*, 147.
60. Weeks, *Greater Love Hath No Man*, 148.
61. Toelle, "A White-Faced Cow," 308. Like most events concerning Bert Hall, the details of this change are sketchy. Hall describes this change as occurring on June 24 in his book *One Man's War*, but he also says this replaced the dollar sign motif. Photos show the plane had "BERT" painted on both sides before this date. There are photos that show "TREB" on one side, but the photos Paul Rockwell took in early July show "BERT" painted on both sides. It's clear that at some point Bert did have "TREB" painted on one side of his plane, but exactly when is questionable.
62. Gordon, *Lafayette Pilot Biographies*, 68.
63. William Charles to Kiffin Rockwell, June 26, 1916, Washington and Lee University.
64. Jim McConnell to Paul Rockwell, June 26, 1916, University of Virginia Archives.
65. Toelle, "A White-Faced Cow," 335.

Chapter 13: July Frenzy

1. Empey, *Over the Top*, 236–38.
2. McConnell, *Flying for France*, 53–55.
3. Jim McConnell to Paul Rockwell, July 1, 1916, University of Virginia Archives.
4. Pardoe, *The Bad Boy*, chap. 5, Kindle location 1767.
5. Mason, *Lafayette Escadrille*, 128.
6. Pardoe, *The Bad Boy*, chap. 6, Kindle location 2095.
7. Hall and Nordhoff, *Lafayette Flying Corps*, 1:83.
8. Flammer, *The Vivid Air*, 73.
9. Mason, *Lafayette Escadrille*, 105. It's not clear that this statement was made during the Fourth of July ceremonies, but his use of the term *Escadrille Américain* makes it clear that it was in this general time frame.
10. Jim McConnell to Paul Rockwell, July 1, 1916, University of Virginia Archives.
11. Loula Rockwell to Kiffin and Paul Rockwell, July 1, 1916, Washington and Lee University.
12. Paul Rockwell to Kiffin Rockwell, July 3, 1916, Washington and Lee University.
13. Paul's camera had a small light leak that "fogged" a spot on the pictures. This was unfortunate from a photography standpoint, but it allowed historians to readily identify the pictures Paul took. Some photographs that for years have been published as "action" pictures of the escadrille are in fact pictures that were posed for Paul.
14. Loula Rockwell to Kiffin and Paul Rockwell, July 6, 1916, Washington and Lee University.
15. Wilberg, *Jean Navarre: France's Sentinel of Verdun*, 74.
16. Guttman, *The Origin of the Fighter Aircraft*, 50.
17. Mason, *Lafayette Escadrille*, 89.
18. Guttman, *The Origin of the Fighter Aircraft*, 59.

19. Guttman, *SPA124 Lafayette Escadrille*, 27.
20. Toelle, "A White-Faced Cow," 318.
21. Flammer, *The Vivid Air*, 50.
22. Jim McConnell to Marcelle Guérin, July 12, 1916, University of Virginia Archives.
23. July 13, 1916, letter from Loula Rockwell to Kiffin and Paul Rockwell, Washington and Lee University.
24. "American Aviators Win in Fight with Germans," *Little Falls (MN) Herald*, July 14, 1916, 5.
25. Paul Pavelka to Jim McConnell, July 11, 1916, Washington and Lee University.
26. Kiffin Rockwell to Paul Rockwell, July 23, 1916, Washington and Lee University.
27. "Third German Plane Sent to the Earth by Kiffin Rockwell," *Atlanta Constitution*, August 14, 1916, 5.
28. "Yankee Fliers Fool Enemy by Diving into Cloud Bank," *New York Tribune*, August 25, 1916, front page.
29. Pardoe, *The Bad Boy*, chap. 5, Kindle Location 1799.
30. Wilberg, *Jean Navarre: France's Sentinel of Verdun*, 52.
31. Jim McConnell to Paul Rockwell, July 25, 1916, University of Virginia Archives.
32. Hall, *One Man's War*, 162.
33. McConnell, *Flying for France*, 68.
34. A burning balloon was a pretty dramatic sight and created a huge plume of smoke that was not likely to be overlooked by ground observers. Some sources have suggested that Prince did shoot down a balloon, but the balloon was so far behind the German lines that its destruction could not be confirmed. This raises the question of why the Germans would fly a balloon that far behind the lines. If ground observers in the French front lines couldn't see the balloon, the observer in the balloon couldn't see the front lines.
35. Ruffin, *The Lafayette Escadrille*, 70.
36. Jim McConnell to Paul Rockwell, July 25, 1916, University of Virginia Archives.
37. Thénault, "The Story of the Lafayette Escadrille," unpublished draft, 76.
38. Parsons, *I Flew with the Lafayette Escadrille*, 134.
39. Franks and Bailey, *Over the Front*, 199. Toelle, "A White-Faced Cow," 318, lists this as Nungesser's twelfth victory, as does Guttman, *The Origin of the Fighter Aircraft*, if you count the victories he describes between pages 54 and 60. The difference between the two numbers depends upon whether Nungesser is given credit for shooting down one or two Aviatiks on June 22, 1916.
40. Hall, *One Man's War*, 160.
41. McConnell, *Flying for France*, 98.
42. Jim McConnell to his mother, July 23, 1916, National Air and Space Museum.
43. Kiffin was recognized as having forced a German plane to land on the following day, July 28, 1916. Kiffin did not mention this in any of his letters and it is not described in squadron histories, so it's possible that somebody finally did say something about his July 27 battle, albeit a day later. Bailey and Cony, *The French Air Service War Chronology*, 62.
44. Kiffin Rockwell to Paul Rockwell, July 27, 1916, Washington and Lee University.
45. Ruffin, "Flying in the Great War." Unless otherwise noted, the descriptions of the medical effects of combat flying are summarized from these articles.

46. Grider, *War Birds*, 267. Although the book is subtitled "Diary of an Unknown Aviator," the aviator was in fact John MacGavock Grider. Grider was killed after flying in combat for one month, and his diary was edited and published after the war by his friend and fellow WWI pilot Elliott White Springs. Springs added two months to the diary and this entry is included with the third month of combat, so it is probably based on the experiences of Springs and the pilots he knew rather than on anything Grider wrote.

47. If a plane fell "over the trenches," it would be seen by ground observers and confirmed as a victory. If a plane fell well behind enemy lines, as Kiffin's fellow pilots said many of Kiffin's victims did, it would not be seen or confirmed.

48. Kiffin Rockwell to Loula Rockwell, July 26, 1916, Washington and Lee University.

49. Hall and Nordhoff, *Lafayette Flying Corps*, 1:343.

50. Paul Rockwell to Kiffin Rockwell, July 25, 1916, Washington and Lee University.

51. Paul Rockwell to Kiffin Rockwell, July 29, 1916, Washington and Lee University.

52. Paul carefully removed that section when he published Kiffin's war letters, but as the official historian of the Lafayette Escadrille, he preserved the complete original letter as well as all of his letters urging Kiffin to talk to Mr. Leygues.

53. Policies and protocol for reporting activities was still evolving at this point in the war. Bailey and Cony's *The French Air Service War Chronology* shows that in the summer of 1916 units such as N3 were routinely reporting "probables"—that is, claims for victories that were not confirmed by ground observers. These did not count as official victories but probably gave some satisfaction to the pilots involved. N124 did not report any probables until November 1916, so it's likely that Captain Thénault was not, in fact, reporting any claims Kiffin or any other pilot in the escadrille made that were not confirmed by ground observers.

54. Kiffin Rockwell to Paul Rockwell, July 31, 1916, Washington and Lee University.

55. Toelle, "A White-Faced Cow," 322.

56. Ibid., 322.

57. Ibid., 335.

Chapter 14: Summer Heat

1. An August 6, 1916, article in the *New York Sun* claimed that daylight began at 2:30 a.m. and pilots were awakened a half hour before then, but the "official" sunrise time for August 6 at Verdun is 5:41 a.m. and civil twilight begins at 4:59 p.m., so this article may have exaggerated a bit. "American Aviators in One Escadrille," *New York Sun*, August 6, 1916, section 2, 6.

2. Wynne, "History of the Escadrille Lafayette," 22.

3. Paul Rockwell to Kiffin Rockwell, August 1, 1916, Washington and Lee University.

4. Kiffin Rockwell to Paul Rockwell, August 4, 1916, Washington and Lee University. The original text of the letter says that "the Lt. went straight down and I thought he had been killed," but the context of the rest of the letter makes it clear Kiffin meant that a German plane went down, not that Lieutenant de Laage went down. Paul Rockwell edited that portion of the letter when he published *War Letters of Kiffin Yates Rockwell*, and his edited text is quoted here.

5. Years later, artist Robert Carlin would paint *Kiffin Saves an Ally*, which illustrated one of these unconfirmed victories. The painting illustrates an incident in which Kiffin reportedly saw a French Voisin being attacked by an Albatros far behind the German lines. Kiffin dove to the rescue, shooting down the Albatros, and the grateful French pilot Lieutenant du Clausonne followed Kiffin back to his airfield to personally thank him. The painting and description of the incident were featured in the Spring 2002 issue of *Over the Front*, but it is not known where Robert Carlin got the information to paint this scene and there is no known documentation to support it.

6. Kiffin Rockwell to Loula Rockwell, August 4, 1916, North Carolina State Archives.

7. Jim McConnell to Marcelle Guérin, August 5, 1916, University of Virginia Archives.

8. Guttman, *SPA124 Lafayette Escadrille*, 29.

9. Whitehouse, *Legion of the Lafayette*, 104.

10. McConnell, *Flying for France*, 135.

11. Paul Rockwell to Kiffin Rockwell, August 10, 1916, Washington and Lee University. The letter is simply dated "Thursday," but it can be dated by Paul's statement that George Rockwell joined Aviation this week. George joined on Tuesday, August 8.

12. Hall, *One Man's War*, 166.

13. Weeks, *Greater Love Hath No Man*, 158.

14. Bailey and Cony, *The French Air Service War Chronology*, 65, indicate this may have taken place on August 13.

15. Hall and Nordhoff, *The Lafayette Flying Corps*, 1:380.

16. Toelle, "A White-Faced Cow," 325.

17. Mason, *Lafayette Escadrille*, 97.

18. Paul Pavelka to Paul Rockwell, August 18, 1916, Washington and Lee University.

19. "Kiffin Rockwell's Letters to His Brother," *Every Week Magazine*, 21.

20. Jim McConnell to Paul Rockwell, August 25, 1916, University of Virginia Archives.

21. The squadron operations log shows that at 9:30 that morning Lieutenant de Laage led a patrol that included Norman Prince, Bert Hall, Dudley Hill, and Paul Pavelka. During this patrol, de Laage attacked one plane, Hall attacked two planes, and Prince seriously damaged a plane near the bois d'Hingrey (Hingrey wood). The log includes the notation "1 plane shot down" next to this patrol. Some sources say that after Prince killed the observer he forced the now nearly defenseless pilot to fly over the lines and land in French territory. This version of events probably originated in Ted Parsons's 1937 book *The Great Adventure*, later reissued as *I Flew with the Lafayette Escadrille*. Parsons wrote a dramatic account of this capture, which included a description of the German pilot standing up in the cockpit and raising his hands over his head to surrender. Capturing an enemy plane in this manner was not unknown during the war, but it was certainly unusual, and it generated a great deal of attention. Sometimes the vanquished pilot was even invited to have dinner with the pilot who captured him before being led off to prison camp. If Norman Prince had indeed forced the German plane to land within the French lines, his victory would certainly have been confirmed and one would expect his fellow pilots to have written about it. Captain Thénault made no mention of Prince capturing an enemy plane in his book, and Bert Hall did not say anything about it in either of the two books he wrote about his wartime adventures. (Hall is not the most

trustworthy source, but he had a flair for the dramatic and an event of this magnitude would certainly have attracted his attention.) The capture of a German plane is also not mentioned in any of the known letters from contemporary American pilots. Ted Parsons was a Lafayette Escadrille pilot, but he did not join the unit until four months after this event, so his account was probably based upon hearsay. While his book is considerably more trustworthy than Bert Hall's books, Parsons wrote for the "pulp fiction" crowd, and he sometimes tended to provide more details than he could have reasonably been expected to know, especially about events that happened before he joined the squadron.

22. Toelle, "A White-Faced Cow," 329.
23. Ibid.
24. Kiffin Rockwell to Paul Rockwell, July 27, 1916, Washington and Lee University.
25. Kiffin Rockwell to Paul Rockwell, September 1, 1916, Washington and Lee University.
26. Wynne, "History of the Escadrille Lafayette," 23.
27. Guttman, *SPA124 Lafayette Escadrille*, 32.
28. Weeks, *Greater Love Hath No Man*, 164; Paul Pavelka to Jim McConnell, August 31, 1916, Washington and Lee University.
29. Toelle, "A White-Faced Cow," 331; Thénault, *Journal de marches et opérations* (N124 Operations Log), September 3–9, 1916.
30. Kiffin Rockwell to Paul Rockwell, September 9, 1916, Washington and Lee University.
31. "One Man's Photo Album," *Over the Front* 5, no. 4 (1990): 319. Thank you to League of WWI Aviation Historians member James Pratt for identifying this encounter as Kiffin's second victory.
32. Toelle, "A White-Faced Cow," 334.
33. It's not clear how Thénault calculated 146 combats. The squadron made 752 combat flights over Verdun. Kiffin made 103 of these flights, Prince made 96 flights, and de Laage was the third-most-active pilot with 75 flights. Kiffin estimated that he had between 30 and 40 individual combats with German planes during the month of July alone, so the total number of combats for the entire squadron must have been higher than 146.
34. Thénault, "The Story of the Lafayette Escadrille," unpublished draft, 76.

CHAPTER 15: DÉJÀ-VU

1. Thénault, "The Story of the Lafayette Escadrille," unpublished draft, 80.
2. Mason, *Lafayette Escadrille*, 104.
3. Newspaper clipping, "Rockwell Captured German and Machine" in a scrapbook presumably compiled by Loula Rockwell. The date and newspaper in which this story ran is not recorded, but details in the clipping make it clear that it was published shortly after the pilots took leave in Paris. North Carolina State Archives.
4. Thénault, "The Story of the Lafayette Escadrille," unpublished draft, 84.
5. McConnell, *Flying for France*, 77.
6. Flammer, *The Vivid Air*, 82.
7. McConnell, *Flying for France*, 77.

8. Thénault, "The Story of the Lafayette Escadrille," unpublished draft, 81.
9. Ibid., 81.
10. Kiffin Rockwell to Loula Rockwell, September 14, 1916, North Carolina State Archives.
11. Hall, *En l'air*, 148.
12. Weeks, *Greater Love Hath No Man*, 166.
13. Flammer, *The Vivid Air*, 85.
14. Mason, *Lafayette Escadrille*, 107.
15. Ibid., 101.
16. Weeks, *Greater Love Hath No Man*, 166.
17. Mason, *Lafayette Escadrille*, 111.
18. Ruffin, *The Lafayette Escadrille*, 78.
19. Thénault, "The Story of the Lafayette Escadrille," unpublished draft, 38.
20. Ibid., 85.
21. Mason, *Lafayette Escadrille*, 112. In 1918, the RNAS would combine with the British Army's Royal Flying Corps (RFC) to form the Royal Air Force (RAF).
22. Miller, *Like a Thunderbolt*, chap. 3, Kindle location 287.
23. Thénault, "The Story of the Lafayette Escadrille," unpublished draft, 87.
24. Ibid., 87.
25. Mason, *Lafayette Escadrille*, 128.
26. Whitehouse, *Legion of the Lafayette*, 38.
27. Thénault, "The Story of the Lafayette Escadrille," unpublished draft, 87.
28. Kiffin Rockwell to Paul Rockwell, September 20, 1916, Washington and Lee University.
29. Kiffin Rockwell to Jim McConnell, September 21, 1916, Washington and Lee University.
30. Thénault, "The Story of the Lafayette Escadrille," unpublished draft, 88.
31. Walthall, "Tangible Links," 81–82.
32. Mason, *Lafayette Escadrille*, 114.
33. Thénault, "The Story of the Lafayette Escadrille," unpublished draft, 88.
34. Ibid., 90. Thénault's account says Kiffin was killed by a bullet that hit his head, but most other accounts, including Captain Thénault's graveside eulogy, say it was a bullet to the throat or the chest.
35. Rockwell, *War Letters of Kiffin Yates Rockwell*, 160.
36. Bill Thaw to Mr. J. A. Susong, September 23, 1916, telegram, Washington and Lee University. The sender is listed as "L Thaw," rather than "W Thaw," and the message reads "tell mother and Paul," rather than "tell mother and Agnes." But these errors probably indicate that the original message was scrawled in haste by a distraught Bill Thaw, who was thinking about what he would say to Paul, and it was perhaps difficult for the telegraph operator to read.
37. "North Carolinian Killed in France," *Pageland (South Carolina) Journal*, front page.
38. "Newport's Kiffin Rockwell Carried on Family's Military Traditions," *Newport Plain Talk*, 2.
39. Thénault, "The Story of the Lafayette Escadrille," unpublished draft, 90.
40. McConnell, *Flying for France*, 96.

41. Unsourced quote among Paul Rockwell's notes, Washington and Lee University.
42. Hall, *One Man's War*, 191.
43. Guttman, *SPA124 Lafayette Escadrille*, 49.
44. Paul Pavelka to Jim McConnell, September 26, 1916, Washington and Lee University.
45. Whitehouse, *Legion of the Lafayette*, 117.
46. Weeks, *Greater Love Hath No Man*, 169.
47. McConnell, *Flying for France*, 99.
48. Wynne, "History of the Escadrille Lafayette," 46.
49. Rockwell, *War Letters of Kiffin Yates Rockwell*, 140.
50. McConnell, *Flying for France*, 96.
51. Paul Pavelka to Jim McConnell, September 27, 1916, Washington and Lee University.
52. Mason, *Lafayette Escadrille*, 122.
53. Lieutenant Zinovi Pechkoff to Loula Rockwell, September 24, 1916 (?), North Carolina State Archives.
54. Letter of condolence to Loula Rockwell, September 24, 1916, North Carolina State Archives.
55. Among the letters of condolence is one vitriolic hate letter from a German sympathizer, proving that bad taste is not solely an attribute of modern generations.
56. Weeks, *Greater Love Hath No Man*, 167.
57. Ibid., 171.
58. Paul Pavelka to Paul Rockwell, October 7, 1916, Washington and Lee University.

Acknowledgments

WHEN AN ENGINEER DECIDES TO STEP OUTSIDE OF HIS FIELD OF EXPERTISE and write a biography, especially one about a man he never met who had experiences the author can barely imagine, the author will need a lot of help and advice. Fortunately for me, many people gave me the help I needed. Without them, I could never have completed this book. At the risk of overlooking many of the people who assisted me, I would like to give special thanks to a few people who were especially helpful.

Noted World War I aviation historians Steve Ruffin and Alan Toelle come immediately to mind. Steve gave me invaluable feedback on my draft manuscript, catching errors, suggesting sources, and challenging me when I strayed too far from the documented facts. He was also extremely helpful in locating photographs to illustrate the book. Steve has continued to provide information, inspiration, and encouragement to me through the publishing process. Alan Toelle similarly provided excellent guidance both on historical details and on the art of telling a story. Alan also freely shared the notes he has compiled over many years of studying the Lafayette Escadrille, including incredibly detailed listings of aircraft, sorties, and weather for the months Kiffin flew with the escadrille.

Historian Marc McClure, who was preparing a documentary on Kiffin as I was writing this book, also freely shared information he gathered during his research. Marc, Steve, and I engaged in many interesting email discussions as we bounced ideas or questions off each other. Dennis Gordon, whose *Lafayette Escadrille Pilot Biographies* was the first source I turned to when I needed information about Kiffin's fellow pilots, was also very helpful in answering emailed questions. Historians and authors Blaine Pardoe, Lance Bronnenkant, Terry Johnson, and David Hanna similarly answered my questions and provided helpful advice as I wrote this book.

I am also very much indebted to the help provided by the archivists and librarians at all the museums and libraries I visited during my research. Thomas Camden, Seth McCormick-Goodhart, and Lisa McCown were especially useful during the several days I spent at Washington and Lee University, and Matthew Peek was most generous with his time and his knowledge during the days I spent combing the State Archives at the North Carolina Department of Cultural Resources.

I would like to extend a special thanks to the relatives and descendants of Paul Rockwell who were gracious enough to share family lore, photographs, and clippings with me and who in many cases took the time to read a preliminary draft of this book and provide feedback. Sybil Rockwell Robb, Paul Rockwell, and Vance Brown were especially helpful in this regard. Katherine Ayres Battle not only shared her time and memories but also took me on a tour of the area around Nichols, South Carolina, where Enoch Shaw Ayres had his farm and where Kiffin spent many happy summers. I am likewise indebted to Paul Rockwell Sr.'s son, Kenneth Rockwell, who shared memories of his father and his uncle Kiffin during a telephone interview early in my research. Kenneth died peacefully in his sleep, in 2014, after a long and productive life.

My great-great aunt, Grace DeWaele Rockwell, provided the inspiration for this book. On my sixteenth birthday, she gave me a copy of Paul Rockwell's book *War Letters of Kiffin Yates Rockwell*, along with a photograph of Kiffin that had a note from Kiffin's mother on the back. I was fascinated by Kiffin's war letters, and I wanted to know more about the people and events he described. I found many excellent books about the Lafayette Escadrille, but I was disappointed that no one had written a biography of Kiffin. Nearly fifty years later, I decided to write one myself.

I owe a special debt of gratitude to my agent, Mr. Joseph Vallely, who is the reason this book is being published. I began this project with no knowledge of the publishing industry and with a naive belief that a book about Kiffin Rockwell and the Lafayette Escadrille would sell itself. I was quickly disabused of this notion when I began approaching literary agents and publishers. Fortunately, I then met Joe. Joe believed in me and in my book, and he guided me through the process of turning my manuscript into a published book. Sadly, Joe passed away before this book was published, and before I could fully express my thanks for his help.

Most of all, I want to thank my wife, Betsy, for her help in creating this book. She was my strongest supporter and my toughest critic as I researched and wrote. She also put up with the fact that for several years I was essentially living in a previous century, monopolizing dinner conversations with tales of people and events that had occurred a hundred years ago. Without her constant support, diligent proofreading, and helpful feedback, I could never have written this book.

Bibliography

ARCHIVES

For conciseness, the names of the following archives have been shortened when used in footnotes and photo attributions. In the following list, the italicized short name is given first, followed by a more complete description of the archive.

Heinz History Center, Thaw Family Papers, Thomas and Katherine Detre Library and Archives, Senator John Heinz History Center, 1212 Smallman Street, Pittsburgh, PA 15222.

National Air & Space Museum, Smithsonian Libraries, National Air & Space Museum, Room 3115, MRC 314, 6th Street & Independence Ave., SW, Washington, DC 20560-0314.

National Museum of the USAF, National Museum of the United States Air Force, Research Division/MUA, 1100 Spaatz Street, Wright-Patterson AFB OH, 45433.

Newport Library, Stokely Memorial Library, 383 E. Broadway, Newport, TN 37821.

North Carolina State Archives, Kiffin Y. Rockwell Papers, WWI Papers, Military Collection, State Archives of North Carolina, Raleigh, NC. Includes "Addenda to Rockwell Material," probably written by Mr. Robert B. House, and an unpublished biography of Kiffin Rockwell written by Loula Rockwell.

Pack Library, North Carolina Collection, Pack Memorial Public Library, Asheville, NC.

University of Virginia Archives, James R. McConnell Collection, Albert and Shirley Small Special Collections Library, University of Virginia.

Virginia Military Institute, VMI Archives, Preston Library, Lexington, VA 24450.

*Washington and Lee Archives,** Paul Ayres Rockwell Collection, WLU Coll. 0301, Special Collections Department, Washington and Lee University, Lexington, VA.

*Washington and Lee Archives,** Dale L. Walker Research Collection, WLU Coll. 0334, Special Collections Department, James G. Leyburn Library, Lexington, VA.

* Paul Rockwell's papers are split into two collections at Washington and Lee University. Mr. Walker is the author of a biography of Lafayette pilot Ted Parsons. Presumably he had borrowed some of Paul Rockwell's papers to write this biography and donated them separately. In any event, to see the complete collection of Paul Rockwell's papers, you need to look at both collections.

Books

Babbitt, George F. *Norman Prince: A Volunteer Who Died for the Cause He Loved*. Boston: Houghton Mifflin, 1917.

Bailey, Frank W., and Christophe Cony. *The French Air Service War Chronology 1914–1918*. London: Grub Street, 2001.

Bentley, W. O. *My Life and My Cars*. New York: A. S. Barnes, 1958.

Blum, Howard. *Dark Invasion*. New York: HarperCollins, 2014.

Boelcke, Oswald. *An Aviator's Field Book*. New York: National Military Publishing, 1919.

Cameron, Lou. *Iron Men with Wooden Wings*. New York: Belmont Books, 1967.

Chapman, Victor. *Victor Chapman's Letters from France*. New York: Macmillan, 1917.

Clark, Alan. *Aces High: The War in the Air over the Western Front 1914–18*. New York: Barnes & Noble Books, 1999.

Clark, Walter, ed. *Histories of the Several Regiments and Battalions from North Carolina in the Great War 1861–1865*. Raleigh: State of North Carolina, 1901.

Dickert, D. Augustus. *History of Kershaw's Brigade*. Newberry, SC: Elbert H. Aull, 1899.

Empey, Arthur Guy. *Over the Top*, New York: G. P. Putnam's Sons, 1917.

Ferguson, Niall. *The Pity of War*. New York: Basic Books, 1999.

Flammer, Philip M. *The Vivid Air*. Athens: University of Georgia Press, 1981.

Flood, Charles Bracelen. *First to Fly: The Story of the Lafayette Escadrille, the American Heroes Who Flew for France in World War I*. New York: Atlantic Monthly Press, 2015.

Fokker, Anthony, and Bruce Gould. *Flying Dutchman: The Life of Anthony Fokker*. 1931. Reprint, New York: Arno Press, 1972.

Franks, Norman L., and Frank W. Bailey. *Over the Front: A Complete Record of the Fighter Aces and Units of the United States and French Air Services, 1914–1918*. London: Grub Street, 2008.

Genet, Edmond C. C. *An American for Lafayette: The Diaries of E.C.C. Genet, Lafayette Escadrille*. Charlottesville: University Press of Virginia, 1981.

Gordon, Dennis, *Lafayette Escadrille Pilot Biographies*. Missoula, MT: Doughboy Historical Society, 1991.

———. *The Lafayette Flying Corps*. Atglen, PA: Shiffer Military History, 2000.

Grider, John MacGavock. *War Birds: Diary of an Unknown Aviator*. 1926. Reprint, College Station: Texas A&M University Press, 1988.

Guttman, Jon. *The Origin of Fighter Aircraft*. Yardley, PA: Westholme, 2009.

———. *SPA124 Lafayette Escadrille: American Volunteer Airmen in World War 1*. Wellingborough, UK: Osprey, 2004.

Hall, James Norman. *High Adventure: A Narrative of Air Fighting in France*. Boston: Houghton Mifflin, 1918.

Hall, James Norman, and Charles Bernard Nordhoff. *The Lafayette Flying Corps*. 2 vols. Boston: Houghton Mifflin, 1920.

Hall, Lieut. Bert. *En l'air (In the Air): Three Years on and above Three Fronts*. New York: New Library, 1918.

———. "Three Months in the Trenches." In *Stories and Letters from the Trenches*, edited by F. B. Ogilvie. New York: J. S. Ogilvie, 1915. http://www.gutenberg.org/files/48636/48636-8.txt.

Hall, Lieut. Bert, and Lieut. John J. Niles. *One Man's War: The Story of the Lafayette Escadrille*. New York: Henry Holt, 1929.

Hart, Peter. *Aces Falling: War above the Trenches, 1918*. London: Orion Books, 2007.

Herwig, Holger H. *The Marne, 1914: The Opening of World War I and the Battle That Changed the World*. New York: Random House, 2011.

Horne, Alistair. *The Price of Glory*. Harmondsworth, UK: Penguin Books, 1978.

Hudson, James J. *Hostile Skies*. Syracuse, NY: Syracuse University Press, 1968.

King, David Wooster. *"L.M. 8046": An Intimate Story of the French Foreign Legion*. New York: Duffield, 1927.

King, Richard. *The Skies over Rhinebeck*. Red Hook, NY: Rhinebeck Aviator's Guild, 1997.

Lafore, Laurence. *The Long Fuse*. Philadelphia: J. B. Lippincott, 1971.

Lamszus, Wilhelm. *The Human Slaughter-House: Scenes from the War That Is Sure to Come*. Translated by Oakley Williams. New York: Frederick A. Stokes, 1913.

Lee, Arthur Gould. *No Parachute: A Classic Account of War in the Air in WWI*. 1968. Kindle edition, London: Grub Street, 2013.

Liddell Hart, B. H. *The Real War 1914–1918*. 1930. Reprint, Boston: Little, Brown, 1964.

MacLanachan, William. *Fighter Pilot*. 1936. Reprint, London: Endeavor Press, 2015.

Mason, Herbert Molloy Jr. *Lafayette Escadrille*. New York: Random House, 1964.

McConnell, James R. *Flying for France: With the American Escadrille at Verdun*. Garden City, NY: Doubleday, Page, 1917.

Miller, Roger G. *Like a Thunderbolt: The Lafayette Escadrille and the Advent of American Pursuit in World War I*. Washington, DC: Air Force History and Museums Program, 2007.

Mosier, John. *The Myth of the Great War*. New York: HarperCollins, 2002.

Mottram, Graham. "Early Aero Engines, 1900–11920." In *The Piston Engine Revolution*, edited by Fred Starr, Ed Marshal, and Brian Lawton, 1–22. Papers from a conference at the Museum of Science and Industry, Manchester, England, April 14–17, 2011. London: Newcomen, 2011. http://www.newcomen.com/the-piston-engine-revolution/.

Pardoe, Blaine. *The Bad Boy: Bert Hall: Aviator and Mercenary of the Skies*. Stroud, UK: Fonthill Media, 2012.

———. *Lost Eagles: One Man's Mission to Find Missing Airmen in Two World Wars*. Ann Arbor: University of Michigan Press, 2010.

Parsons, Edwin C. *I Flew with the Lafayette Escadrille*. Indianapolis, IN: E. C. Seale, 1963.

Pershing, General John J. *My Experiences in the World War*. 1931. Reprint, Blue Ridge Summit, PA: TAB Books, 1989.

Reynolds, Quentin. *They Fought for the Sky*. New York: Bantam, 1963.

Rickenbacker, Eddie V. *Fighting the Flying Circus*. 1919. Reprint, New York: Avon Books, 1969.

Roberts, E. M., R.F.C. *A Flying Fighter: An American above the Lines in France*. 1918. Kindle edition, San Francisco: Pickle Partners Publishing, 2013.

Rockwell, Paul Ayres. *American Fighters in the Foreign Legion, 1914–1918*. Boston: Houghton Mifflin, 1930.

———. *Three Centuries of the Rockwell Family in America, 1630–1930*. Paris: Author, 1930.

———. *War Letters of Kiffin Yates Rockwell*. Garden City, NY: Country Life Press, 1925.

Ruffin, Steven A. *The Lafayette Escadrille: A Photo History of the First American Fighter Squadron*. Havertown, PA: Casemate, 2016.

Seeger, Alan. *Letters and Diary of Alan Seeger*. New York: Charles Scribner's Sons, 1917.

Strange, Lieutenant Colonel Louis A. *Recollections of an Airman*. 1933. Reprint, London: Greenhill Books, 1980.

Sumner, Ian. *German Air Forces, 1914–18*. Wellingborough, UK: Osprey, 2005.

Taylor, A. J. P. *The First World War*. New York: Capricorn Books, 1972.

Thénault, Captain George. *Journal de marches et opérations pendant la campagne du 14/8/16 au 9/9/17* (Escadrille N124 combat log). Washington, DC: Smithsonian Libraries, National Air and Space Museum. https://archive.org/details/Journaldesmarch00.

———. *The Story of the Lafayette Escadrille*. Boston: Small, Maynard, 1921.

———. "The Story of the Lafayette Escadrille." (Typewritten draft—unpublished). Washington and Lee University Archives.

Tuchman, Barbara W. *The Guns of August*. New York: Macmillan, 1962.

Virginia Military Institute. *Official Register 1904–1905*. Lexington: Virginia Military Institute, 1905.

Wake Forest College. *Bulletin of Wake Forest College, Seventy-Third Session, 1907–1908*. Winston-Salem, NC: Trustees of Wake Forest College, 1908.

Washington and Lee University. *Washington and Lee University Catalog*. Lexington, VA: Washington and Lee University, 1909, 1910, and 1911.

Weeks, Alice S. *Greater Love Hath No Man*. Boston: Bruce Humphries, 1930.

Wellesley College. *Legenda, 1912* (Wellesley Class Yearbook). Wellesley MA: Wellesley College, 1912.

Werner, Johannes. *Knight of Germany: Oswald Boelcke, German Ace*. 1933. Reprint, London: Greenhill Books, 1985.

Whitehouse, Arch. *Legion of the Lafayette*. Garden City, NY: Doubleday, 1962.

Wilberg, Jim. *Jean Navarre: France's Sentinel of Verdun and the First French Fighter Pilots*. N.p: Aeronaut Books, 2010.

Winslow, Carroll Dana. *With the French Flying Corps*. New York: Charles Scribner's Sons, 1917.

PERIODICALS

Balsley, Clyde. "The Diary of H. Clyde Balsley." *Cross & Cockade Journal, Society of WW1 Aero Historians* 18, no. 2 (1977). http://www.overthefront.com/over-the-front-journal/cross-cockade-issues.

"Kiffin Rockwell's Letters to His Brother." *Every Week Magazine* 5, no. 23 (December 3, 1917).

Nolan, William F. "The Bitter Bird Man." *Sports Illustrated*, February 5, 1962, M4.

Olley, Jonathan. "The Forbidden Forest." *Orion Magazine*, March–April 2009. https://orionmagazine.org/article/the-forbidden-forest/.

"Paul Ayres Rockwell: War Correspondent, Author, Aviator, World Traveler." *Sigma Phi Epsilon Journal*, November 1930. Washington and Lee University Archives.

Ruffin, Steven A. "Flying in the Great War: Rx for Misery." *Over the Front* 14, no. 2 (1999) and 17, no. 2 (2002). http://www.overthefront.com/over-the-front-journal/back-issues.

Toelle, Alan D. "A White-Faced Cow and the Operational History of the Escadrille Americaine." *Over the Front* 24, no. 4 (Winter 2009). http://www.overthefront.com/over-the-front-journal/back-issues.

Walthall, Charles. "Tangible Links: Exploring the Material Culture of World War I." *Over the Front* 33, no. 1 (Spring 2018): 81–82.

Wynne, H. Hugh. "History of the Escadrille Lafayette." *Cross & Cockade Journal* 2, no. 1 (1961).

NEWSPAPERS

"American Flyer Thought He Was Native of France." *Harrisburg Telegraph*, October 20, 1916.

"Another Veteran Crosses." *Dillon (SC) Herald*, July 30, 1914.

"Atlanta Boy, Wounded on French Battlefield, Paints Graphic Pen Picture of European War." *Atlanta Constitution*, May 2, 1915.

"Aviators from America Soar over Lines of German Troops." *Albuquerque Morning Journal*, May 19, 1916, 1.

"Coolness of Americans Saves Outpost in France." *New York Post*, February 2, 1915.

Craig, Britt. "Paul Rockwell Tells Story of Kiffin's Death." *Atlanta Constitution*, November 11, 1916.

"Dr. Loula Rockwell Dies Here at Age 92." *Asheville Citizen*, July 29, 1959.

"Drop Polite Notes between Air Fights." *Leavenworth (WA) Echo*, November 26, 1915.

"Fliers Can't Drink Says Lieut. Thaw." *New York World* (?), December 31, 1915 (Heinz History Center archives).

"German Machine Brought Down." *Twin City Daily Sentinel*, May 19, 1916.

Herring, Kate M. "If I Had a Dozen Sons I Should Want Them to Fight for France." *Philadelphia Public Ledger*, May 26, 1918, Magazine Section, 1.

"History of First Baptist Church." *Cocke County Banner*, March 2, 1972 (Stokely Library, Newport, Tennessee).

"Intern American Flyers, His Cry." *New York Tribune*, December 25, 1915, 4.

"Lincoln Opposed by Three Generations." Undated clipping from unknown newspaper (Marion, SC, Library).

"Local Happenings." *Newport Plain Talk*, May 4, 1901.

"Local Happenings." *Newport Plain Talk*, July 13, 1901.

"Local Happenings." *Newport Plain Talk*, July 10, 1902.

"Local Happenings." *Newport Plain Talk*, December 4, 1902.

"Local Happenings." *Newport Plain Talk*, September 21, 1905.

"Madison Historical Society Pumpkin Blaze and Ghost Walk!" *Madison (CT) Patch*, October 10, 2011. https://patch.com/connecticut/madison-ct/madison-historical -society-pumpkin-blaze-and-ghost-walk.

"Mountain Topics." *Asheville Citizen-Times*, September 21, 1952.

"New Demand Made for the Internment of William Thaw." *New York World* (?), December 29, 1915 (Heinz History Center archives).

"Newport's Kiffin Rockwell Carried on Family's Military Tradition." *Newport Plain Talk*, January 28, 2010.

"North Carolinian Killed in France." *Pageland (South Carolina) Journal*, September 27, 1916.

"Paul Pavelka, Soldier of Fortune." *New York Sun*, December 30, 1917.

"Skill in Riding Bucking Pony Revealed Kiffin Rockwell's Will to Fly." *Newport Plain Talk*, undated (Stokely Library, Newport, Tennessee).

"Three Young Atlantians Would Shoulder Arms in Defense of France." *Atlanta Journal*, August 4, 1914.
"With the French Foreign Legion." *Norwich Bulletin*, December 9, 1916.

INTERVIEWS

Battle, Katherine Ayres (Loula Rockwell's grand-niece). Interviewed by the author, September 22, 2016.
Brown, Vance (Kiffin Rockwell's grand-nephew). Interviewed by Marc McClure, May 9, 2017.
Brown, Vance (Kiffin Rockwell's grand-nephew). Interviewed by the author, May 30, 2017.
Rockwell, Paul. Interviewed by the Cross & Cockade Society, 1962 (USAF Oral History Program Interview #550, IRIS Number 0090450).
Rockwell, Paul. Interviewed by Dr. Louis D. Silveri, Southern Highlands Research Center, University of North Carolina at Asheville, July 22, 1976 (http://toto.lib.unca.edu/findingaids/oralhistory/SHRC/rockwell.html).
Rockwell, William James Kenneth (Paul Rockwell's son). Telephone interview by the author, March 6, 2010.

ONLINE RESOURCES

Fryer, Jane. "Bravery of British WWI 'Suicide Club' Whose Fighter Pilots Took on Germany and the Red Baron with Only 15 Hours' Training and Lasted on Average Just 11 Days." *Daily Mail*, June 4, 2010. https://www.dailymail.co.uk/news/article-1283972/Bravery-British-WWI-suicide-club-fighter-pilots-took-Germany-Red-Baron-15-hours-training-lasted-average-just-11-days.html.
Garvin, Karen S. "British Air Raids on Zeppelin Sheds, September to December 1914." Academia, 2013. http://www.academia.edu/3202752/British_Air_Raids_on_Zeppelin_Sheds_September_to_December_1914.
Hale, Julian. "A Few of the First: The RFC, August 1914." Royal Air Force Museum, 2014. http://www.rafmuseum.org.uk/blog/a-few-of-the-first-the-rfc-august-1914/.
House, Robert Burton. "Kiffin Yates Rockwell." *Documenting the South*. Originally published in *The North Carolina Booklet*, April–July 1920. http://docsouth.unc.edu/wwi/house/house.html.
Rogers, Lieutenant Colonel Philipe D., USMC. *L'Escadrille Lafayette: Unité volontaire de combat oubliée de l'Amérique* (chapter 3: "A Short History of the Lafayette Escadrille"). Ecole Pratique des Hautes Etudes, 2005. http://www.institut-strategie.fr/Arogers_3.htm.
Trouillard, Stephanie. "August 22, 1914: The Bloodiest Day in French History." *France 24*, August 22, 2014. https://www.france24.com/en/20140822-august-22-1914-battle-frontiers-bloodiest-day-french-military-history.
Tucker, Glen. "Rockwell, James Chester." *NCpedia*, 1994. https://www.ncpedia.org/biography/rockwell-james-chester.
———. "Rockwell, Kiffin Yates." *NCpedia*, 1994. http://ncpedia.org/biography/rockwell-kiffin-yates.

Photo Credits

In addition to photos from the author's collection and those graciously made available by Ms. Sybil Robb, Kiffin's grand-niece, photos are used with permission from the following sources:

State Archives of North Carolina: Kiffin Y. Rockwell Papers, WWI Papers, Military Collection, State Archives of North Carolina, Raleigh, North Carolina

University of Virginia Archives: James R. McConnell Collection, Albert and Shirley Small Special Collections Library, University of Virginia

Virginia Military Institute: VMI Archives, Preston Library, Lexington, Virginia

Washington and Lee University: Paul Ayres Rockwell Collection, Special Collections Department, Washington and Lee University, Lexington, Virginia

Wikimedia Commons: Links to the Wikimedia Commons images used in this book are given below; full details on the public domain status are provided in the linked pages:

British FE-2 Pusher: https://commons.wikimedia.org/wiki/File%3ABuddeckes_FE2b.jpg (public domain)

Fokker Eindekker: https://commons.wikimedia.org/wiki/File%3AFokker_M5K-MG_E5-15.jpg (public domain)

World War 1 Inline Engine: https://commons.wikimedia.org/wiki/File:LIberty_L-6_engine_installed_in_captured_Fokker_D.VII.jpg (public domain)

World War 1 Rotary Engine: https://commons.wikimedia.org/wiki/File:Le_rhone.jpg (public domain)

Additional Public Domain Image: The photo of the Bleriot Penguin is from Hall and Nordhoff's *The Lafayette Flying Corps* (this book is in the public domain)

Index

aces, 259n53; Boelcke as, 165, 182, 257n19; Fonck as, 198; Guynemer as, 198; Immelmann as, 182; Nungesser as, 154; Wintgens as, 265n56
advertising, Rockwell, K., in, 14
aerial barrage, by Germans, 139, 141, 165
airplanes: artillery spotting by, 95, 96; at Battle of the Somme, 203–4; bombing by, 94; combat between, 44, 97–107; confirmed victories by, 103–4; dead-reckoning navigation for, 119–20; deflection shooting from, 97, 98–99; development of, 91–107; fléchettes from, 94–95; for flight training, 109–27; at front lines, 41; of Germans, 91, 100; identification markings of, 154–55; inline engines for, 92; night flying of, 159–60; over trenches, 96; parachutes for, 104–6; pusher, 101; radio of, 95–96; for reconnaissance, 28, 93–94, 96, 101, 165, 224; rotary engines for, 92–93, 198; shot down, 94, 96–97, 142, 162, 186; specialization of, 93; tail skids on, 110; two seats in, 95–96, 98; at Verdun, 141; winters in, 125–26. *See also specific topics*
air temperature, pilots and, 207
altitude sickness, 207

American Escadrille. *See* Lafayette Escadrille
American neutrality, in World War I, 19, 23, 55, 63, 81–82, 137, 144
anti-aircraft guns, 95, 155–56; with balloons, 201; Thaw and, 228; at Verdun, 141, 175; Zeppelins and, 256n9
Army Aviation Department, 21
Army of Counani, 61
artillery: balloons and, 95, 201; at Battle of Artois, 66; at Battle of the Somme, 192; kitchen and, 41; Rockwell, K., on, 49; spotting of, by airplanes, 95, 96; at Verdun, 139–40
Atlanta Constitution, 2, 13, 14
Ayres, Enoch Shaw, 3–4, 15
Ayres, Loula. *See* Rockwell, Loula
Ayres, Thomas, 4

Bach, Jim: flight training of, 44, 46, 132–33; as prisoner of war, 133–34
balloons: artillery and, 95, 201; hydrogen in, 201; at Luxeuil, 154; parachutes for, 104, 154; Prince, N., and, 202–3, 267n34; in World War I, 104–5. *See also* Zeppelins
Balsley, Clyde, 145, 173; promotion of, 189; at Verdun, 175, 183–85; wounds of, 183–85, 186, 192, 195–96